THE PERSONAL INFORMATION PROTECTION AND ELECTRONIC DOCUMENTS ACT

AN ANNOTATED GUIDE

THE PERSONAL INFORMATION PROTECTION AND ELECTRONIC DOCUMENTS ACT

AN ANNOTATED GUIDE

STEPHANIE PERRIN

HEATHER H. BLACK

DAVID H. FLAHERTY

T. MURRAY RANKIN, Q.C.

IRWIN LAW

A Quicklaw Company

The Personal Information Protection and Electronic Documents Act:
An Annotated Guide

Published in 2001 by
Irwin Law Inc.
Suite 930, Box 235
One First Canadian Place
Toronto, Ontario
M5X 1C8

ISBN: 1-55221-046-4

National Library of Canada Cataloguing in Publication Data

Main entry under title:
    The Personal Information Protection and Electronic Documents Act

Includes bibliographical references and index.
ISBN 1-55221-046-4

1. Canada. Personal Information Protection and Electronic Documents Act.
2. Privacy, Right of – Canada.   3. Public records – Law and legislation – Canada.
4. Electronic records – Law and legislation – Canada.   5. Electronic data interchange
– Law and legislation – Canada.   I. Perrin, Stephanie (Stephanie E.).

KE4422.A31P47 2001   342.71'0662   C00-933304-5
KF4483.C524P46 2001

The opinions expressed in this book are those of the authors and not those of the Department of Justice, the Department of Industry, or the Office of the Privacy Commissioner of Canada.

Printed and bound in Canada.

1 2 3 4 5   05 04 03 02 01

CONTENTS

FOREWORD BY BRUCE PHILLIPS *ix*

INTRODUCTION *xi*

CHAPTER 1: Background to the Act *1*

CHAPTER 2: Part 1: Schedule 1 *13*

A. The Incorporation of the CSA Standard as the Schedule *13*
B. Commentary to Schedule 1 *15*
Principle 1: Accountability *15*
Principle 2: Identifying Purposes *18*
Principle 3: Consent *22*
Principle 4: Limiting Collection *32*
Principle 5: Limiting Use, Disclosure, and Retention *33*
Principle 6: Accuracy *35*
Principle 7: Safeguards *36*
Principle 8: Openness *38*
Principle 9: Individual Access *40*
Principle 10: Challenging Compliance *44*

CHAPTER 3: Part 1: The Act *47*

Section 1: Short Title *47*

Part 1: Protection of Personal Information in the Private Sector *48*

Section 2: Interpretation *48*
Section 3: Purpose *55*
Section 4: Application *56*

Division 1: Protection of Personal Information   *61*

Section   5: Compliance with Obligations   *61*
Section   6: Effect of Designation of Individual   *62*
Section   7: Collection, Use, and Disclosure without Consent   *62*
Section   8: Access Procedures   *85*
Section   9: Exceptions to the Right of Access   *88*
Section 10: Sensory Disability   *94*

Division 2: Remedies   *94*

Section 11: Filing of Complaints   *94*
Section 12: Investigations of Complaints   *97*
Section 13: Commissioner's Report (including Commentary on
      Terms to Designate a Finding)   *100*
Section 14: Review by the Federal Court   *104*
Section 15: Commissioner's Application for Review   *106*
Section 16: Remedies   *107*
Section 17: Summary Hearings by Federal Court   *107*

Division 3: Audits   *109*

Section 18: Audits   *109*
Section 19: Audit Reports   *111*

Division 4: General   *111*

Section 20: Confidentiality   *111*
Section 21: Competent Witness   *113*
Section 22: Protection of the Commissioner   *114*
Section 23: Consultation with Provinces   *115*
Section 24: Promoting the Purposes of the Part   *116*
Section 25: Annual Reports to Parliament   *117*
Section 26: Regulations   *118*
Section 27: Whistleblowing   *120*
Section 27.1: Discipline of Employees   *120*
Section 28: Offence and Punishment   *121*
Section 29: Review of Part by Parliamentary Committee   *122*

Division 5: Transitional Provisions   *122*

Section 30: Transitional and Coming into Force   *122*

CHAPTER 4: Parts 2 to 5: Moving Federal Legislation Out of the "Age of Paper"   *125*

A. Introduction   *125*
B. Part 2: Electronic Documents   *126*
    1) Filing Documents and Making Payments by Electronic Means   *127*
    2) Electronic Alternatives   *128*
    3) Secure Electronic Signatures   *129*
    4) Public Key Cryptography   *130*
    5) Retention of Documents   *131*
    6) Regulations and Orders   *132*
C. Part 3: Amendments to the *Canada Evidence Act*   *133*
    1) Media-Neutral Documents   *134*
    2) *Uniform Electronic Evidence Act*   *134*
    3) Authentication   *135*
    4) Best Evidence Rule   *135*
    5) Presumption of Integrity   *135*
    6) Electronic Record Keeping   *136*
D. Part 4: Amendments to the *Statutory Instruments Act*   *137*
E. Part 5: Amendments to the *Statute Revision Act*   *137*

CHAPTER 5: Critical Privacy Issues   *139*

A. Introduction   *139*
B. Definition of Personal Information and the Concept of Anonymity   *139*
C. Publicly Available Information   *142*
D. Regulations   *142*
E. Comments on Investigative Bodies   *150*
F. Comments on Publicly Available Information   *151*
G. Organizations and Their Affiliates   *153*
H. Scholarly, Historical, and Market Research   *154*
I. Medical Information   *155*

CHAPTER 6: Frequently Asked Questions   *159*

A. Scope and Application   *159*
B. Collections, Uses, and Disclosures   *162*
C. Access   *163*

D. Complaints   *164*

E. Lawful Investigations   *165*

F. Commissioner's Powers and Operations   *166*

G. Federal Court   *167*

H. Research   *167*

    1) Medical Research and Information   *167*

    2) Genealogical Research   *168*

    3) The Standard   *169*

I. Technology-Related Issues   *169*

APPENDIX 1:

The *Personal Information Protection and Electronic Documents Act*   *173*

APPENDIX 2:

Guidelines of the OECD Governing the Protection of Privacy and Transborder Flows of Personal Data   *221*

APPENDIX 3:

Directive 95/46/EC of the European Parliament   *227*

APPENDIX 4:

Federal Court of Canada Registry Offices   *261*

APPENDIX 5:

Privacy Impact Assessments: An Essential Tool for Data Protection   *265*

APPENDIX 6:

Examples of Privacy Codes   *275*

A — Sample Privacy Code for a Small Enterprise   *275*

B — TELUS Privacy Code   *285*

C — AIR MILES® Privacy Code   *299*

TABLE OF CASES   *307*

INDEX   *311*

ABOUT THE AUTHORS   *317*

FOREWORD

It is a truism that some of the most profound and far-reaching factors affecting social change frequently are little noticed or discussed while they are occurring, and it is only in the afterlight of experience that people look back to identify historic turning points that were apparent to only a few at the time.

I do not think it is an exaggeration to include in that category the passage last April by Parliament of Bill C-6, the *Personal Information Protection and Electronic Documents Act.* This statute, which came into effect on 1 January 2001, constitutes the first determined effort to place a check upon, and ultimately to reverse, the massive erosion of individual privacy rights brought about by the application of computer and communications technology in the commercial world.

The phenomenon of computer technology and its impact on personal information management of course has been widely recognized for several years, but despite pervasive public uneasiness, there was a widely held opinion among respectable authorities that nothing could be done to rein in the technological juggernaut. Bill C-6 has changed all that. It is an honourable, even courageous, initiative by Canada's Parliament, enacted in the face of substantial opposition by special interest groups. It comes not a moment too soon, given the long and unimpeded run the commercial world has enjoyed largely free of any legal restraints upon its usage of personal information.

It is my belief that this guide to the new statute soon will become a well-thumbed, standard reference for Canadian business, the legal profession, consumer groups, the academic community, and, given the care taken to ensure clarity and easy understanding, among the lay public as well. No one is better qualified to author such a volume than the persons who collaborated to produce it.

Heather Black was the legal adviser to the Department of Industry for the preparation of Bill C-6. Stephanie Perrin was the department's policy adviser on privacy issues. Between them, they have an unmatched knowledge of the bill. They were there — at the conception, gestation, and the final production of Bill C-6.

Many other fingerprints can be found upon this piece of legislation, of course. It could not be otherwise concerning a statute with such a long reach as this one. But it is only right and just to say that without the participation of Ms. Perrin and Ms. Black, the end result might well have been less satisfactory, particularly with respect to the provision of a mechanism for independent oversight.

The *Personal Information Protection and Electronic Documents Act* is by no means the end of problems associated with harnessing technology to serve social values such as privacy, as well as those of efficiency, economy, and public safety. Many issues, such as video surveillance and drug testing, to mention just two, remain mostly untouched. But it is an excellent beginning. I have no doubt it will be seen in time as a critical milestone in the long, hard march along the road towards the recognition and full restoration of the right to a private life as a foundation stone in a free and civilized society. All honour to those such as Black and Perrin who first set their feet upon it.

Bruce Phillips
Privacy Commissioner of Canada
1991–2000

INTRODUCTION

The title of this Act is the *Personal Information Protection and Electronic Documents Act,* and it received Royal Assent on 13 April 2000. Although its title focuses on electronic documents, Part 1 is entitled "Protection of Personal Information in the Private Sector" and in fact is about the protection of personal information in all formats. The Act is the culmination of a long history of research, consultation, and collaborative effort between the private sector, the Department of Industry and the former Department of Communications, and the Department of Justice. The privacy advocacy community and federal, provincial, and territorial privacy commissioners and ombudsmen were also involved in this long process of developing data protection for the private sector in Canada.

The issue of the protection of personal information first rose to prominence in the late 1960s and early 1970s, when computers were starting to become important tools for government and the large industries such as banking and credit reporting. The Department of Communications, newly formed in 1969, teamed up with the Department of Justice in 1972 to study the issue, and they subsequently published the report *Privacy and Computers*.[1] The authors of the report recommended that the *Human Rights Act* be extended to include the protection of personal information, and that eventually separate legislation might be necessary. In 1977 the *Canadian Human Rights Act*[2] was extended to include the protection of personal information in the public sector.

In the United States, the issues became important at about the same time, although the context was slightly different. During the early 1970s, the United States was in the throes of the Watergate investigation and the Pentagon Papers, and the emphasis in information policy was definitely on the side of the journalists and on access to information. The Privacy Pro-

---

[1] Department of Communications and Department of Justice, *Privacy and Computers: A Report of a Task Force* (Ottawa: Information Canada, 1972).

[2] R.S.C. 1985, c. H-6.

tection Study Commission was established in 1975 and recommended a federal privacy act with oversight in its 1977 report. The legislation was viewed more in the context of the need to protect personal information when releasing information subject to the new *Freedom of Information Act.*[3] As a result, the U.S. administration was less decisive in its commitment to privacy and established legislation for the federal public sector only, without an oversight body to supervise the implementation by government of the law.

In Europe, meanwhile, the Council of Europe had begun to address the issue because of the emergence of various federal and state data protection laws in the 1970s. Much of Europe had painful and recent memories of the abuses that could be made of personal information held in centralized registries, as had happened in the Nazi occupation during the Second World War. Therefore, Europeans had a natural desire for strong human rights protection that embraced all forms of personal information. In 1980 the Council of Europe passed Convention 108,[4] a binding convention that committed all signatory member states to introduce data protection legislation that contained a set of common principles. At the same time, the Organization for Economic Cooperation and Development (OECD) formed a committee to develop data protection principles and published in 1980 the OECD *Guidelines Governing the Protection of Privacy and Transborder Flows of Personal Data.*[5] These guidelines have become the root document for many privacy laws and codes of practice around the world, and they were used by Canada in the drafting of the federal *Privacy Act* of 1982.

When the federal *Privacy Act* [6] was passed, it applied only to records held by the federal government, just as in the United States. Regulating the public sector was seen as a bold enough step for the federal government, at a time when none of the provinces had taken even that basic step. Unlike most European data protection laws, the Act did not apply to the private sector. Canada did, however, establish a Privacy Commissioner and staff, separate from the Office of the Information Commissioner. Such a Privacy Commissioner, of course, had in effect existed since Part IV of the *Canadian Human Rights Act* had gone into effect in 1978. The federal departments of Justice and Foreign Affairs took the initiative to write to leading organizations in the private sector and urged them to adopt the OECD Guidelines in voluntary codes of practice. It is fair to say, however,

---

[3]   *Freedom of Information Act 1974,* 5 U.S.C. § 552.

[4]   *Convention for the Protection of Individuals with regard to the Automatic Processing of Personal Data,* E.T.S. No. 108, Strasbourg, 1981 [Convention 108]; see <http://conventions.coe.int/treaty/EN/cadreprincipal.htm>.

[5]   See Appendix 2 of this book.

[6]   R.S.C. 1985, c. P-21.

that most organizations at that time paid little more than lip service to privacy protection. Throughout the 1980s, the issue grew in importance, but it was not until the 1990s and the rapid expansion of telecommunications services, the interconnection of voice and data networks, and the emergence of the personal computer that privacy protection in the private sector became a number one public concern. Governments at all levels were unwilling to address the issue in the face of strong deregulatory pressures from industry, a reliance on market forces during expanding global free trade, and hard economic times.

At the end of the eighties, the European Community took stock of the compliance it had achieved through Convention 108,[7] assessed the emerging European Single Market where border controls and internal tariffs were to be dropped, and decided that it needed a new instrument to harmonize data protection legislation. The European Commission tabled a tough draft data protection directive, which demanded that member states implement data protection legislation to meet this new higher standard or suffer the directive to be applied by the European Community. It also provided that they must not transfer data to jurisdictions where there was inadequate data protection.

This directive sparked a huge controversy over the merits of self-regulation versus legislation, and whether a state had the right to insist on this kind of harmonization of legal and policy matters; this question may yet wind up being settled at the World Trade Organization. The principal protagonists in this discussion are the United States and the European Commission, although there is hardly a country in the world that will not ultimately be affected by the outcome, given the extent to which global data flow is necessary in today's economy.

In the light of this development, a very timely suggestion was made by David McKendry of Price Waterhouse to the Canadian Standards Association (CSA) to set up a technical committee to develop a standard for data protection, similar to the management standards that were being developed under ISO 9000. The committee was struck according to the fixed matrix composition that CSA follows for all its work, whether concerning fireproof pyjamas or reliable medical devices. This matrix was composed of consumer representatives, government at both federal and provincial levels, business representatives, and other organizations such as labour unions and professional associations.

The committee took the OECD Guidelines, divided itself into three groups, and set to work to update the guidelines and adapt them to Canadian realities. At this time, the Quebec government was just starting to hold parliamentary hearings about its own legislation, so the committee

---

[7]   Above note 4.

also factored in the work being done in Quebec, which ultimately culminated in Bill 68, an *Act Respecting the Protection of Personal Information in the Private Sector* in 1993.[8] Quebec has, in fact, been the leader in fashioning privacy protection for its citizens, including constitutional protection for "a right to respect for his private life" in section 5 of the *Quebec Charter of Human Rights and Freedoms.*[9]

In 1994 the Minister of Industry, John Manley, created the Information Highway Advisory Council to advise him on how Canada could most benefit from the Information Highway. In response to a public discussion paper, most consumer representatives, privacy commissioners, and privacy advocates replied that they wanted legislated privacy protection, while most businesses stated that they could self-regulate to the CSA Standard.[10] The draft standard was tabled for public comment in 1995 and was passed unanimously by the CSA Committee in September 1995. By this time, the Advisory Council had recommended to government that they develop flexible framework legislation based on the CSA Standard and work with the provinces to harmonize their efforts. This recommendation was accepted by the government in May 1996,[11] and the federal Department of Industry, in consultation with Justice, started work on the legislation.

A consultation paper was released in January 1998,[12] and once again the resounding cry from business was to use the CSA Standard as the basis for legislation. Many consumer representatives agreed this would be a good approach, although they generally also focused on some of the weaknesses of the CSA Standard. Everyone agreed on the need for harmonization from coast to coast, with the same rules for all, but there was not much useful advice on how to achieve this unity in Canada's challenging jurisdictional environment. When the government sifted through this advice and its policy imperatives, it arrived at the following requirements:

- The law must be based on the CSA Standard, which was a carefully crafted consensus document, with every clause negotiated but not drafted in legislative language.

---

[8] R.S.Q., c. P-39.1.

[9] R.S.Q., c. C-12, s. 5.

[10] *Privacy and the Canadian Information Highway: Building Canada's Information and Communications Infrastructure* (Ottawa: Industry Canada, 1994); see the summary of comments in *Privacy and the Canadian Information Highway: Review of Comments Received on the Industry Canada Discussion Paper* (Carleton Place, ON: Akay Information Consulting, 1995).

[11] *Building the Information Society: Moving Canada into the 21st Century* (Ottawa: Minister of Supply and Services Canada, 1996).

[12] *The Protection of Personal Information — Building Canada's Information Economy and Society* (Ottawa: Industry Canada/Justice Canada, 1998).

- The same marketplace rules must hold for the entire country, in a period where markets were rapidly converging and competitors who were historically under different jurisdictions were now entering each other's markets (banks and insurance, telecommunications carriers and Internet service providers, direct marketers in all sectors).
- The law must not set up new unjustified barriers to internal and international trade, and must not disadvantage responsible players by allowing data havens or offshore rivals to escape regulation.
- The Privacy Commissioner would be responsible for oversight, in a light flexible model. Not only should the implementation of the legislation be amenable to audit by independent third parties, but the Commissioner should also have authority to audit practices independent of any complaint.
- The heart of successful privacy protection lies in awareness of all parties of rights, expectations, responsibilities, and the actual facts of data processing and dataflow. There is a tremendous need for public education and awareness, and a vital role for the Privacy Commissioner to play.

Both the Department of Industry and the Department of Justice had various historical avenues for consulting with the provinces about how to achieve a harmonized approach to this problem. Industry Canada had used the Information Highway exercise to establish a working group of Information Highway Ministers, and the issue of how to address privacy had arisen. There was agreement that the CSA Standard was a useful approach, although Quebec had already legislated. The Minister of Industry had also led an initiative to dismantle internal barriers to trade, and there were ongoing meetings of this group. Consumer Ministers met regularly to discuss various matters, and privacy had arisen as an issue.

The concept of incorporating a standard within legislation is relatively rare. It is not unusual to regulate to a standard by specifying that organizations shall meet requirements of a standard (e.g., electrical wiring, polluting effluents, food and drugs). However, the notion of incorporating a management standard for the protection of personal information in a law is unique and has resulted in a law that many find difficult to understand at first glance. The policy reasons for this approach are addressed in chapter 1.

This guide addresses the legislation in logical order, namely by examining Schedule 1 first because the basic requirements for the protection of personal information are all contained in the standard, and the Act itself addresses exceptions and elaborations that are not self-explanatory without the core concepts of the standard being thoroughly understood first. The drafters of the Act had to provide more precision where the language was too general for a statute, and delete certain definitions and notes when policy had been introduced in non-statutory language. These issues are described in some detail in chapters 2 and 3.

CHAPTER 1

BACKGROUND TO THE ACT

The *Personal Information Protection and Electronic Documents Act* represents only the second use of the broad branch of the federal trade and commerce power in the last sixty-five years. Its use generated a storm of controversy in the provinces and prompted the provincial Ministers of Justice unanimously to ask the federal Minister of Justice, at a meeting in November 1998, to withdraw the bill. With juvenile crime and gun control legislation on the agenda, this was the only item on which the provincial Ministers achieved unanimity. It may well be imagined that this level of reaction was not unanticipated by the federal government, so the reasons why the government took this step are worth examining.

The federal government has been involved in the examination of the protection of privacy since 1971 when the Task Force on Privacy and Computers was struck by the then Department of Communications and the Department of Justice. The task force studied the information-handling practices of companies in Canada, as well as the federal government, and published the report *Privacy and Computers*[1] in 1972, recommending that the federal government regulate its own use of data banks before prescribing for the private sector. Although Part IV of the *Canadian Human Rights Act*[2] was an initial step in 1977, full coverage did not occur until 1982 when the federal *Privacy Act*[3] was passed. By this time, there was somewhat more pressure to regulate the private sector because many European states had developed data protection legislation for the private sector, but as free trade negotiations started around the world, there was a strong deregulatory push from industry that dissuaded at least North American governments from acting in any way to discourage the free flow of information.

---

[1] Department of Communications and Department of Justice, *Privacy and Computers: A Report of a Task Force* (Ottawa: Information Canada, 1972).

[2] R.S.C. 1985, c. H-6.

[3] R.S.C. 1985, c. P-21.

Prior to the 1970s, various international human rights documents had been produced that attempted to protect civil liberties and the protection of privacy. The *Universal Declaration of Human Rights* had been published in 1948,[4] and the *European Convention for the Protection of Human Rights and Fundamental Freedoms* followed in 1950.[5] The *International Covenant on Civil and Political Rights* was adopted in 1966 by the United Nations.[6] However, human rights experts recognized that these documents were too vague — particularly in the face of the growing sophistication of data processing — to ensure adequate protection of civil liberties in the area of personal data protection. The Council of Europe developed the *Convention for the Protection of Individuals with regard to the Automatic Processing of Personal Data*[7] to provide more specificity and harmonize developing data-protection legislation. It was largely in response to the development of this document, and to studies on data banks and data processing in a more economic sense, that the OECD member states decided to act.

The OECD Guidelines were in many ways a victory for the forces in favour of the free flow of information. A committee was established in 1978, chaired by the Honourable Mr. Justice Michael Kirby, Chairman of the Australian Law Reform Commission, to develop guidelines on basic rules governing transborder dataflow and the protection of personal data and privacy. The committee met over a series of meetings at the OECD offices in Paris and developed a set of eight principles that are still regarded as the fundamentals of fair information practices. The document that they produced also detailed the problems and issues they encountered, and it is well worth reading even now, twenty years later, to develop an understanding of the complexity of harmonizing differing country approaches to the treatment of personal information. The guidelines were developed in close consultation with the experts working at the Council of Europe on Convention 108, but the thrust of the OECD activity was non-regulatory, while the Council of Europe developed a set of similar principles that were to be implemented in national law.

This friction between the "free flow of data" and the legislated protection of human rights continued through the eighties and nineties, especially after the European Community tabled its proposal for a Council Directive concerning the protection of individuals in relation to the processing of per-

---

4   GA Res. 217 A(111), 10 December 1948, UN Doc. A/810 at 71 (1948); see <www.hrweb.org/legal/udhr.html>.

5   Rome, 4.XI.1950; see <http://conventions.coe.int/treaty/EN/cadreprincipal.htm>.

6   GA Res. 2200 A (XXI) 16 December 1966, 21 UN GAOR Supp. (No. 16) at 52, UN Doc. A/6316 (1966), 999 U.N.T.S. 171; see <www.hrweb.org/legal/cpr.html>.

7   E.T.S. No. 108, Strasbourg, 1981 [Convention 108]; see <http://conventions.coe.int/treaty/EN/cadreprincipal.htm>.

sonal data[8] in 1990. The draft directive threatened to oblige member states to implement tough data protection legislation that would be harmonized throughout the growing European Community, and to block data transfers to states that did not have "adequate protection." A vigorous debate commenced (and continues to this day) on what constituted "adequate protection." A final version of the directive was passed by the Council of Ministers in October 1995, coming into force in October 1998, and obliging all member states to block the flow of personal data to states without "adequate protection," subject to the derogations listed in Article 26.

The tensions of this debate were felt keenly in Canada, sitting as we do between the United States and Europe. As long as the United States maintained that self-regulation was the preferred approach to dealing with privacy issues, there was a strong view held by most of Canadian industry — particularly those industries controlled through head offices in the United States — that privacy legislation would be bad for business. Quebec followed the lead of Europe and in 1994 passed privacy legislation for the private sector, founded on a rather far-reaching right of privacy that had been entrenched in articles 35 to 41 of the *Civil Code*. The Quebec bill had originally contained provisions similar to those of the Directive to block the flow of data within Canada, if there were not adequate data protection, but these provisions were dropped in the final legislation. The direct marketing industry secured a broad exemption for the exchange of nominative lists, which tended to mitigate some of the biggest concerns of industry. Nevertheless, when the parties had clustered around the drafting table at the CSA back in 1992, there had been a certain amount of tension among them since none of these outcomes had been resolved as yet.

Bruce Phillips, the Privacy Commissioner of Canada appointed in 1991, was one of the early supporters of the CSA Code. In a letter dated 4 February 1992 to the president of the Canadian Standards Association, John Kean, Phillips warmly endorsed the initiative, recognizing the need to put more discipline into the codes of practice of the time. For several years, the previous commissioner, John Grace, had reported in his annual report to Parliament that self-regulation would suffice. In the first years of his office, Phillips also supported self-regulation, and his office was always willing to assess voluntary privacy codes that parties such as the Canadian Bankers Association and the Canadian Direct Marketing Association would bring to them. But by 1994, Bruce Phillips had reached the conclusion that self-regulation was not enough, and he started calling on the government to legislate broadly at the national level in his 1993–94 report:

---

8   Directive 95/46/EC of the European Parliament and of the Council of 24 October 1995 on the protection of individuals with regard to the processing of personal data and on the free movement of such data; OJ L281 (1995) at 0031–0050. See Appendix 3 of this book.

"What is desperately needed is national privacy legislation to establish the principles and framework for all the players."[9] By this time, Quebec had regulated, and it was clear that Canada would soon be experiencing the same kinds of harmonization issues that Europe had been undergoing for at least ten years.

The following year, Bruce Phillips stated:

> The greatest significance of the CSA Code may lie, not in its proposed form as a voluntary code for business, but in its embodiment into national framework legislation — a national standard of privacy protection against which all sectors can be held accountable. The Information Highway Advisory Council has recognized the code's place as the basis for legislation, coupled with an effective oversight mechanism. The Commissioner can only applaud.[10]

The drafting of the CSA Code took place largely during the two-year period from 1993 to 1995, when the lobbying against the European Directive was at its height, the Quebec law was going through the National Assembly, and the Information Highway exercise was taking place not just in Canada but around the world. It was a remarkable compromise. A discussion draft was circulated in 1995, and the final text was voted through unanimously in September 1995. The Office of the Privacy Commissioner of Canada abstained from voting for reasons relating to the protocol of the office, but not from applauding the passage of the code into the final accepted standard. Immediately afterwards, on 3 October 1995, the Canadian Direct Marketing Association became the first direct marketing association in the world to endorse privacy legislation. It issued a press release in which President John Gustavson stated:

> Fundamental changes in our society are taking place in an era of information technology . . . More and more we are seeing the inter-relation of databases and growth in the accumulation of transactional data. All Canadians have the right to know about and consent to the collection of personal information about them. And CDMA believes legislation is the most effective means of ensuring all private sector organizations adhere to the same basic rules in handling this information.[11]

---

9   *Annual Report of the Privacy Commissioner of Canada, 1993–94* (Ottawa: Canada Communication Group, 1994) at 6 (Cat. No. IP 30-1/1994 ISBN 0-662-61245-0).

10 *Annual Report of the Privacy Commissioner of Canada, 1994–95* (Ottawa: Canada Communication Group, 1995) at 15 (Cat. No. IP 30-1/1995 ISBN 0-662-61956-0).

11 CDMA, Press Release, "Direct marketers call for national privacy legislation" (3 October 1995).

The monkey was squarely on the federal government's back now. There were several reasons the CDMA may have chosen to call for legislation, but regardless of which were paramount, the move was politically astute. The CDMA itself was composed of a broad mix of members, some federally regulated, such as the banks and the telecommunications carriers; some provincially regulated, such as mailing list brokers and video rental chains. Sectoral regulation of privacy issues had already started to creep in, and the various members were already subject to differing rules about the use of personal information.

There had been a significant scandal in Canada concerning telemarketing calls, which had prompted various governments and consumer ministries to get together to try to regulate to protect consumers. The CDMA was well aware that another such scandal, perpetrated in all likelihood by a player who was not a member of its association and therefore not bound by its voluntary code, could prompt governments to legislate sectorally in a way that could be unpredictable and discriminatory to direct marketers. Furthermore, the CDMA was well aware from its many efforts to educate consumers on how to protect themselves from telemarketing fraud that the cost of education is enormous, and industry groups that need such public education are well served in a legislated environment where the costs are distributed among all players, including government. Finally, the CDMA had reached consensus on a standard that it could live with, and it was aware that the Information Highway Advisory Council had recommended legislating that standard. The CDMA was unlikely to get a better opportunity to achieve legislation harmonized to a standard it could live with.

In 1996, the Standards Council of Canada published the model code as a national standard for Canada: CAN/CSA-Q830-96.

In the meantime, the federal government had accepted the recommendation of the Information Highway Advisory Council to develop federal legislation based on the standard and to discuss harmonization with the provinces. One of the activities that was already in progress was a working group of the Uniform Law Conference of Canada (ULCC), headed by a member of the Information Law and Privacy section of the Department of Justice. They started work on a draft law that would serve as a model law and would reflect the CSA Standard. This process, being public, was very useful to get the advice and input of legal experts from the provinces and from the private sector, and the early drafts were used as discussion drafts by the Departments of Industry and Justice in their development of a draft bill. Incorporating the standard proved to be a tricky process, however, and the first drafts produced by the drafters were in fact based on the Quebec legislation, incorporating the principles of the CSA Code loosely. This incorporation was in fact so loose that the private sector members of the CSA Committee were quite agitated when the draft was circulated in the spring of 1998, largely because they had some difficulty detecting the standard in the text.

In January 1998 the Departments of Industry and Justice distributed a consultation paper on how best to legislate. Many parties endorsed the now current proposition of incorporating the CSA Standard, without fully appreciating the drafting challenges that this entailed. When the controversy erupted over the draft ULCC law that attempted to do precisely this, various positions became more clear. There is nothing like draft text to focus the mind on detail. Incorporating a standard in legislation that was written originally as a voluntary instrument is inherently difficult for a number of reasons.

First, the standard was a mix of recommendations and requirements, usually written as "shoulds" and "shalls." In the regime of voluntary standards, a "should" is often regarded as best practice and treated as a necessity unless there are strong reasons not to do so, but this kind of flexibility is not recognized in legal drafting.

Second, the definitions used in the standard do not follow legal drafting style, and in some cases (for instance, "consent"), they embodied policy decisions that would have been more appropriately addressed in the text of the code.

Third, there was a certain amount of repetition and cross-referencing in the code of practice that is problematic in legislation.

Fourth, two of the more difficult issues to decide were dealt with in the code as notes. These were the exceptions to the requirement for consent and the exceptions to the right of access. General statements using examples were incorporated as notes, partly because it was very difficult to reach agreement on text in the context of a voluntary exercise. These notes were too vague for the law, but since they contained very important exceptions, they had to be dealt with somehow. All these issues made the incorporation of the code in its totality an unattractive option from a legal drafting point of view. The ULCC drafters did not have to face the challenge of the scope of application because model laws do not deal with the issue, but that additional challenge certainly awaited the drafters of the federal law.

Why bother incorporating the standard at all, given these rather substantial obstacles? Why not just reflect the basic fair information practices, and rewrite them in legal drafting language? There are many critics of the bill who felt that this is what should have been done. Industry groups who participated in the drafting of the code, however, strongly felt otherwise, having fought hard for the compromises achieved in the code. Consumer groups sought stronger protections. Human rights groups wanted language that spoke of privacy as a fundamental human right. The government objectives for this legislation were several, however, and they were largely met by attaching the standard intact. Before addressing these objectives, let us examine the problems of scope and application.

The constitutional scope for federal action in protecting privacy is somewhat limited. Discussion of the issue in *Privacy and Computers*[12] pointed out the extensive power that the provinces have over property and civil rights, the ability of the federal Parliament to regulate banks, and the potential to regulate databank operators by imposing standards through the *Criminal Code*. It also pointed out the federal powers for regulating national undertakings such as telecommunications activities for matters of interprovincial and international dimensions, for trade and commerce, and for peace, order, and good government. The Department of Justice commissioned a study in 1994 by René Laperrière of the Groupe de Recherche, Informatique et Droit of the University of Quebec at Montreal. He explored various sectoral possibilities, mentioning rather briefly the same possibilities for a more expansive approach. In 1994 the Department of Industry commissioned a study on the possibilities for federal regulation because of the fundamental importance of communications in today's society.[13] That study recommended harmonized action but based on peace, order, and good government.

It is clear that the federal government has no power to legislate with respect to property and civil rights, so the kind of approach used by Quebec, based on a strong Civil Code, is out of the question. This does not mean that a right of privacy entrenched in the *Canadian Charter of Rights and Freedoms* would not be useful, but it is important to remember that the *Charter* only applies to Crown actions and so would hardly be useful in protecting the citizen in exchanges of personal information in the private sector.

A piece of human rights legislation that applied only to the federally regulated companies, notably banks and telecommunications companies, would do little to harmonize privacy protection in the marketplace, given that their competitors would be free of regulation. Furthermore, the biggest areas of concern at the time the legislation was contemplated were direct marketing and the Internet. It was not clear at the time that either of these players were predominantly federally regulated.

The trade and commerce powers of the federal government are broad and based on the concept that only Parliament can regulate matters that transcend provincial boundaries and cannot be regulated in a satisfactory manner by one or more provinces. It was the position taken by the federal government that the protection of personal information falls into this category for a number of reasons.

First, personal information and its use and exchange have become a fundamental part of doing business and indeed are the lifeblood of electronic

---

[12] Department of Communications and Department of Justice, *Privacy and Computers: A Report of a Task Force* (Ottawa: Information Canada, 1972).

[13] *Privacy and the Information Highway: Regulatory Options for Canada—A Study*, prepared by Ian Lawson in association with David Woods (Ottawa: Industry Canada, 1995).

commerce. Companies that cannot have access to customer and employee information, and process it where and when necessary, are at a disadvantage in today's highly competitive global economy. A credit card company may be collecting applications by printed forms mailed in or on an Internet site, and it may be processing the data in the Caribbean for a fraction of the cost of such transactions in Canada. It may be transmitting the data back electronically to other points in Canada. How can a province regulate such activities, relying on powers within the province? How can companies compete if they are unable to take advantage of global data-processing resources that cut costs?

Second, companies are unable to control dataflows within networks. When an employee of a company accesses a Web site, or sends an e-mail to a colleague who works at home, the data could be travelling around the world because of the nature of the Internet. In a world of dynamic communications, it is hard to predict where data will flow. This is an entirely different world than we had twenty years ago when most data still flowed in either paper format or on magnetic tapes. In the year 2000, most data flow electronically, through increasingly complex networks and chains of operators that were not dreamt of ten years ago.

Other federal states have addressed privacy issues at the national level also, basing their actions on other powers. Australia, for instance, has strong federal powers for international matters, and the issue of widespread transborder personal dataflows validates federal action in this area. The United States has not exercised much federal power in this area, but it is worth noting that after the states had regulated in various ways the issue of caller identification, the Federal Communications Commission stepped in and harmonized legislation by imposing its standards on the states. It is clear that this is not the optimal way to regulate, both from the perspective of industry, who have to change their observance of law, which usually involves cost, or from the perspective of federal-provincial relations.

The use of the trade and commerce powers facilitates the capture in the scope of the law of all commercial activity. Given the convergence of players in each other's markets, this is a good thing because it imposes the same rules on all parties, which is cheaper from a regulatory point of view and fairer from a competitive perspective. Furthermore, the exercise of the trade and commerce power, which covers goods involved in interprovincial and international trade, fills a gap in coverage that the provinces are unable to address. When personal data flow outside of a province, only the federal government has the power to intervene and regulate their collection, use, and disclosure. At the time of the tabling of this legislation as C-54 in 1998, Quebec companies were already subject to strong sanctions under the Quebec Bill 68 if they failed to protect the information of Quebeckers when it left the province, but the Commissioner was unable to investigate outside the province or correct the practices of the non-Quebec companies involved. Personal data that are used in commerce flow through a number of complex relationships, mostly protected by contract but often several steps from the original organization that has the relationship with the customer. It is vital that someone be able to follow the chain of interactions.

Given that data flow around the world, often in the most trivial day-to-day transactions, and that only the federal government has the power to regulate in these international matters, it was important that the government act. However, large quantities of sensitive personal information are collected in several areas where the federal government does not have the power to act. The first is health information, which is largely a provincial matter because the information is generated and held in publicly funded hospital and medical systems. The second is education, squarely a provincial responsibility except in the matter of commercial training enterprises. The third is employee data, with the exception of federally regulated employees. The question naturally arose: How do we incite action that will protect these data?

Quebec had already legislated to protect this information, but no other province had taken notice; and it was unlikely that they would follow the Quebec formula, based on the *Civil Code*, because of the inherent differences between the civil and common law systems. At the time of the announced decision to legislate, there was no sign of imminent provincial action; in fact, several provinces had not even legislated to protect personal information held in the public sector. If it takes over fifteen years to follow the federal lead to protect the privacy of your citizens when you are the custodian and have a fiduciary responsibility, how long would it take before provinces would move to curb the abuse of information in the private sector, where there are strong competitive and trade reasons to create data havens? Given the Canadian federal provincial landscape, this is akin to asking one of those "How long does it take to screw in a light bulb?" questions.

Returning to the policy objectives of the federal government, there were a number of sound reasons for incorporating the standard intact. First, much of the data that Canadians felt strongly about didn't fall under the jurisdiction of the federal government, either because these data were intrinsically provincial, as in the case of educational records, or because they were being held in a foreign country, usually the United States. Having watched the efforts of the European Union to impose harmonization on its members, and to prevent the unfair competition that would ensue if foreign competitors could remove data from the territory without obligations to protect, it seemed clear that agreeing on the foundation of protection was a vital first step. Using the standard — an updated version of the OECD Guidelines — could not only avoid endless debate over redrafting the principles in a law, but could be transferred across jurisdictions and legal regimes far more easily.

International standards are the agreed method of resolving trade disputes in many areas, from food labelling to telecommunications equipment, so why not focus on a data protection standard? It is important in
trade disputes to have a mechanism to prove that you are not imposing
conditions on your trade partners that exceed those you impose on your
own companies, or that force them to adapt your approach to issues. Con-
forming to a standard, either through regulatory action or through contractual obligation that is capable of independent assessment through
internationally recognized audit systems, seems an eminently sensible way
to approach this problem. It is unfortunate that international discussion of
the issues, dating apparently from the early days of the OECD Guidelines
and Convention 108, has tended to get hung up on the issue of self-regulation versus legislation. In this respect, recent progress in the "Safe Harbor" discussions between the European Commission and the United States
is heading in the direction of clearly defined obligations and independent
oversight. A standard might be more useful as an instrument than the "frequently asked questions" that they have employed to provide precision.

Second, the mechanism of harmonization would have to be multivalent,
capable of being referenced in regulatory regimes, in sectoral legislation, or in
contract. A standard provides that flexibility, but only if you leave it intact.
Once rewritten or incorporated into law in a changed format, the natural
human tendency to try and improve on another's text and rewrite to suit the
circumstances takes over. Empirically, this may make for better data protection legislation, and a better fit to each unique environment, but it raises hur-
dles and expense for business. Consumer advocates, perhaps naively, always
are optimistic that they will make progress in getting better protection at each
new regulatory skirmish, but there is plenty of evidence to suggest the oppo-
site would hold true, especially as data mining and customer relationship
management become more entrenched in the information economy.

Third, there is a huge challenge in applying standards in the technological arena that give voice to the principles of privacy protection iterated in
legal fora. Lawyers and technical standards-setting bodies, usually peopled
with engineers and technologists, often have a hard time translating each
other's objectives and detailed requirements at the ground level; in fact, in
many cases in the privacy arena, there simply has not even been a dialogue.
Technical standards for cryptographic systems, digital signatures, public
key architectures, call signalling systems, and wireless law enforcement
access are usually made without the benefit of privacy and human rights
experts contributing to the product. The emergence of privacy standards
at the management level can only help illuminate standards at the technical level, by at least providing reference documents that may be reflected in
specific technical requirements. It would be better if this dialogue grew
and a more multidisciplinary approach to standards setting were to evolve.

The reverse is equally true. When the European Directive concerning the processing of personal data and the protection of privacy in the tele-communications sector[14] first saw the light in 1990 as draft directive SYN 287, there was an outcry from the telecommunications companies in North America that the legal requirements for protecting privacy had been developed with no regard to developing standards in switching equipment. There was some grumbling that the directive was a thinly disguised trade barrier to keep newer switches out of Europe. Whether or not there was any truth to this allegation, it is certainly equally important for legal experts to avail themselves of a spectrum of technical expertise when they develop requirements that must be implemented in technology.

Fourth, to return to the question of how to incite the provinces to move in this area, the standard is a politically neutral instrument, having been developed largely by industry, with representation from provinces, consumer groups, and provincial privacy commissioners. The federal gov-ernment made the decision to invoke the trade and commerce power but decided to encourage the provinces to act by exempting intraprovincial collection, use, and disclosure where a province had acted in a "substan-tially similar" manner. The standard forms the basis for determining whether protection is substantially similar.

For all these reasons, with the full support of the industry players who contributed to the CSA Standard, but to the great bewilderment of pri-vacy experts and legal scholars everywhere, the drafters of this legislation set about the task of incorporating the text of the standard intact in the law. It was decided to incorporate it as a Schedule and make the modifica-tions in the body of the law that would inevitably be required to retrofit the language of the code to a legal text.

---

14   Directive 97/66/EC of the European Parliament and of the Council of 15 December 1997, available at <http://158.169.50.95:10080/legal/en/dataprot/protection.html>.

CHAPTER 2

PART 1: SCHEDULE 1

A. The Incorporation of the CSA Standard as the Schedule

The opening sections of the Act, after the title in section 1, deal with the definitions (section 2), the purpose (section 3), and the scope and application (section 4). These sections are dealt with in chapter 3. In this chapter, we will discuss the principles and commentary in the CSA Model Code for the Protection of Personal Information, found in Schedule 1 of the Act. The code is the heart of the Act, and it is essential that it be read first to understand the operation of the provisions in the body of the legislation.

Subsection 5(1) of the Act provides that subject to the provisions stipulated in sections 6 to 9, every organization shall comply with the obligations set out in Schedule 1. The Schedule states that these are the principles set out in the National Standard of Canada entitled the Model Code for the Protection of Personal Information, CAN/CSA-Q830-96. The Schedule starts at clause 4 of the CSA Standard, omitting the overview at the beginning and the definitions. The definitions as drafted in the standard were not appropriate for legislation because they incorporated policy and guidance. To more thoroughly understand how the standard works as an instrument for the management of personal information, we will examine it in detail here.

The standard was conceived as a voluntary instrument to guide business and other organizations in the management of personal information, and in respecting the rights of the individuals with whom they deal. There was great diversity in the membership of the CSA Technical Committee, so it was natural that there would be many conflicting goals. Industry members, tasked with managing the privacy issue for their organizations, were generally keenly interested in achieving an instrument that would forestall regulation, that would be easy to understand and apply, and that would allow their organizations to continue to function with information assets they currently held.

It is fair to say that consumer representatives regarded the exercise of drafting a voluntary standard as inferior to law, but worthwhile in getting decent practices in place and drawing attention to the issue. Most of the consumer representatives were from the province of Quebec, and during the drafting process they were busy working on the Quebec legislation, eventually Bill 68, *An Act Respecting the Protection of Personal Information in the Private Sector,*[1] so there was a lively cross-fertilization of the concepts that business wished to see in the code versus the protections that consumer advocates and government representatives were introducing from the European Directive[2] or the Quebec legislation.

Privacy experts and academics, accustomed to the concepts of data protection law and the language and rhetoric of human rights, were initially quite sceptical of the utility of the exercise; some still are. The standards community were interested, particularly those involved in security and information technology because they were being asked to build systems that respected privacy or that respected legislation, and they needed an intermediary document that explained what those basic specifications were in the form of fair information practices. Auditors, in the form of accounting firms, were interested in the process because they could foresee eventual new revenue streams from the auditing of information practices.

The process involved the committee as a whole dividing into three groups, each one examining a portion of the OECD Guidelines with a view to updating them and adapting them to the Canadian legal environment and to the scope of the exercise. Then a drafting committee was struck to boil this down into a new document. Although the process took two years, it was not a simple task to draft a code that could achieve consensus in this group, and all members were satisfied that although not perfect, the final product was very good.

The code comprises ten interrelated principles that should not be read in isolation from each other. Each principle is followed by explanatory paragraphs that give further detail, impose further distinct obligations, and in some cases provide guidance in both interpretation and procedures. In addition to this, two principles have explanatory notes, which qualify the binding nature of the obligation. These notes have been dispensed with in the Act through the use of the phrase "despite the note" in those sections of the Act which deal with the exceptions to the obligations (see subsections 7(1), (2), & (3), and subsection 9(3)). However, when the code was drafted, the notes were necessary to incorporate and illuminate concepts that could not be agreed upon in any other way — that is, within

---

[1]   R.S.Q., c. P-39.1.

[2]   Directive 95/46/EC of the European Parliament and of the Council of 24 October 1995 on the protection of individuals with regard to the processing of personal data and on the free movement of such data; OJ L281 (1995) at 0031–0050. See Appendix 3 of this book.

the primary principles or as subparagraphs. Although not useful as a tool for legal interpretation, they have been left in the Schedule to keep the standard intact.

Incorporating the standard intact was a major challenge for the drafting team, but it was considered worth doing for the following reasons:

- There was considerable support for the standard, from both consumer advocates and business.
- Some businesses had already developed company codes based on the standard.
- It was recognized that focusing on a recognized set of fair information practices that were relatively easy to communicate decreased the very significant education costs of compliance for both staff and the public.
- Standards are the method of choice for promoting harmonization of international trade practices. Promoting common adherence to a standard is more palatable and ultimately more successful than insisting other jurisdictions apply the first party's legislation extraterritorially.

B. Commentary to Schedule 1

SCHEDULE 1	COMMENTARY

Principle 1 — Accountability

4.1
An organization is responsible for personal information under its control and shall designate an individual or individuals who are accountable for the organization's compliance with the following principles.

4.1.1
Accountability for the organization's compliance with the principles rests with the designated individual(s), even though other individuals within the organization may be responsible for the day-to-day collection and processing of personal information. In addition, other individuals within the organization may be delegated to act on behalf of the designated individual(s).

The first decision of the committee was to make accountability the first principle and the cornerstone of the code. Each organization is responsible for the personal information in its care and must name someone who will be accountable for compliance. Although others are responsible for the collection and processing of personal information, and the designated officer may delegate his powers to others to act for him, the designated officer is accountable.

4.1.2
The identity of the individual(s) designated by the organization to oversee the organization's compliance with the principles shall be made known upon request.

The name and coordinates of that designated officer must be available on request.

4.1.3
An organization is responsible for personal information in its possession or custody, including information that has been transferred to a third party for processing. The organization shall use contractual or other means to provide a comparable level of protection while the information is being processed by a third party.

Clause 4.1.3 is important because it is the only area in the Act where transborder dataflow issues are addressed. An organization remains responsible for information in its possession or custody, including information that has been transferred to a third party for processing. The concept of custody and transfer is an important one, as opposed to disclosure, because when an organization discloses information, it must assure itself that it has the right to disclose, and once that is fulfilled and the disclosure has taken place securely, its responsibility is at an end.

However, if the information has been transferred for processing of any kind, and the organization expects to maintain an interest in the data, it retains responsibility and must use contractual or other means to provide a comparable level of protection.

Although this clause was drafted before the development of the Internet as the engine of electronic commerce, it works particularly well in the new global environment of the collection and sharing of data through Internet browsers. The word "processing" was chosen because it was as technologically neutral as possible, and when used in the sense that it is used in the British *Data Protection Act*[3] to refer to all kinds of data use and manipulation, it provides a simple broad rule. Contracts referring to the obligations of the standard would be appropriate when dealing with business partners, contractors, or data processing operations, while "other" anticipates the possibility that in cases of parent companies or affiliates, all parties may be required to comply with the same data protection code so that separate contracts between parties are not necessary.

---

[3]   *Data Protection Act 1984*, c. 35.

4.1.4

Organizations shall implement policies and practices to give effect to the principles, including

(a) implementing procedures to protect personal information;

(b) establishing procedures to receive and respond to complaints and inquiries;

(c) training staff and communicating to staff information about the organization's policies and practices; and

(d) developing information to explain the organization's policies and procedures.

Clause 4.1.4 is an unusual innovation in a data protection statute. It requires organizations to implement policies and practices to give effect to the principles, including the key areas of implementing actual procedures to protect personal information, establishing complaints and enquiries procedures, training staff, and developing information materials that provide transparency about policies and procedures.

Although it may sound burdensome to those unaccustomed to concepts of data protection, those with experience in trying to ensure compliance to privacy policies know all too well that the organization that does not know what its practices are is unlikely to be adhering to the commitments it has made, whether those commitments are in the form of adherence to national law, to customer service standards, or to a Web privacy policy.

This requirement is a key provision of the standard and of the legislation, not simply because it represents workload and obligations. If properly done, a good privacy policy, based on this standard, will lead logically to the development of sound information management procedures, clearer security procedures and practices, and ultimately cost savings in the area of reduction of the collection and management of unnecessary information.

When the clause was crafted at the CSA Standards Committee, it was novel, but now, largely as a result of the growing role of auditors in verifying compliance to self-regulation and professed policies, the requirement to actually operationalize fair information practices is recognized. The agreement between the European Union and the United States to accept the "Safe Harbor" principles and the oversight of the Federal Trade Commission will add a further impetus to the need for verifiable practices and procedures.

Principle 2 — Identifying Purposes

4.2

The purposes for which personal information is collected shall be identified by the organization at or before the time the information is collected.

4.2.1

The organization shall document the purposes for which personal information is collected in order to comply with the Openness principle (Clause 4.8) and the Individual Access principle (Clause 4.9).

4.2.2

Identifying the purposes for which personal information is collected at or before the time of collection allows organizations to determine the information they need to collect to fulfil these purposes. The Limiting Collection principle (Clause 4.4) requires an organization to collect only that information necessary for the purposes that have been identified.

The standard requires that organizations identify the purposes for which they are collecting, using, and disclosing personal information, but is silent on the issue of whether those purposes are legitimate, fair, lawful, or acceptable to the individuals whose information is involved.

The determination of this issue, which is at the heart of many information privacy conflicts, was relegated to the consent clause. Rather than attempt to dictate what types of purposes were acceptable, or find a way to constrain them in a voluntary codes environment, the committee agreed that the decision to consent to the collection, use, and disclosure of information rested with the individual. Emphasis was placed on the openness provisions and accountability clauses, which were made rigorous enough to ensure that the individual would have ample opportunity to find out what was being done with his information, and thus could make an informed decision.

The rationale was that if an organization was prepared to state its purposes, and felt it could justify a purpose for collection, use, and disclosure to its customers and the public at large, it should be free to proceed with the management of information to achieve that purpose.

There was a great deal of criticism of this looseness of purpose from privacy advocates at the time, but the OECD Guidelines on which the code is based were less strict, and the public sector Acts in Canada do not impose constraints on purpose on a file either. The Quebec private sector legislation[4] deals with the issue in the following way:

---

[4]   R.S.Q., c. P-39.1, s. 8.

8. A person who collects personal information from the person concerned must, when establishing a file on that person, inform him

(1) of the object of the file;

(2) of the use which will be made of the information and the categories of persons who will have access to it within the enterprise;

(3) of the place where the file will be kept and of the rights of access and rectification.

The only constraint on purpose appears in section 23 when an enterprise must provide an opt-out to individuals who do not wish their information on a "nominative list" to be used "for purposes of commercial or philanthropic prospection."

The Industry Committee of the House of Commons, which was charged with reviewing Bill C-54 after introduction in the House in October 1998, decided that in a legislative framework with oversight, it was quite appropriate to impose further restraint on the identification of purposes, and added subsection 5(3) of the Act, the purpose justification section. The operation of this section will be discussed later. The obligations of this clause with respect to purposes are thus limited to the following rather narrow obligations:

- The purposes must be identified by the organization at or before the time of collection, but there is no mandatory time constraint in documenting them mentioned in this principle.
- It is not mandatory to inform the individual of the purposes of the collection, use, and disclosure at the time of collection, although it is recommended. This flexibility allows for the reality that not all information is collected directly from the individual in a conscious way, and that there is considerable burden in discussing the purposes of each information item with the individual.

4.2.3
The identified purposes should be specified at or before the time of collection to the individual from whom the personal information is collected. Depending upon the way in which the information is collected, this can be done orally or in writing. An application form, for example, may give notice of the purposes.

For instance, if an individual orders a videotape at 1:00 A.M. while watching a late movie (by dialing a 1-800 number), it is likely that the call centre will time-stamp that order in some way, or that the transaction logs would enable someone to determine that the individual had made the call at a certain time from a certain telephone. This is certainly personal information: it is gathered for legitimate accountability purposes, but it is unlikely that the average individual would want to discuss this collection over the telephone at that hour.

Information that is gathered through an application form is another matter, however, and it is recommended and in fact anticipated by the individual that some reason be given for the collection of the data elements on a form. On Internet forms today, it is common to have mandatory fields and other optional ones, such as income and family size. All the purposes behind those collections would have to be documented, and since it would be trivially easy to link to the policy and practices that explain the collection, it would be expected that this opportunity should be offered to the individual.

New Purpose

4.2.4
When personal information that has been collected is to be used for a purpose not previously identified, the new purpose shall be identified prior to use. Unless the new purpose is required by law, the consent of the individual is required before information can be used for that purpose. For an elaboration on consent, please refer to the Consent principle (Clause 4.3).

When information that has been gathered for one purpose is to be used for a different purpose, that new purpose must be identified, and unless the purpose is to comply with a law, the consent of the individual must be sought. For instance, in the above example of the videotape purchase, it is entirely possible that during the investigation of a crime, a law enforcement official might want to ascertain the content of a particular phone call made from a residence, and might subpoena the logs of the call centre and attempt to find the individual who took the call or any records indicating the duration of the call. Clearly, the disclosure of the records to the law enforcement official was not anticipated and is a new purpose for the records, but consent would nevertheless not be sought from the individual.

We are now living through times of rapidly expanding uses of data mining techniques. There are many large databases of customer information gathered from loyalty cards or other types of transactional data gathering, and rarely, if ever, do the owners of such databases seek consent for the use of that data for anything but further direct marketing opportunities. Usually those statements refer to "similar quality organizations" or some other euphemism for their list clients. Not every individual who ticks off the box to agree to receive other offers would anticipate that the government, credit grantors, or other perhaps hostile groups might be able to purchase the information.

These statements will have to be much more detailed, explicit, and particular to comply with this clause (4.3.2), or the organization will have to go back and seek a fresh consent from the individual to release the information.

4.2.5
Persons collecting personal information should be able to explain to individuals the purposes for which the information is being collected.

Clause 4.2.5 is not mandatory; it merely states that those gathering the information should be able to explain the purposes of the information collection to the individual. This recognizes the economic reality that often the uses of information can be detailed and subtle, yet the individuals gathering data are unlikely to be senior in the organization, or best able to express company policies and procedures. The organization is accountable to be transparent about its purposes and practices, but it may designate particular individuals to perform that task.

4.2.6
This principle is linked closely to the Limiting Collection principle (Clause 4.4) and the Limiting Use, Disclosure, and Retention principle (Clause 4.5).

Clause 4.2.6 underscores the interlinkage of the principles and the need to limit collection, use, and disclosure to the stated purposes.

Principle 3 — Consent

4.3
The knowledge and consent of the individual are required for the collection, use, or disclosure of personal information, except where inappropriate.

Note: In certain circumstances personal information can be collected, used, or disclosed without the knowledge and consent of the individual. For example, legal, medical, or security reasons may make it impossible or impractical to seek consent. When information is being collected for the detection and prevention of fraud or for law enforcement, seeking the consent of the individual might defeat the purpose of collecting the information. Seeking consent may be impossible or inappropriate when the individual is a minor, seriously ill, or mentally incapacitated. In addition, organizations that do not have a direct relationship with the individual may not always be able to seek consent. For example, seeking consent may be impractical for a charity or a direct-marketing firm that wishes to acquire a mailing list from another organization. In such cases, the organization providing the list would be expected to obtain consent before disclosing personal information.

Those who are unfamiliar with data protection law are inclined to regard clause 4.3 as weak; in fact, during the debate in the Industry Committee of the House of Commons, this allegation was made numerous times. It is useful to review just how much consent actually exists in data protection statutes to appreciate the strides that were made by the CSA Committee in crafting this clause.

To begin with, the OECD Guidelines on which the code is based have only this to say about consent, under the collection limitation principle:

> There should be limits to the collection of personal data and any such data should be obtained by lawful and fair means and, where appropriate, with the knowledge or consent of the data subject.

The Use Limitation principle of the OECD Guidelines states that personal data should not be disclosed or used for purposes other than those originally specified, unless with the consent of the data subject or by authority of law.

The CSA Code, on the other hand, while not going so far as to demand "informed consent," insists on both knowledge of the data subject and consent, for collection, use, and disclosure. The note seeks to explain the expression "where appropriate," and though this is helpful in comprehending the intent of the code, it is not sufficient for a law, and thus section 7 of the Act instructs us to disregard the note. The only situations where an organization may collect, use, or disclose without the consent of the data subject are specified in subsections 7(1), 7(2), and 7(3), respectively.

A law that is based on consent creates a number of tensions for those responsible for its implementation: How can you ensure that the individual has an opportunity to exercise his or her free will in providing personal data? How do you provide for those situations when you are in an adversarial situation vis-à-vis the individual, as in a fraud investigation? Is there some information that is so sensitive that it should be protected from voluntary disclosure, by forbidding organizations to gather it? For instance, in Canada we do not allow people to sell their kidneys — should there be similar limits to prevent them from selling their DNA? How do you ensure that basic rights are always protected, particularly when the individuals are not aware of the value, sensitivity, or interpretations that are being placed on the data?

These are not easy questions to answer, and a decision in one direction often requires exemptions or exceptions to provide for all situations. The CSA Committee decided that consent would be the cornerstone of the code, and that there would be no differentiation between "sensitive" data and other kinds of data. It is extremely difficult to determine *a priori* what is sensitive information, for people tend to have different views on what they consider most sensitive, and the matter can vary from one context to another.

Medical information, often recognized as the most sensitive information, provides an excellent example. If an individual suffers from a plantar's wart and from high blood pressure, he might freely tell his employer about the plantar's wart, but not the high blood pressure, and yet do the reverse with his dinner date ... and feel strongly about his privacy in both situations. It was thought safest to let individuals decide what is sensitive in which circumstances by giving them control of the information based on the right of consent.

4.3.1

Consent is required for the collection of personal information and the subsequent use or disclosure of this information. Typically, an organization will seek consent for the use or disclosure of the information at the time of collection. In certain circumstances, consent with respect to use or disclosure may be sought after the information has been collected but before use (for example, when an organization wants to use information for a purpose not previously identified).

Clause 4.3.1 points out that the consent for collection, use, and disclosure should be sought at the time of collection, but that in certain circumstances the consent for a use or disclosure may be sought afterwards, for instance when a new purpose has been identified. In most circumstances when one becomes a new customer, the organization does not immediately seek consent for marketing a whole range of services; they wait for the relationship to grow and ask for permission to use the information for marketing or further analysis later.

The note gives an example of marketing lists, stating that it would be impractical for an organization such as a charity that was purchasing a mailing list, to seek the consent of each individual on the list before mailing information to him or her. It says: "In such cases, the organization would be expected to obtain consent before disclosing the information." This is an important and at times confusing concept: the consent is transferable. An organization can obtain the consent of the individual for its own use of the data, and for anticipated uses of the data by the immediate recipients to whom they intend to disclose the data. This consent for subsequent use and disclosure then travels with the data, or is transferable.

Obviously, the restriction of collection, use, and disclosure for the same purpose applies, and the need to obtain consent as described in 4.2.4 is triggered once again by any change in purpose between the two organizations.

In summary, every organization must have the consent of individuals for the collection, use, and disclosure of their information for the stated purposes. If they are unable to get the consent of the individuals themselves because they do not have a relationship with them, the third party from whom they are getting the information must obtain the consent of the individuals. The consent would cover the purposes for which the second organization plans to use the information, as well as the disclosure to that organization.

Most of the transparency clauses that appear in marketing information, data collection instruments, and contracts are first or second generation — that is, they have been put in to comply with rather basic privacy policies or fair information practices. This Act will force organizations to examine their data sharing arrangements and make sure not only that they are obtaining a valid consent, but also that they have been fully transparent to their clients so that the consent may be considered sufficient for further disclosures and uses by their business partners.

4.3.2

The principle requires "knowledge and consent." Organizations shall make a reasonable effort to ensure that the individual is advised of the purposes for which the information will be used. To make the consent meaningful, the purposes must be stated in such a manner that the individual can reasonably understand how the information will be used or disclosed.

Clause 4.3.2 amplifies the concept of "knowledge" and ties it to purpose by stating that organizations must make "a reasonable effort" to ensure that the individual is advised of the purposes for which the information is used. These purposes "must be stated in such a manner that the individual can reasonably understand how the information will be used or disclosed." This is an obligation that goes beyond purpose, to ensuring that the individual understands what is happening to his information.

Although the code avoids using the expression "informed consent," in fact this clause imposes an obligation that comes very close to the notion of informed consent. For example, it would not suffice to describe the purpose of collecting and mining all of a customer's purchase details as "marketing products and services" if in fact a company used the information to create complex profiles that were not related to selling items of their inventory, and made these profiles available to others, such as government agencies.

4.3.3

An organization shall not, as a condition of the supply of a product or service, require an individual to consent to the collection, use, or disclosure of information beyond that required to fulfil the explicitly specified, and legitimate purposes.

Clause 4.3.3 was dubbed the "refusal to deal clause" by the CSA Committee and was the subject of much debate. Consumer advocates were adamant that if there were to be no "relevancy" requirement, or test to determine whether each data element was in fact required and therefore its collection and use permissible, then there must be a clause to stop organizations from asking for information that is not necessary, and refusing service if the individual did not comply. In fact the collection limitation clause (4.4) is very strict, but the problem in the code stems from the lack of restraint on the purpose clause, to which collection is strongly linked.

This particular linkage is a good example of what has been described as the "fugue-like" nature of the CSA Code; particular themes are carried from one principle to another and are reinforced in one section whereas they might appear to be rather weak in another section where they were introduced. This characteristic was well recognized by the Committee, and was reinforced in clause 3.1, General Requirements (of the Code): "The ten principles that make up this Standard are interrelated. Organizations adopting this Standard shall adhere to the ten principles as a whole."

The refusal to deal clause is clear and quite strong. An organization shall not require an individual to consent to the collection, use, or disclosure of information beyond that which is necessary to fulfil the *explicitly specified, and legitimate purposes.* This language in fact does not appear in the purpose specification clause, which is very neutral with respect to purposes and in fact offers no rationale to evaluate them as legitimate or otherwise. The message is clear: if you are planning to deny a service to someone for failure to provide information, the information must be necessary to fulfil a legitimate and specific purpose, not an overly broad or inflated one. Subsection 5(3) of the Act now provides further means of determining what is a "legitimate" purpose by establishing the reasonable person test.

In light of these issues, clause 4.3.5 would have followed more logically at this point because it discusses the expectations of the individual as to the uses and possible disclosure of her or his information.

4.3.4

The form of the consent sought by the organization may vary, depending upon the circumstances and the type of information. In determining the form of consent to use, organizations shall take into account the sensitivity of the information. Although some information (for example, medical records and income records) is almost always considered to be sensitive, any information can be sensitive, depending on the context. For example, the names and addresses of subscribers to a newsmagazine would generally not be considered sensitive information. However, the names and addresses of subscribers to some special-interest magazines might be considered sensitive.

Clause 4.3.4 discusses the form of the consent and permits variance depending on sensitivity. Examples are given of when information might be considered sensitive, and the importance of context is emphasized. The example cited is that of a magazine subscription, where a news magazine would generally not be considered sensitive. Specialty magazines, such as newsletters on certain diseases, religious periodicals, or gambling would likely be considered sensitive.

4.3.5

In obtaining consent, the reasonable expectations of the individual are also relevant. For example, an individual buying a subscription to a magazine should reasonably expect that the organization, in addition to using the individual's name and address for mailing and billing purposes, would also contact the person to solicit the renewal of the subscription. In this case, the organization can assume that the individual's request constitutes consent for specific purposes. On the other hand, an individual would not reasonably expect that personal information given to a health-care professional would be given to a company selling health-care products, unless consent were obtained. Consent shall not be obtained through deception.

Certainly, the reasonable expectations of the individual described in clause 4.3.5 are important to these evaluations. This section is purely discursive, giving examples of what an individual might expect to have happen to his information. The last line, however, is an obligation not to obtain information through deception.

4.3.6

The way in which an organization seeks consent may vary, depending on the circumstances and the type of information collected. An organization should generally seek express consent when the information is likely to be considered sensitive. Implied consent would generally be appropriate when the information is less sensitive. Consent can also be given by an authorized representative (such as a legal guardian or a person having power of attorney).

Clause 4.3.6 discusses the method of obtaining consent. The code had definitions for express and implied consent that were omitted from the law because they embodied policy. The clause states that express consent is "generally" required when the information is considered sensitive, whereas implied consent would "generally be appropriate" when the information is less sensitive.

We have discussed the problems of determining what is sensitive above in clause 4.3.4. The problem is: What is express consent? What is implied consent? Absent the definitions, and given that this clause contains no obligations (shalls) but only provides advice, organizations relying on the concept of implied consent should be very diligent in ensuring that they are fully transparent and in compliance with the openness principle.

Express consent means that the individual has explicitly indicated his consent to the collection, use, or disclosure of the information. Note that these actions are separate, and consent is required for each. This consent could be in writing or orally, but there has to be a substantive "yes, you may use my information." Implied consent means that the individual can reasonably be assumed to have consented to the use of his information, and that reasonable assumption usually rests on how well informed the individual was about the collection, use, or disclosure of the personal information. Absent express consent, the organization would have to be able to demonstrate that the individual had every opportunity to know that his information was going to be collected and used, and for what purposes, and that armed with this information, the individual persisted with the action that resulted in the information flow.

Good examples of clear implied consent are rare, but one which came up during the drafting of the code was the use of a debit card that was mailed to an existing customer of a bank. The customer had a first-generation debit card that only allowed him access to his savings account, and the second-generation cards were mailed out when the old ones were about to expire. The new cards offered additional features, such as the ability to pay a credit card using the card at a new and improved automated bank machine. Does the customer need to complete a signed consent to the matching of his banking data with his credit card data, or can he simply use the new card at the machine and thereby imply his consent for the release of the information to fulfil the new purpose?

Most customers would prefer to have the new service immediately; they do not want to fill out more forms. The code and the law allow this, but the problem then becomes one of ensuring that the individual is well enough informed that one can reasonably construe conscious consent. Sometimes it is easier to ask for a signature than to build an information structure around an action that is rigorous enough to prove knowledge on the part of the actor.

Clause 4.3.6 also allows consent through an authorized person, such as a legal guardian. Who may act for another person is not addressed in this law because this matter falls under provincial jurisdiction. There are also no particular provisions for children.

4.3.7

Individuals can give consent in many ways. For example:

(a) an application form may be used to seek consent, collect information, and inform the individual of the use that will be made of the information. By completing and signing the form, the individual is giving consent to the collection and the specified uses;

(b) a checkoff box may be used to allow individuals to request that their names and addresses not be given to other organizations. Individuals who do not check the box are assumed to consent to the transfer of this information to third parties;

(c) consent may be given orally when information is collected over the telephone; or

(d) consent may be given at the time that individuals use a product or service.

4.3.8

An individual may withdraw consent at any time, subject to legal or contractual restrictions and reasonable notice. The organization shall inform the individual of the implications of such withdrawal.

Clause 4.3.7 provides four examples of how individuals can give consent.

The first is the standard application form, with explanations of the purpose of the collection and a signature box.

The second is a checkoff box where an individual may deny permission to disclose or use information for specific purposes, or what is commonly known as opt-out. This should be read with clauses 4.3.4 and 4.3.5, and not be used for sensitive or important data or recipients.

The third example is the obtaining of consent over the telephone, and the fourth is consent when the individuals use a service.

A good example of consent through use is the use of the debit card as described above. It is counter-intuitive that an action such as using a product or service is only an implied consent, but since many individuals do not understand or think about the flows of information necessary for transactions, you cannot call this an express consent even though the action is express.

There has been considerable debate over whether the CSA Code was too weak on its consent provisions, or whether it was so vague that companies are unable to determine the rules. There is a huge range of information elements, uses, and disclosures, and it is very difficult to draw lines and make meaningful distinctions. If you decide to draw lines and delineate what is acceptable, and what is not, inevitably much escapes despite best efforts to contain it.

For instance, in the province of Quebec, the direct marketing industry was successful in lobbying for an exemption from the requirement to get consent for the collection and exchange of nominative lists (lists of names and addresses, with the reason for inclusion on the list) for the purposes of marketing. This is a much broader exemption than in the

CSA Code, with the result that all companies engaged in marketing may freely traffic in customer information unless the communication "does not infringe upon the privacy of the persons concerned."[5]

This is as difficult and subjective an evaluation as that which is required in the CSA Code to determine what the threshold of consent should be for your particular information collection.

Article 7 of the European Directive[6] says that "Member States shall provide that personal data may be processed only if (a) the data subject has unambiguously given his consent;" and Article 8, para. 2(a), which deals with the processing of special categories of data (formerly "sensitive data") forbids processing in the absence of the explicit consent of the data subject.

The CSA Code is technology-neutral — it attempts to deal with all media. In the context of electronic commerce, where many organizations now have the benefit of an Internet interface with their customers and e-mail, it is much easier both to inform and to ensure that the customer reads the message, through the use of pop-up windows and other such annoyances. No doubt it will not be long before we have mechanical voices seeking our agreement online, refusing to be silent until we have ticked a choice. This may not feel like progress but it will likely satisfy the requirements of informed consent, at minimal cost to both parties.

---

[5]   R.S.Q., c. P-39.1, s. 22.

[6]   See above note 2.

Principle 4 — Limiting Collection

4.4

The collection of personal information shall be limited to that which is necessary for the purposes identified by the organization. Information shall be collected by fair and lawful means.

This key provision is short and self-explanatory and means that there is an obligation to show that the information is necessary for the purposes, the purposes must be specified. Those purposes are now constrained by the reasonable person test.

4.4.1

Organizations shall not collect personal information indiscriminately. Both the amount and the type of information collected shall be limited to that which is necessary to fulfil the purposes identified. Organizations shall specify the type of information collected as part of their information-handling policies and practices, in accordance with the Openness principle (Clause 4.8).

Even if the reasonable person test had not been added, the requirement of clause 4.4.1 places a rather heavy burden on the organization. The clause goes on to say that the amount and the type of information collected *shall* be limited to that which is necessary to fulfil the stated purposes. This really closes off wholesale collection of information, with or without consent, unless the purposes have been stated broadly enough to permit the collection.

If we take current Internet information collection practice, for instance, the vacuuming up of all transactional data and matching it with user profiles will be terminated through the application of this clause.

4.4.2

The requirement that personal information be collected by fair and lawful means is intended to prevent organizations from collecting information by misleading or deceiving individuals about the purpose for which information is being collected. This requirement implies that consent with respect to collection must not be obtained through deception.

4.4.3

This principle is linked closely to the Identifying Purposes principle (Clause 4.2) and the Consent principle (Clause 4.3).

Collection by fair and lawful means is an expression straight from the OECD Guidelines, and it should go without saying. Clause 4.4.2 links it with the purpose for which the information is collected, but in fact it is broader than that. In this age of keystroke counting, hidden backup tapes, video surveillance, one-pixel "Web bugs," and the myriad electronic devices that now have imbedded intelligence or connectivity, fair and lawful also refers to fair notice, and whether the actual collection or surveillance is acceptable. There are very few legal protections from surveillance and intrusive data gathering, so the inclusion of the concept of fairness is important and may offer some legal redress where there has been none, although the Act will not be able to control the activities of organizations outside Canada.

Principle 5 — Limiting Use, Disclosure, and Retention

4.5

Personal information shall not be used or disclosed for purposes other than those for which it was collected, except with the consent of the individual or as required by law. Personal information shall be retained only as long as necessary for the fulfilment of those purposes.

Clause 4.5 echoes closely the language of the OECD Guidelines in limiting use to that which is envisaged in the specified purposes. It also introduces the distinction between use and disclosure, which although not defined is central to the Act. Use refers to any processing and treatment of data within the organization, whereas disclosure refers to the release of the information to third parties. This distinction begs further elaboration of what an organization is, and whether affiliates, subsidiaries, and divisions are part of the organization and therefore may "use" the information, or whether they are outside and the information must be "disclosed" to them. In terms of the law, it is clear what these entities are, and while divisions may be part of an organization, subsidiaries and affiliates are separate legal entities and thus are not part of the organization.

In the context of a voluntary code, these were difficult distinctions to make, and the CSA Committee decided to refrain from attempting to define where the boundaries of a single organization fell because the code was intended to be applied universally across the country and across sectors. A more relevant question is whether the individuals in another division of a company have a need to know the information and the answer to that question is usually "no," except that if the purpose of collecting the information is to generate marketing prospects, there may be many divisions who would have a similar desire to see the information. The same could be said of affiliates, but it is quite clear they are not part of the organization.

4.5.1

Organizations using personal information for a new purpose shall document this purpose (see Clause 4.2.1).

Organizations using the information for a new purpose must document that purpose, and must also seek the consent of the individual (see 4.2.1). This clause provides a strong incentive to companies to think of all the possible uses of the information before they gather it, which is not only good discipline but is required by the collection limitation principle.

4.5.2
Organizations should develop guidelines and implement procedures with respect to the retention of personal information. These guidelines should include minimum and maximum retention periods. Personal information that has been used to make a decision about an individual shall be retained long enough to allow the individual access to the information after the decision has been made. An organization may be subject to legislative requirements with respect to retention periods.

4.5.3
Personal information that is no longer required to fulfil the identified purposes should be destroyed, erased, or made anonymous. Organizations shall develop guidelines and implement procedures to govern the destruction of personal information.

The principle states that information shall be retained for only as long as necessary for the fulfilment of the stated purposes. Clause 4.5.2 provides guidance on the need to develop guidelines for retention schedules and procedures. It also introduces the obligation to retain information that has been used to make a decision about an individual for as long as may be necessary to allow the individual access to the information. This will be a variable determination depending on the circumstances; a pizza delivery system would hardly be expected to keep an order for three weeks, let alone years (as opposed to its receipts), but a bank is obliged to keep many of its records for seven years. The clause ends by pointing out that there may be mandatory retention periods to which the organization is subject.

There has been much debate about the usefulness of the "shoulds" in the Schedule. Many have argued that the only useful material is in the obligations; any recommendations ought to be deleted. Clause 4.5.3 is a good example of how the balance has been struck between the obligations and the recommendations.

Remembering that the principle clause places an obligation on organizations to retain information "only as long as is necessary" to fulfil the purposes, this means it must be disposed of when it is not necessary. However, if the code were to say, "Organizations shall destroy data that are no longer necessary," a heavy obligation would be placed on companies to locate and purge information as soon as it had served its purpose. This would be really problematic if the data were held in a large legacy database, and the organization was expected to regularly identify the information that was no longer necessary and purge it. Indeed, it would be no less expensive, in all probability, if the data were buried in paper files, particularly if they had been transferred to long term-storage.

Instead, the code creates an obligation to develop guidelines and implement procedures to govern the destruction of data, with a recommendation that information which is no longer required be destroyed, erased, or made anonymous.

4.5.4

This principle is closely linked to the Consent principle (Clause 4.3), the Identifying Purposes principle (Clause 4.2), and the Individual Access principle (Clause 4.9).

Clause 4.5.4 points out the linkages with other principles, but omits the link to the safeguards principle (4.7.5). In fact, a great many privacy scandals have occurred through the careless destruction, dumping, or recycling of documents containing personal information, so it is worth reiterating the importance of having policies and procedures in place which ensure that information which is no longer to be retained is being disposed of in a secure manner.

Principle 6 — Accuracy

4.6

Personal information shall be as accurate, complete, and up-to-date as is necessary for the purposes for which it is to be used.

Once again, there is a direct linkage of this clause (4.6) with the stated purposes: information must be as accurate, complete, and up to date as is necessary for the purposes for which it is to be used. If a bank has gathered information about a customer to grant a loan, and the customer fulfils her part of the bargain and regularly makes payments on time, there is no reason to go back and refresh the data about income and financial obligations, however useful that might be to the marketing department.

4.6.1

The extent to which personal information shall be accurate, complete, and up-to-date will depend upon the use of the information, taking into account the interests of the individual. Information shall be sufficiently accurate, complete, and up-to-date to minimize the possibility that inappropriate information may be used to make a decision about the individual.

Clause 4.6.1 points out that the interests of the individual must be taken into account, and therefore, if there is a possibility that inappropriate information might be used to make a decision about the individual, there is a justification for checking the accuracy and completeness of the data.

4.6.2
An organization shall not routinely update personal information, unless such a process is necessary to fulfil the purposes for which the information was collected.

4.6.3
Personal information that is used on an ongoing basis, including information that is disclosed to third parties, should generally be accurate and up-to-date, unless limits to the requirement for accuracy are clearly set out.

Clause 4.6.2 states that organizations shall not routinely update the data unless it is necessary to fulfil the original purpose, although the following clause states that if the information is used on an ongoing basis or is disclosed to third parties, it should be accurate unless the limits to accuracy have clearly been set out. All the sections of this clause stress the interests of the individual in having the information accurate, not those of the organization.

Principle 7 — Safeguards

4.7
Personal information shall be protected by security safeguards appropriate to the sensitivity of the information.

Clause 4.7 states that information shall be protected by safeguards appropriate to the sensitivity of the information. This raises the requirement to evaluate the sensitivity of the information.

4.7.1
The security safeguards shall protect personal information against loss or theft, as well as unauthorized access, disclosure, copying, use, or modification. Organizations shall protect personal information regardless of the format in which it is held.

4.7.2
The nature of the safeguards will vary depending on the sensitivity of the information that has been collected, the amount, distribution, and format of the information, and the method of storage. More sensitive information should be safeguarded by a higher level of protection. The concept of sensitivity is discussed in Clause 4.3.4.

Clause 4.7.1 goes further and imposes a specific obligation to protect against loss, theft, unauthorized access, disclosure, copying, use, or modification, and that this shall be regardless of the format. These are clear obligations, and there is a requirement to put in place specific security safeguards to meet them. Unfortunately, security is one of the most underfunded and least understood aspects of many organizations, and the lack of security is a major cause of privacy breaches. Statistics from the major audit companies show generally that the vast majority of security breaches originate within an organization, despite the press surrounding Internet hackers and risks online.

4.7.3
The methods of protection should include

(a) physical measures, for example, locked filing cabinets and restricted access to offices;

(b) organizational measures, for example, security clearances and limiting access on a "need-to-know" basis; and

(c) technological measures, for example, the use of passwords and encryption.

Clause 4.7.3 provides guidance on how to achieve this security by listing the methods of physical, organizational, and technical measures, including the use of passwords and encryption. Security includes the need to limit access to those who need to know, even beyond the use limitation principle. It will require industry standards for encryption, secure transmissions, password systems, and the use of virus screens and firewalls to prevent tampering with data. It will also include, where appropriate, computer-generated audit trails, which track the use of and access to the file.

Although these audit systems are not deployed as often as security systems experts might wish, they are now much more affordable than in the past and should be considered for all new systems, in the light of the new requirements of this legislation.

4.7.4
Organizations shall make their employees aware of the importance of maintaining the confidentiality of personal information.

Clause 4.7.4 imposes an obligation to train personnel about the importance of maintaining confidentiality. This obligation adds to and provides specificity to the obligation expressed in 4.1.4 to establish procedures and to train staff. This obligation has received little focus in the debate about the legislation, but it is a substantive one and no doubt will be the focus of investigations where a security breach results in the release of personal information. This requirement will be important in the investigation of complaints, but also in the context of the Privacy Commissioner's audit powers.

During the Parliamentary debate, concern was expressed over whether or not the audit powers of the Commissioner were intrusive, and the Act requires the Privacy Commissioner to have reasonable grounds to believe that the obligations of the Act are not being observed before he embarks on an audit of an organization.

The Dutch Data Commissioner observed at a recent conference[7] that the way they go about doing their informal audits is by calling the company and asking a few questions of company staff concerning their policies and procedures. In the event that staff fails to get a passing grade on these questions, they say, "Well, that is not really a good answer. I think we will come in and have a look at your practices."

Clauses 4.7.3 and 4.7.4 will give the Privacy Commissioner of Canada ample justification to do the same thing, and given the state of awareness of security measures generally and the likelihood most staff would fail such a test, it is an area that should receive immediate attention in compliance plans.

4.7.5
Care shall be used in the disposal or destruction of personal information, to prevent unauthorized parties from gaining access to the information (see Clause 4.5.3).

Once again, this is an obligation to take care in the destruction of documents, and it is a frequent issue in privacy scandals that reach the press.

Principle 8 — Openness

4.8
An organization shall make readily available to individuals specific information about its policies and practices relating to the management of personal information.

This obligation is transformative and far-reaching but has received very little publicity. The principle states the obligation to make specific information available about policies and practices relating to the management of personal information. European data protection law often contains obligations of "notification," but this provision goes much further by imposing an obligation to document policies and procedures concerning the handling of personal information, and make those policies available to the individual. The Openness principle of the OECD Guidelines merely states:

> There should be a general policy of openness about developments, practices, and policies with respect to personal data. Means should be readily available of establishing the existence and nature of personal data, and the main purposes of their use, as well as the identity and usual residence of the data controller.

The standard is much more explicit.

---

7   Computers' Freedom and Privacy Conference (Washington, D.C., April 1999).

4.8.1

Organizations shall be open about their policies and practices with respect to the management of personal information. Individuals shall be able to acquire information about an organization's policies and practices without unreasonable effort. This information shall be made available in a form that is generally understandable.

Organizations must be open about their policies; they must make the information available without unreasonable effort on the part of the individual, and they must make it available in a form that is generally understandable. This may necessitate the explanation of information systems protocols, for instance.

4.8.2

The information made available shall include

(a) the name or title, and the address, of the person who is accountable for the organization's policies and practices and to whom complaints or inquiries can be forwarded;

(b) the means of gaining access to personal information held by the organization;

(c) a description of the type of personal information held by the organization, including a general account of its use;

(d) a copy of any brochures or other information that explain the organization's policies, standards, or codes; and

(e) what personal information is made available to related organizations (e.g., subsidiaries).

Clause 4.8.2 provides a list of information which must be made available, but it is not an exhaustive list. The list includes:

a) the particulars of the person who is accountable for the organization's policies and practices;

b) the means of getting access to one's own personal information;

c) the description of the type of personal information held by the organization, including a general account of its use. Although this is fairly high level, the individual access principle provides a more specific right to more detailed data. If an organization wishes to minimize formal requests for detailed information, it is in its own interests to have information about its policies and practices available on request;

d) a copy of any brochures or other information that explain the organization's policies, standards, or codes; and

e) what personal information is made available to related organizations.

4.8.3

An organization may make information on its policies and practices available in a variety of ways. The method chosen depends on the nature of its business and other considerations. For example, an organization may choose to make brochures available in its place of business, mail information to its customers, provide online access, or establish a toll-free telephone number.

The example given is subsidiaries, but it would certainly also include business partners, service providers such as Web site operators or carriers, and any number of partners in the information food chain. The use of the word "related" would preclude the necessity of being transparent about practices concerning organizations that are not related, such as law enforcement and regulatory bodies, or legal counsel acting for third parties in cases such as defamation, copyright violation, and divorce.

Nevertheless, these are rights of access that are not generally understood by individuals, and the organization has a choice of disclosing these particular release possibilities under this provision or in the consent applications. It is probably preferable to do it here, because these policies should provide the educational tools that will be used for training staff.

Principle 9 — Individual Access

4.9
Upon request, an individual shall be informed of the existence, use, and disclosure of his or her personal information and shall be given access to that information. An individual shall be able to challenge the accuracy and completeness of the information and have it amended as appropriate.

Note: In certain situations, an organization may not be able to provide access to all the personal information it holds about an individual. Exceptions to the access requirement should be limited and specific. The reasons for denying access should be provided to the individual upon request. Exceptions may include information that is prohibitively costly to provide, information that contains references to other individuals, information that cannot be disclosed for legal, security, or commercial proprietary reasons, and information that is subject to solicitor-client or litigation privilege.

Clause 4.9 goes much further in granting rights to the subject of the information than most public sector data protection laws, by requiring organizations to inform the data subject, on request, of the information that the organization holds, and about what use is being made of it. It also provides the individual the right to find out to whom the information has been disclosed. The subclauses provide further detail about the obligations involved here, as well as guidance.

The note in principle 9 was the subject of great debate in the CSA Committee and was important to certain members, notably those who made use of marketing lists. It notes that there are certain situations where it is not possible to give access to the information, but that these exceptions are to be limited and specific.

Section 9 of the Act instructs us to disregard this note, and lists the only permissible circumstances when an organization is permitted to deny access to information. Two situations offered as examples in the note are not repeated in the Act: information that is prohibitively costly to provide, and information that is subject to litigation privilege. A provision allowing access to be denied if it was prohibitively expensive was removed on the recommendation of the Industry Committee.

4.9.1

Upon request, an organization shall inform an individual whether or not the organization holds personal information about the individual. Organizations are encouraged to indicate the source of this information. The organization shall allow the individual access to this information. However, the organization may choose to make sensitive medical information available through a medical practitioner. In addition, the organization shall provide an account of the use that has been made or is being made of this information and an account of the third parties to which it has been disclosed.

Clause 4.9.1 describes the obligations of an organization to inform the individual upon request of whether or not the organization holds information about the individual. Note that this is not the same as a right of notification because the individual must enquire. The code does not specify that this request must be in writing, but the Act does, for greater legal certainty. Organizations "are encouraged" to indicate the source of the information, but this is not stated as an obligation. Nevertheless, since the collection must be done with consent, it would be difficult to imagine too many situations other than those involving the investigation of an offence or breach of an agreement where it would not be necessary to state where the information came from to establish that the information had been gathered with consent.

This clause also permits an organization to allow access to sensitive medical information through a medical practitioner. Jurisdictions vary in their use of this provision, and in North America it is becoming much more common for the individual to have direct access to her own medical information except in unusual circumstances.

Finally, the clause obliges an organization to provide "an account" of both the use of the information and the third parties to whom it has been disclosed.

4.9.2

An individual may be required to provide sufficient information to permit an organization to provide an account of the existence, use, and disclosure of personal information. The information provided shall only be used for this purpose.

Clause 4.9.2 allows the organization to require more information to locate the individual's data, but does not permit the organization to use it for any other purpose than to locate the information. If, for instance, a customer of a large hotel wanted to obtain a record of all his transactions with the hotel, he might have to provide an estimate of the time periods when he might have visited and the services he used, such as the barber, the restaurant, and the fitness club. If he had used the fitness club in the past, the hotel would not be permitted to use this information to market current services.

4.9.3

In providing an account of third parties to which it has disclosed personal information about an individual, an organization should attempt to be as specific as possible. When it is not possible to provide a list of the organizations to which it has actually disclosed information about an individual, the organization shall provide a list of organizations to which it may have disclosed information about the individual.

Clause 4.9.3 provides guidance as to how to assist the individual in understanding the possible disclosure of his information. It introduces the requirement that when it is impossible to provide a complete list of the disclosures of the personal information, the organization shall provide a list of organizations to whom it may have disclosed the information.

Examples of such circumstances that arose in the discussion of the CSA Committee include a compilation of the customers of a list broker, who would regard that information as a commercial confidence but who would nevertheless have a duty under this clause to provide generic references such as magazine publishers, loyalty organizations, hotels, and so forth.

Another example would be non-retention of the information, again relevant in the context of direct marketing practices where the lists drawn up for a given marketing campaign are volatile, and duplicating the mailing list would require rerunning the computer search at enormous cost. This is a situation where the requirement to retain information so that the data subject has time to access it is clearly outweighed by the interests of everyone in not retaining the information.

It is counter-intuitive to suggest that an organization can use information without collecting it, but current data management practices and network realities are such that the language developed to deal with data processing seems rather rusty. Organizations often do not actually bring information under their control — they may have arranged viewing or analysis rights on a distributed basis. This certainly makes it more problematic for the individual to exercise his access rights.

The Europeans had anticipated this when they included article 15 in the directive, relating to automated processing.

4.9.4

An organization shall respond to an individual's request within a reasonable time and at minimal or no cost to the individual. The requested information shall be provided or made available in a form that is generally understandable. For example, if the organization uses abbreviations or codes to record information, an explanation shall be provided.

Clause 4.9.4 deals with the cost and time deadlines for providing access to information, which were thorny issues in the crafting of a voluntary code. The compromise reached was "a reasonable time" and "at minimal or no cost." The Act has provided further specification by requiring the information to be delivered within thirty days, with a possible further thirty days' extension. It allows companies to charge a fee, and the constraint on those fees is the requirement stated here that it be "minimal."

The information must be made available in a form that is generally understandable, which provides ample scope for interpretation in terms of language, format, and terms used. The last sentence clarifies that if an organization uses codes to record information, an explanation must be provided.

There are always issues in the area of payments and credit information as to what information belongs to the individual and which information is the company's commercial confidential information, and this will be exacerbated as more organizations get into data mining and personalization. The drafters of the legislation believed the expansiveness of this right of access would tend to favour the rights of the individual.

4.9.5

When an individual successfully demonstrates the inaccuracy or incompleteness of personal information, the organization shall amend the information as required. Depending upon the nature of the information challenged, amendment involves the correction, deletion, or addition of information. Where appropriate, the amended information shall be transmitted to third parties having access to the information in question.

Clause 4.9.5 requires the organization to amend the information when the individual successfully demonstrates the inaccuracy or incompleteness of the information. It also states that "where appropriate," the organization shall transmit the information to third parties having access to the information in question. This is a good example of one of the most frequent criticisms of the code: the juxtaposition of a mandatory requirement with the qualifier "where appropriate."

Because most of the drafters of the CSA Code had experience in the real-life implementation of privacy legislation or codes of practice, they tended to rely on good judgment when there were conflicts. In a situation where erroneous information may have resulted in poor decisions about the individual, it is imperative that the correct information be sent to all those concerned.

If the data are merely incomplete but the substantive impact of refreshing them would be nil, it is sometimes more likely that errors would creep in if the information is sent off without an operational requirement. Furthermore, setting up an administrative operation that emphasizes sending out information that is not required would favour the development of more intensive data gathering and "live" data management, which goes against the principle of collection limitation.

4.9.6
When a challenge is not resolved to the satisfaction of the individual, the substance of the unresolved challenge shall be recorded by the organization. When appropriate, the existence of the unresolved challenge shall be transmitted to third parties having access to the information in question.

In circumstances where the organization is not prepared to amend the information, it is required to record the substance of the unresolved challenge. Once again, there is a requirement to transmit the information concerning this unresolved challenge to third parties having access to the information in question, where appropriate.

Principle 10 — Challenging Compliance

4.10
An individual shall be able to address a challenge concerning compliance with the above principles to the designated individual or individuals accountable for the organization's compliance.

Clause 4.10 is probably the broadest basis for complaint in any data protection code. An individual has the right to address a challenge concerning an organization's compliance with any of the principles, and the individual complaining does not have to be the subject of the data in question. The remaining subclauses detail an organization's responsibilities in investigating such complaints, and these obligations are extensive.

4.10.1
The individual accountable for an organization's compliance is discussed in Clause 4.1.1.

The requirements concerning the designating of the accountable individual are described in the first principle, in 4.1.1.

4.10.2

Organizations shall put procedures in place to receive and respond to complaints or inquiries about their policies and practices relating to the handling of personal information. The complaint procedures should be easily accessible and simple to use.

Organizations are required to put in place procedures for the handling of complaints and inquiries about their policies. This might seem an obvious thing to do, but it is in fact rare to find a company that responds positively and in an informed way to detailed questions about its information policies. Surveys conducted by consumers' groups[8] have shown that even in areas where regulation is already in effect, awareness among staff leaves much to be desired. This clause puts the onus on the organization to get organized and provide simple, accessible systems.

4.10.3

Organizations shall inform individuals who make inquiries or lodge complaints of the existence of relevant complaint procedures. A range of these procedures may exist. For example, some regulatory bodies accept complaints about the personal-information handling practices of the companies they regulate.

Clause 4.10.3 provides that the organization must also inform the individual of relevant complaint mechanisms, such as the regulatory agencies responsible for certain sectors. Since this code was drafted for voluntary compliance, this requirement was put in to ensure that companies did not waylay the unhappy client at their customer service department and neglect to make him aware of any rights he might have to complain to regulatory authorities, such as the Canadian Radio-television and Telecommunications Commission (CRTC) or the Banking Ombudsman.

Since subsection 13(2) gives the Commissioner the power to decline to report on matters that could more appropriately be dealt with through other procedures provided by the laws of Canada or a province, this clause is still very relevant. Organizations must inform the individual of these other avenues, and the simplest way to ensure this obligation is met is to include the relevant information in the complaints handling procedures.

---

[8] *The 1998 Personal Data Protection and Privacy Review: A Report by PIAC and Action Réseau Consommateurs* (Ottawa: PIAC, 1998).

4.10.4

An organization shall investigate all complaints. If a complaint is found to be justified, the organization shall take appropriate measures, including, if necessary, amending its policies and practices.

Clause 4.10.4 requires that organizations investigate all complaints, and that they must take "appropriate measures" if the complaint is found to be justified. This includes amending their policies and procedures if necessary. If, for instance, a customer complained that a Web site was not secure and did not protect customer files from hacking, an organization ought to amend and improve its security procedures if they find on investigation that the individual is correct.

CHAPTER 3

PART 1: THE ACT

This chapter builds on the previous one by examining in detail how the *Personal Information Protection and Electronic Documents Act*[1] adds to, modifies, and clarifies the code discussed in chapter 2.

The Act	Commentary

Bill C-6, An Act to support and promote electronic commerce by protecting personal information that is collected, used or disclosed in certain circumstances, by providing for the use of electronic means to communicate or record information or transactions and by amending the *Canada Evidence Act*, the *Statutory Instruments Act,* and the *Statute Revision Act*, 2d Sess., 36th Parl., 48–49 Elizabeth II, 1999 –2000, assented to 13th April 2000.

Section 1: Short Title

1. This Act may be cited as the *Personal Information Protection and Electronic Documents Act.*

---

[1] S.C. 2000, c. 5.

PART 1: PROTECTION OF PERSONAL INFORMATION IN THE PRIVATE SECTOR

Section 2: Interpretation

Definitions

2.(1) The definitions in this subsection apply in this Part.

"alternative format," with respect to personal information, means a format that allows a person with a sensory disability to read or listen to the personal information.

The term "alternative format" is used in section 10, with reference to the right of an individual to access information in a format that a person with a hearing or seeing disability can understand. It is subject to a "reasonable and necessary" test.

"commercial activity" means any particular transaction, act or conduct or any regular course of conduct that is of a commercial character, including the selling, bartering or leasing of donor, membership or other fundraising lists.

The definition of "commercial activity" is key to understanding the scope of the Act. The definition has been criticized as being too broad and essentially circular. Read carefully, it is not circular and defines what commercial activity is by virtue of its nature or character. The amendment adopted at third reading clarifies that notion by adding the phrase, "including the selling, bartering or leasing of donor, membership or other fundraising lists."

The breadth of the definition was intended to capture as broad a range of transactions involving the collection, use, or disclosure of information as possible. The Constitution limits federal jurisdiction under the trade and commerce power to commercial activities, and any attempt to limit the activities that might be covered under a broad definition would be counter-productive from Parliament's perspective.

The definition covers particular transactions and regular courses of conduct. Hence, any organization that is in business and that collects, uses, or discloses personal information in the course of doing business would be bound by the law for all its activities. On the other hand, if an organization is not in business (such as a charitable or an educational organization), its regular activities would not be subject to the law because they are not of a commercial character. However, if that organization from time to time engages in the selling of its membership lists, for example, or a graduate list in the case of an educational institution, that particular transaction would be subject to the Act.

Determining what is commercial activity is fundamental to understanding the Act. It defines the scope of the Act, as set out in paragraph 4(1)(a):

> This Part applies to every organization in respect of personal information that (a) the organization collects, uses or discloses in the course of commercial activities.

This paragraph contains the only mention of this term in the Act.

There is no particularly useful jurisprudence with respect to the meaning of commercial activity. It was applied in *Windsor-Essex County Real Estate Board* v. *Windsor (City)*[2] to determine whether an entity was carrying on a business and thus subject to a business tax. The commercial activity test in Windsor-Essex was rejected by the Supreme Court of Canada in the *Hearst* case[3] as not being useful in determining whether an organization is carrying on a "business." The Court adopted a preponderant purpose test: if the preponderant purpose is not the making of a profit, then the organization is not carrying on a business.

In the new Act, there is no reference to business and the definition clearly contemplates that non-profit organizations may be engaged in a commercial activity.

"Commissioner" means the Privacy Commissioner appointed under section 53 of the *Privacy Act*.

The word "Commissioner" is used throughout Part 1 of the Act and means the Privacy Commissioner of Canada who is appointed under section 53 of the *Privacy Act*, the federal public sector law. The Privacy Commissioner is appointed by the Governor in Council after approval by resolution

---

[2]   (1974), [1975] 51 D.L.R. (3d) 665 (Ont. C.A.) [*Windsor-Essex*].

[3]   *Re Regional Assessment Commissioner and Caisse Populaire de Hearst Ltee.* (1983), 143 D.L.R. (3d) 590 (S.C.C.) [*Hearst*].

of the Senate and the House of Commons. The Commissioner is appointed to hold office during good behaviour for a term not to exceed seven years, and is eligible to be reappointed for a further term not exceeding seven years.

Section 56 of the *Privacy Act* allows the appointment of one or more Assistant Privacy Commissioners by the Governor in Council on the recommendation of the Privacy Commissioner. Section 57 states that the Assistant Privacy Commissioner shall perform any duties or functions of the Office of Privacy Commissioner under the *Privacy Act* or any other Act of Parliament as are delegated by the Privacy Commissioner.

"Court" means the Federal Court— Trial Division.

The "Court" refers to the Trial Division of the Federal Court of Canada.

"federal work, undertaking or business" means any work, undertaking or business that is within the legislative authority of Parliament. It includes

This term is defined only for the purposes of paragraph 4(1)(b) so as to extend the Act to personal information about employees of federal works and, for purposes of subsection 30(1), to describe the application of the Act in the first three years of its coming into force. Otherwise, federal works are covered by the broad definition of "organization" as in paragraph 4(1)(a) where the scope of the Act extends to "every organization in respect of personal information that the organization collects, uses, or discloses in the course of commercial activities." For a bank, to use an obvious example, personal information about its customers is covered under paragraph (a) while information about its employees is covered under paragraph (b).

Jurisdiction over federal works flows from subsections 91(29) and 92(10) of the *Constitution Act, 1867,* and the Peace, Order and Good Government residual power in the opening words of section 91, as well as the specific enumerations of power in section 91, which encompass banks and the postal service, for example. In the past few years alone, jurisprudence under subsections 91(29) and 92(10) has confirmed federal jurisdiction over telecommunications systems,[4] railways,[5] nuclear electrical generating facilities,[6] and gas pipelines.[7]

Following is a list of examples of works that are covered by the definition:

(a) a work, undertaking or business that is operated or carried on for or in connection with navigation and shipping, whether inland or maritime, including the operation of ships and transportation by ship anywhere in Canada;

a) inland and maritime shipping, including the operation of lighthouses (e.g., Canada Steamship Lines)

(b) a railway, canal, telegraph or other work or undertaking that connects a province with another province, or that extends beyond the limits of a province;

b) railways, telecommunications undertakings, cable operators, interprovincial transportation undertakings (e.g., Via Rail, Canadian Pacific, Rogers Cable, Bell Canada, Télécable Videotron, Toronto Terminals Railway, AMJ Campbell Van Lines)

(c) a line of ships that connects a province with another province, or that extends beyond the limits of a province;

c) interprovincial and international shipping (e.g., companies operating shipping in the Great Lakes)

(d) a ferry between a province and another province or between a province and a country other than Canada;

d) interprovincial and international ferries (e.g., Marine Atlantic, Quyon Ferry)

(e) aerodromes, aircraft or a line of air transportation;

e) airports, aircraft, and airlines (e.g., Air Canada, NAVCANADA, Pearson International Airport)

(f) a radio broadcasting station;

f) radio and television broadcasting undertakings (e.g., CBC, CTV, Global TV Network)

(g) a bank;

g) the banks listed in Schedules 1 and 2 of the *Bank Act* (e.g., Bank of Montreal, Royal Bank, Banque Nationale, Amex Bank of Canada, Chase Manhattan Bank of Canada, Citibank; it does not include "authorized foreign banks" within the meaning of section 2 of the *Bank Act*)

---

[4] *Alberta Government Telephones* v. *Canada (Radio-Television & Telecommunications Commission)*, [1989] 2 S.C.R. 225.

[5] *U.T.U.* v. *Central Western Railway*, [1990] 3 S.C.R. 1112.

[6] *Ontario Hydro* v. *Ontario (Labour Relations Board)*, [1993] 3 S.C.R. 327.

[7] *Westcoast Energy Inc.* v. *Canada (National Energy Board)*, [1998] 1 S.C.R. 322.

(h) a work that, although wholly situated within a province, is before or after its execution declared by Parliament to be for the general advantage of Canada or for the advantage of two or more provinces;

h) grain elevators, local railways, dams, and works declared by Parliament to be for the general advantage of Canada (e.g., Devco)

(i) a work, undertaking or business outside the exclusive legislative authority of the legislatures of the provinces; and

i) atomic energy (e.g., Atomic Energy of Canada Ltd., Ontario Hydro nuclear generating facilities) and all other matters not within provincial jurisdiction, such as municipal governments and local works and undertakings in the three territories

(j) a work, undertaking or business to which federal laws, within the meaning of section 2 of the *Oceans Act*, apply under section 20 of that Act and any regulations made under paragraph 26(1)(k) of that Act.

j) offshore drilling operations (e.g., Hibernia)

"organization" includes an association, a partnership, a person and a trade union.

"Organization" is a key word used extensively throughout the Act, which is binding on organizations as defined. The definition itself is inclusive and based on the CSA Model Code, which defines organization as follows:

> A term used in the model Code that includes associations, businesses, charitable organizations, clubs, government bodies, institutions, professional practices, and unions.

The definition in the Act includes an association, a partnership, a person, and a trade union. The *Interpretation Act*[8] defines "person" as including legal persons.

---

[8]   R.S.C. 1985, c. I-21, s. 35.

"personal health information", with respect to an individual, whether living or deceased, means

(a) information concerning the physical or mental health of the individual;

(b) information concerning any health service provided to the individual;

(c) information concerning the donation by the individual of any body part or any bodily substance of the individual or information derived from the testing or examination of a body part or bodily substance of the individual;

(d) information that is collected in the course of providing health services to the individual; or

(e) information that is collected incidentally to the provision of health services to the individual.

"personal information" means information about an identifiable individual, but does not include the name, title or business address or telephone number of an employee of an organization.

An amendment made by the Senate and accepted by the House of Commons to defer the application of the Act to personal health information necessarily added a new definition of personal health information to the Act. The definition is taken from *The Saskatchewan Health Information Protection Act*[9] with only minor changes. The term is not used anywhere in the Act except in subsection 30(1.1), which is transitional. Subsection 30(2.1) provides that 30(1.1) will cease to have effect on 1 January 2002.

It hardly seems worthwhile to try to decipher what the relationship is between the personal health information definition and the definition of personal information in subsection 2(1) of the Act for a one-year stay of execution, unless of course the sale of personal health information affects the organization's bottom line in a big way. The definition of "personal information" is broad enough to include all sorts of information including medical or health information. Once subsection 30(1.1) is spent, it would be reasonable to assume that the definition of personal health information would be deleted in a Miscellaneous Statute Law Amendment sometime in the future.

The definition of "personal information" reflects a departure from traditional definitions, such as that found in the federal *Privacy Act*, in that it does not limit personal information to information that is recorded. It therefore includes tissue information and bodily fluids such as blood and urine samples that may not be recorded and cannot easily be defined as body parts yet contain intensely personal information.

The definition excludes from the scope of the Act basic business information such as the title and business address of an employee of an organization. This does not mean that an organization must release that information if it wishes to main-

---

[9]   S.S. 1999, c. H-O.021, s. 2.

tain its confidentiality, but it does mean that a purchasing clerk, for instance, cannot refuse to have her name and phone number included in a purchasing directory on the grounds that they are her personal information. Similar provisions exist in the federal *Privacy Act* to prevent public servants from claiming similar privacy rights.

The definition is open-ended and does not include a list of examples such as can be found in the federal *Privacy Act.* Regardless of what legislation may say about such lists being non-exhaustive, they tend to have the effect of limiting thinking as to what personal information can be. The definition in the Act is limitless in terms of what can be information about an identifiable individual. The key is that the individual must be identifiable, so truly anonymous information is not "personal information."

However, caution should be exercised in determining what is truly "anonymous" information since the availability of external information in automated format may facilitate the re-identification of information that has been made anonymous. Sometimes elements or details hidden deep within a file also will serve to authenticate the identity of an individual.

"record" includes any correspondence, memorandum, book, plan, map, drawing, diagram, pictorial or graphic work, photograph, film, microform, sound recording, videotape, machine-readable record and any other documentary material, regardless of physical form or characteristics, and any copy of any of those things.

The term "record" is used only in connection with the powers of the Commissioner to investigate complaints and carry out audits, where he has powers to compel the production of records. The Act throughout relies on the term "personal information" because, unlike other legislation such as Quebec's *Act Respecting the Protection of Personal Information in the Private Sector,*[10] this Act provides to the individual a right of access to information, not files or records. Given the transformation of the nature of information flows that has taken place with the development of the Internet and technologies such as Javascript, this is entirely appropriate.

---

[10]   R.S.Q., c. P-39.1.

Notes in Schedule 1

(2) In this Part, a reference to clause 4.3 or 4.9 of Schedule 1 does not include a reference to the note that accompanies that clause.

Subsection 2(2) deals with the notes that are found in clauses 4.3 and 4.9 of Schedule 1, the consent principle and the individual access principle. Each of these principles is followed by a note that sets out, in the case of 4.3, the circumstances where having to obtain the consent of the individual for collection, use, or disclosure may be "inappropriate," and, in the case of 4.9, situations where an organization would not be required to provide an individual with access to information about himself.

This is the first reference in the Act to modifications that are necessary to turn the CSA Code into law. The notes are both reasonably vague and, more important, open-ended in the examples they give of the respective circumstances where consent is not necessary or the situations where an individual cannot be given access to personal information. To provide greater certainty to both organizations and individuals, sections 7 and 9 of the Act detail specific and limited circumstances and situations.

The notes remain in the CSA Code to guide anyone using it as a voluntary standard, or where it is imposed on a third party by contract, but they have no legal effect as far as the interpretation of the law is concerned.

Section 3: Purpose

3. The purpose of this Part is to establish, in an era in which technology increasingly facilitates the circulation and exchange of information, rules to govern the collection, use and disclosure of personal information in a manner that recognizes the right of privacy of individuals with respect to their personal information and the need of organizations to collect, use or disclose personal information for purposes that a reasonable person would consider appropriate in the circumstances.

Purpose clauses are not uncommon in federal legislation, but certainly every law does not have one. They can be useful, but they can also be dangerous, if not carefully drafted, as courts tend to rely on them to try to understand the underlying policy objectives of legislation.

In the purpose clause, we find the first reference to the "reasonable person," the famed "man on the Clapham Omnibus" so familiar to generations of law students. The test of reasonableness in this context is an objective one. What would a reasonable person consider is a necessary collection, use, or disclosure of personal information about himself or herself in the circumstances? What is the nature of the information collected? What is the business of the organization? Why is this information necessary?

There is a heavy weighting here on the side of privacy. The interests of individuals and the interests of organizations are not in fact balanced in the traditional sense. The "right" of privacy of individuals is balanced against the "need" of organizations. Organizations must then demonstrate that they "need" the information. Such language will likely be critical in the judicial interpretation of this legislation.

Section 4: Application

4.(1) This Part applies to every organization in respect of personal information that

(a) the organization collects, uses or discloses in the course of commercial activities; or

Section 4 is critical to an understanding of the scope and application of the law. It brings together three of the key definitions: "organization," "personal information," and "commercial activity."

Paragraph (a) states that the law applies to every organization in respect of personal information that it collects, uses, or discloses in the course of commercial activities. This is the crucial statement in the law of the exercise by the federal Parliament of the general branch of the trade and commerce power.

Subsection 91(2) of the *Constitution Act, 1867,* provides that Parliament has jurisdiction over "the regulation of trade and commerce." Given the breadth of that language, the exercise of the trade and commerce power has the potential to encroach on provincial jurisdiction over property and civil rights. Notwithstanding the language, the courts have over the years taken a fairly conservative approach to the use of the trade and commerce power in an attempt to maintain a balance between federal and provincial powers.

There are two branches of the trade and commerce power: (1) the international/ interprovincial or narrow branch, and (2) the general or broad branch.[11]

---

[11] This distinction was first drawn by the Privy Council in *Citizens' Insurance Co.* v. *Parsons* (1881), 7 App. Cas. 96 (P.C.).

Part 1 of the Act relies on both branches at different points of its implementation. In the first three years following coming into force, in addition to applying to federal works, undertakings, and businesses, it will apply to international/interprovincial trade in personal information where the information is the subject of the trade — relying on the narrow branch.

In the third year following coming into force, it will apply to organizations in the private sector in the provinces and more broadly to international/interprovincial flows of personal information in the course of commercial activities generally — relying on the broad branch.

The narrow branch of the trade and commerce power has generated a large number of decisions that can be summed up as standing for the propositions that

1. the key criterion is not whether the transaction in question crossed provincial or national borders but whether the goods in question form part of an international/inter-provincial flow of trade;[12] and

2. for federal jurisdiction to reach into a transaction otherwise completed entirely within the province, there must be an overall scheme of regulation of interprovincial trade and the economy as a whole into which the transaction falls.[13]

Following a fifty-year hiatus, the general branch of the power was revived by the Supreme Court of Canada in *General Motors of Canada Ltd.* v. *City National Leasing*,[14] which was a challenge to the validity of a civil remedy under the *Combines Investigation Act* (now the *Competition Act*) introduced in legislative amendments in 1975. In a unanimous decision by Dickson C.J., the Court upheld the amendment as a valid exercise of the general trade and commerce power and essentially

---

[12] *Reference re Farm Products Marketing Act (Ontario)*, [1957] S.C.R. 198.

[13] *Caloil Inc.* v. *Canada (A.G.) (No. 2)*, [1971] S.C.R. 543.

[14] [1989] 1 S.C.R. 641 [*General Motors*].

authorized the regulation of intraprovincial trade by the federal Parliament.

The Court enunciated a five-part test for the valid exercise of the power:

1. the presence of a general regulatory scheme;
2. the oversight of a regulatory agency;
3. a concern with trade as a whole rather than a particular industry;
4. the legislation should be of a nature that the provinces jointly or severally would be constitutionally incapable of enacting; and
5. the failure to include one or more provinces in the legislative scheme would jeopardize the successful operation of the scheme in other parts of the country.

The Court cautioned that the five criteria are not exhaustive, nor will any one of them be determinative, in and of itself.

The five criteria appear to be satisfied in Part 1 of the Act.

- Part 1 qualifies as a "general regulatory scheme."
- The role of the Privacy Commissioner provides the necessary oversight.
- The CSA Code is concerned with trade as a whole.
- Although the provinces could enact similar rules, the rules would not be effective if enacted only on a provincial basis because the flow of information cannot be contained for regulatory purposes within any one province.
- The failure to include a province or locality in Part 1 would cause information to flow and leak out of the regulated area, thereby undermining the scheme in the regulated area.

Some provinces have indicated publicly that they may consider mounting a constitutional challenge of the use of the trade and commerce power in Part 1 of the Act. It will be interesting to see what the courts will make of the application of the tests in *General Motors* to a data protection law.

(b) is about an employee of the organization and that the organization collects, uses or discloses in connection with the operation of a federal work, undertaking or business.

Paragraph (b) states that the law also applies to personal information about an employee of a federal work, undertaking, or business that is collected, used or disclosed in connection with the operation of the federal work. It is necessary to specifically state this because employee information, labour relations, and modification of the employment relationship are within the jurisdiction of the provinces as falling under property and civil rights, and that relationship is not considered as coming within the meaning of "commercial."[15]

Therefore paragraph (a), which relies on the trade and commerce power cannot include employee information. Notwithstanding provincial jurisdiction over labour relations, the federal Parliament does have jurisdiction to regulate employment in works, undertakings, and businesses within the legislative authority of the federal Parliament.[16]

Limit

(2) This Part does not apply to

Subsection 4(2) provides that the Act does not apply to

(a) any government institution to which the *Privacy Act* applies;

a) government institutions to which the *Privacy Act* applies. Schedule II of the *Privacy Act*, which covers the public sector, has an extensive list of government bodies other than government departments to which the Act applies. Examples include Canada Post and the National Gallery.

In paragraph 26(2)(a), there is a power for the Governor in Council to pass an order to provide that the Act will be binding on agents of Her Majesty in right of Canada to which the *Privacy Act* does not apply. Examples of this

---

[15] *Toronto Electric Commissioners* v. *Snider*, [1925] A.C. 396; *A.G. Canada* v. *A.G. Ontario* (Labour Conventions), [1937] A.C. 326; *Reference re Application of Hours of Work Act (British Columbia) to Employees of the Canadian Pacific Railway in Empress Hotel, Victoria (City)*, [1950] A.C. 122 (B.C.P.C.); *Oil, Chemical and Atomic Workers International Union, Local 16-601* v. *Imperial Oil Limited and A.G. British Columbia*, [1963] S.C.R. 584; and *A.G. Canada* v. *A.G. Ontario* (Unemployment Insurance), [1937] A.C. 355 (P.C.).

[16] *Reference re Validity of the Industrial Relations and Disputes Investigation Act, R.S.C. 1952, c. 152, and as to its applicability in respect of certain employees of the Eastern Canada Stevedoring Company Limited*, [1955] S.C.R. 529.

(b) any individual in respect of personal information that the individual collects, uses or discloses for personal or domestic purposes and does not collect, use or disclose for any other purpose; or

(c) any organization in respect of personal information that the organization collects, uses or discloses for journalistic, artistic or literary purposes and does not collect, use or disclose for any other purpose.

would be the CBC, Atomic Energy of Canada Limited, and Enterprise Cape Breton.

b) individuals who collect, use, or disclose personal information for purely personal or household purposes, such as Christmas card lists.

c) organizations that collect, use, or disclose personal information solely for journalistic, artistic, or literary purposes. The purpose of this exception is to preserve the *Charter* right of freedom of expression. Any attempt to bring organizations such as newspapers or other news organizations, publishing houses, or writers and artists into a legislative scheme that provides regulation and oversight on collection, use, and disclosure of information would raise serious, legitimate, and ultimately insurmountable *Charter* problems.

Although the effect of this paragraph is that none of the provisions of the Act apply to information collected, used, or disclosed for journalistic, artistic, or literary purposes, individuals may still be able to challenge the organization on the purposes of its collection, use, or disclosure. If the Privacy Commissioner receives such a complaint, he has an obligation to investigate the complaint unless he believes it to be outside his jurisdiction. If an individual can make a compelling case that the organization collected, used, or disclosed information that enjoyed this journalistic privilege for purposes other than those related to free expression, such as marketing, the Privacy Commissioner is empowered to investigate.

Other Acts

(3) Every provision of this Part applies despite any provision, enacted after this subsection comes into force, of any other Act of Parliament, unless the other Act expressly declares that that provision operates despite the provision of this Part.

Subsection 4(3) is a primacy section that was recommended by the Industry Committee of the House of Commons. It provides that any provision in Part 1 of the Act takes precedence over any provision of a subsequent Act of Parliament, including any amendment to an existing Act, unless the provision in the new law, or amendment, states specifically that the provision in the new law or amendment overrides a provision in Part 1 of the Act.

Such a primacy section prevents any confusion between the Act and subsequent legislation as to which law applies. It does not operate that way in respect of existing legislation, leaving the primacy issue to the usual rules of legislative interpretation. It also serves to focus Parliament's attention on privacy issues in subsequent legislation should that legislation seek to override the Act.

DIVISION 1: PROTECTION OF PERSONAL INFORMATION

Section 5: Compliance with Obligations

5.(1) Subject to sections 6 to 9, every organization shall comply with the obligations set out in Schedule 1.

Section 5 provides that subject to the provisions set out in sections 6 to 9 of the Act, all organizations to which the Act applies shall comply with the obligations set out in Schedule 1. Those obligations are expressed in the code by the use of language such as "shall" and "must."

Meaning of "should"

(2) The word "should", when used in Schedule 1, indicates a recommendation and does not impose an obligation.

Subsection 5(2) goes on to provide that where the code uses the word "should," the recommendation — for that is what it is — is not an obligation.

Appropriate purposes

(3) An organization may collect, use or disclose personal information only for purposes that a reasonable person would consider are appropriate in the circumstances.

Subsection 5(3), which was added on the recommendation of the Industry Committee, is a very important provision. It picks up the notion of the "reasonable person" originally found in section 3.

In the view of many privacy advocates, one of the major flaws of the code is that it does not contain a "justification principle" — that is, it does not oblige an organization to justify why it is collecting, using, or disclosing personal information. In the code, it is simply enough for an organization to state its purposes in collecting, using, and disclosing personal information. Subsection 5(3) attempts to close that gap with a reasonable person test.

Since the test is an objective one that has a long history of judicial application, it is unlikely that the "reasonable person" will be either an avid privacy advocate or a prying data miner. It will be interesting to see what elements the courts ultimately consider under the notion of "appropriate in the circumstances."

Section 6: Effect of Designation of Individual

6. The designation of an individual under clause 4.1 of Schedule 1 does not relieve the organization of the obligation to comply with the obligations set out in that Schedule.

Section 6 merely provides greater clarity that if an individual has been designated as the responsible person under the accountability principle, it does not remove the obligation from the organization as a whole. This clause was added to ensure that liability would not be transferred to one person in the organization.

Section 7: Collection, Use, and Disclosure without Consent

Principle 3 of the CSA Code says that "[t]he knowledge and consent of the individual are required for the collection, use or disclosure of personal information, except where inappropriate."

The open-ended character of the phrase, "except where inappropriate," does not lend itself to statutory interpretation, largely because of the uncertainty as to the scope of what is or is not appropriate. The note to clause 4.3 of Schedule 1 attempts to establish what inappropriate may mean, but it too, being a mere list of examples, is also open-ended.

The solution for the drafters of the Act was to set out, in section 7, three lists that are finite in nature, defining the circumstances where it might not be appropriate to seek consent. Thus, in each of subsections 7(1), (2), and (3), the Act states that "despite the note," for the purposes of clause 4.3 of Schedule 1, these are the *only* circumstances where an organization does not need consent to collect (7(1)), use (7(2)), or disclose (7(3)) personal information.

There are important differences between the exceptions to consent envisaged by the note and those that are actually permitted by section 7. These will be dealt with under each subsection. A further and very important distinction is that there are separate lists for collection, use, and disclosure without consent, underlining the different thresholds of the three activities.

The essential feature of a data protection bill is to provide to the individual the right to control the treatment of his own personal information. The Germans have referred to this as "informational self-determination," a term that is perhaps more elegant in German than when rendered into English. The cutting edge of individual control of information therefore has to be at the collection stage because it is more difficult to exert control once the data have been collected. This Act very strongly links the data collected to the purposes that have been stated by the organization and requires thorough documentation of the organization's information practices to ensure that the individual may be well informed of the eventual use and disclosure of his information.

With this in mind, subsection 7(1) contains a much shorter and more circumscribed list of permissible collections without consent than appears in subsections 7(2) and 7(3). Once an organization has satisfied an individual that it has a legitimate need to gather his information, an entirely different debate then occurs as to what uses and disclosures without consent are permissible.

For instance, once an individual has established a relationship through contract with his Internet service provider, that organization has a number of public responsibilities that might require it to use or disclose information for purposes that may have been unforeseen at the time of collection, or that might not have been specified to the individual. This would include the disclosure of transactional data if a law enforcement agency produced a warrant for the investigation of possession of child pornography.

Throughout the debate over this legislation while it was being considered by Parliament, there was a view more often assumed than expressed, that if organizations did not have a specific exception from the requirement to get consent, they would be unable to collect, use, and disclose the information that they were in the habit of processing. This is evidence that organizations are not now in the habit of asking for consent, but it does not mean that consent would be impossible to obtain.

For instance, cellular telephone companies were interested in being able to share information on clients who were "skipping," or signing up with a company long enough to run up a huge bill, then moving on to the next provider. It would be rather easy to include consent for the sharing of unpaid debt information with other cellular providers. In some cases organizations are quite right in saying that extensive "mouse print" consent forms that list every possible use or release discourages customers from signing a contract, but in this case the kind of customers who would be disinclined to agree with this provision are exactly the kind an organization wants to discourage.

Collection without knowledge or consent

7.(1) For the purpose of clause 4.3 of Schedule 1, and despite the note that accompanies that clause, an organization may collect personal information without the knowledge or consent of the individual only if

(a) the collection is clearly in the interests of the individual and consent cannot be obtained in a timely way;

There are two elements that must be present to meet the test in paragraph 7(1)(a): the collection must be clearly in the interests of the individual concerned, *and* consent cannot be obtained in a timely way.

A key element here is the notion of timeliness. The issue isn't that consent cannot be obtained but that it cannot be obtained in time to be useful. This suggests that an after-the-fact notice to the individual would be a good practice for an organization to adopt.

> **Example**: Mary Smith is travelling on business and staying at the Hotel Vancouver. Her son is away at camp, falls from a rock, and is rushed to hospital with injuries. The camp director calls her place of business and is directed to the hotel. The hotel establishes that she is out for dinner with a friend, but the concierge made the reservation and is able to contact the restaurant. The camp is permitted to collect this information under 7(1)(a) because the collection is clearly in the interests of Mary Smith. Her consent could not be obtained in a timely manner. The disclosure by either her workplace, the restaurant or the hotel of where she is, who she is with, and any other information necessary to find her and contact her, such as cellular phone numbers, would be permitted under 7(3)(e): "made to a person who needs the information because of an emergency that threatens the life, health or security of an individual."

This example also demonstrates a different threshold for collection and disclosure for the benefit of the individual: you may collect information for somebody's benefit, and you may use it under paragraph 7(2)(d). Lest this be abused, there is no equivalent clause in subsection 7(3) that permits you to disclose it "clearly in the interests of the individual" but you may disclose it when the safety or health of an individual are in jeopardy.

An organization is bound to respect the confidentiality of the information it collects, but once it discloses the information, it may well be out of its control as well as out of the control of the individual, so it was felt that the ability to disclose "in the interests of the individual" would lead to abuse.

(b) it is reasonable to expect that the collection with the knowledge or consent of the individual would compromise the availability or the accuracy of the information and the collection is reasonable for purposes related to investigating a breach of an agreement or a contravention of the laws of Canada or a province;

In paragraph 7(1)(b) there are two principal tests to meet before information can be collected without consent under this provision:

1. There is a reasonable expectation that collection with the knowledge or consent, but primarily with the knowledge of the individual, would compromise either the availability or the accuracy of the information.
2. The collection itself is reasonable for purposes related to investigating a breach of an agreement or a contravention of federal or provincial laws.

This paragraph is not meant to create an open season on collecting all kinds of information under the guise of investigating lawbreakers; the information collected must be reasonably linked to the purposes for which the investigation is being carried out.

The concept of reasonableness is important here. First, the organization must determine that it would be reasonable to expect that collection with consent would compromise the availability or accuracy of the information, and second, that the information being collected is reasonable for the purposes of the investigation. Both these tests of reasonableness are to be applied by the organization in this paragraph but are also subject to challenge by the individual under subsection 5(3). In any challenge to collections under this paragraph, the courts will apply an objective reasonableness test as well.

Example: John Doe is a passenger in Mary Smith's car during an accident that involves injuries. John Doe claims that he is permanently unable to work and claims for long-term disability under Mary's policy. The insurance company does not have a contract with John Doe, and so has not secured his consent to verify his claim. Once he files for the insurance benefits, he is reluctant to give consent for anything other than verifying his medical information, but the company wishes to check into his employment history to verify that he does not have a history of malingering.

At first glance there does not appear to be any substantial reason why the insurance company cannot get a consent that would cover their investigation, but it is possible in some circumstances that an organization might be limited in what it can demand of an injured party. In such circumstances, it would have to be able to show that there were reasonable grounds to believe that John Doe was perpetrating insurance fraud, which is a contravention of the laws of Canada.

> **Example:** Bob Smith runs a small video store in a large city. There is a video camera set up by the front door which is trained on the cash register to deter robberies. While cleaning up one night, Bob has moved the video camera about so that it is pointing into the street, and he notices what appears to be evidence of drug dealing going on outside his store. He decides to leave the camera going at this angle and gives the tape to the police the next day.

Clearly, Bob is unlikely to get the consent of the individuals concerned. Is the collection reasonable for the purpose of investigating a violation of the law? If he has seen enough to satisfy himself of the likely nature of the activity on the street, he may rest assured that this collection of information would satisfy the test.

(c) the collection is solely for journalistic, artistic or literary purposes; or

Although information collected, used, or disclosed for journalistic, artistic, or literary purposes is not subject to the Act, paragraph 7(1)(c) is necessary to deal with the situation where information collected for a journalistic purpose is used for another purpose, which requires consent.

This provision protects the collector of that information for the original purpose and collection, which may have been done without the knowledge or consent of the individual.

> **Example:** A journalist writes an article about the low vacancy rate in the Ottawa rental housing market, interviewing numerous new hires in the high-tech sector who are stuck in hotels while they try to find permanent accommodation. A property manager and a hotel chain both contact the newspaper to ask if they can offer discounts and free service to the interviewees. The newspaper contacts a list of twenty people whose names it obtained from high-tech companies, not all of whom were contacted for the article, and asks for their consent to release their information. Most agree, but several question how the newspaper had collected the information in the first place.

The newspaper is protected by this paragraph in the event that one of those individuals complains to the Privacy Commissioner about collection without consent.

(d) the information is publicly available and is specified by the regulations.

Other than in section 7, the Act is silent on the issue of publicly available information, or information that has been made available on public records, such as the land titles registry or the telephone book. Over the years a great deal of information has been released from such records, and with the advent of electronic records and scanners, it is now easy to collect and disseminate information for purposes totally unrelated to the original collection, usually without the knowledge and consent of the individual. However, a total prohibition on the collection and use of publicly available information is as undesirable as its continued unrestricted collection and use.

The Act attempts a compromise, which is found here in paragraph 7(1)(d). An organization may collect publicly available information without the knowledge or consent of the individual, if the information or the class of information is specified in the regulations, as provided in paragraph 26(1)(a.1). (See chapter 5 for a discussion of the regulations.)

The idea here is that limitations to the requirement for consent should be limited and *specific*. The provision in section 26 states that the "Governor in Council may make regulations . . . specifying information or classes of information for the purposes of 7(1)(d), 2(c.l) or 3(h.1)."

The notion here is not to define publicly available information — as in a definition such as "all information placed on a public register by a government agency" — but rather to list the data elements that when placed on a public register may be collected, used, or disclosed without the consent of the data subject. Given the sensitive nature and the vast breadth of information available to the public, if no attempt is made to restrict the practice, there would be scant point in this legislation.

> **Example**: A province makes available its property assessment rolls. Joe Quickbuck wants to collect the names, addresses, phone numbers, and all other information he can find on owners of property valued at over $200,000. In the event that a regulation is developed to exempt the name, address, and value of the property for all owners of property listed in the assessment rolls, he will be able to purchase this information in bulk format from the province.[17]

It should be noted that Joe Quickbuck still must satisfy the reasonableness test for collection, which is described in subsection 5(3), and the collection must be justified by his stated purposes. Thus, if his plan were to target wealthy old ladies to sell

---

[17] See B.C. Information and Privacy Commissioner's Investigation Report # P98-011, "An Investigation concerning the disclosure of personal information through public property registries," 31 March 1998: <http://www.oipcbc.org/investigations/reports/invrpt11.html>. This report states that in 1997, B.C. Assessment generated approximately $2.3 million in revenue through the sale of information from the assessment roll, including name and address of the property owner, description and classification of the property, actual value of the land and improvements.

intrusion detectors, the collection would probably be found to be reasonable for the purpose, and the purpose would probably pass the reasonable person test in subsection 5(3).

Use without knowledge or consent

(2) For the purpose of clause 4.3 of Schedule 1, and despite the note that accompanies that clause, an organization may, without the knowledge or consent of the individual, use personal information only if

(a) in the course of its activities, the organization becomes aware of information that it has reasonable grounds to believe could be useful in the investigation of a contravention of the laws of Canada, a province or a foreign jurisdiction that has been, is being or is about to be committed, and the information is used for the purpose of investigating that contravention;

Paragraph 7(2)(a) is intended to allow organizations to carry out internal investigations using either in-house or contract investigators. The information may be used only for the purposes of the investigation, and the organization must have reasonable grounds to believe that the information could assist in the investigation of a contravention of federal, provincial, or foreign law. The contravention must have been committed, be about to be committed, or be in the course of being committed. The incorporation of the objective standard of reasonable belief should ensure that this provision is not subject to abuse.

> **Example**: Harry Younger complains to his ISP that he is having trouble downloading large files from the Internet. His ISP help-desk, at his invitation, opens a couple of files and discovers that Harry is downloading obscene material. They go and retrieve his old e-mail files from backup tapes to see if he has any huge files there, and open them to see if they are the same type of material. They find that the information appears to be obscene and therefore may violate the *Criminal Code*, so they decide to disclose the material that they have collected to the police under paragraph 7(3)(d).[18]

(b) it is used for the purpose of acting in respect of an emergency that threatens the life, health or security of an individual;

Paragraph 7(2)(b) states that information about an individual can be used by an organization in an emergency that threatens the life of either that individual or another individual.

> **Example**: The management team of a telecommunications company is on a team-building exercise in rural Quebec, and one of the team has what

---

18 This example is borrowed rather loosely from *R. v. Weir*, [1998] 8 W.W.R. 228 (Q.B.).

appears to be a either a seizure, a heart attack, or a stroke while on a small island without transportation. His colleagues call back to the office to the human resources department to check the records of his executive medical checkup to find out what conditions he might be suffering from so they could administer the appropriate first aid.

(c) it is used for statistical, or scholarly study or research, purposes that cannot be achieved without using the information, the information is used in a manner that will ensure its confidentiality, it is impracticable to obtain consent and the organization informs the Commissioner of the use before the information is used;

Paragraph 7(2)(c) defines a multipart test that must be met before information can be used by an organization:

1. The information must be used for statistical purposes, or scholarly study, or scholarly research.
2. The statistical purpose, study, or research cannot be achieved without using the information (i.e., the purposes could not be fulfilled using anonymous data).
3. The organization uses the information in a way to ensure it remains confidential.
4. It is impracticable for the organization to obtain consent, which usually occurs where there are large numbers of persons involved, or the information is old and individuals are hard to trace.
5. The organization informs the Privacy Commissioner of the use before it occurs.

The obligation to inform the Privacy Commissioner before use gives the Commissioner the opportunity to recommend protective measures to the organization and thus provides a degree of oversight. It also will serve to keep the Commissioner apprised of industry practices with regard to uses of information.

> **Example**: A grain elevator company in rural Saskatchewan has decided to celebrate its business by publishing the history of the Saskatchewan Wheat Pool and its own part in the history of prairie grain. The editor of this project digs into all the old personnel records, sifts through the records of grain shipments, and uses customer information to contact farmers who might have historical records or memories to share in the production of the book.

All these instances are uses of personal information — one being of personnel and the other of customer data — and are for scholarly or historical study. If an independent researcher had come in and looked at the records, it would have been a disclosure under paragraph 7(3)(f).

Walking through the five-part test, then:

1. It is clear the information is being used for historical research. Scholarly is a broader term than historical and would also include medical, scientific, and economic research.
2. The purposes cannot be achieved without using the information, because the appeal of the book will be based partly on the stories of the people involved.
3. Although this appears counter-intuitive when one is publishing the information, it is clear that there is much information in the records that would not be suitable to publish, that could be very sensitive, and that must be kept confidential. For the information that the company seeks to publish, it would only be good sense to check with the individuals or next of kin before proceeding, but note that this section concerns use and provides that all the information may be *used* for the research necessary to produce the book.

    Maintaining confidentiality also entails such things as doing the work in-house or providing adequate security, clearing a limited number of personnel for the project, and ensuring that information not used is returned to its former storage.
4. If the personnel records stretch back over seventy-five years, it is highly unlikely that the individuals concerned are alive or that the addresses in the files are still valid. It would be impracticable to try to get consent to use this information.
5. Informing the Commissioner may be as simple as sending a letter explaining that the organization plans to publish its history and will be reviewing all its files to find interesting stories to use. It should also indicate who will have

access, the terms and conditions of that use, procedures to be followed in the event of subsequent disclosure, and how the confidentiality of the records will be maintained.

(c.1) it is publicly available and is specified by the regulations; or by that section;

Paragraph 7(2)(c.1) allows organizations to use publicly available information. See discussion under 7(1)(d) above.

(d) it was collected under paragraph (1)(a) or (b).

Paragraph 7(2)(d) states that information that was collected under paragraphs 7(1) (a) or (b), without the knowledge or consent of the individual, may be used by the organization without consulting or informing the individual, for the purposes for which it was collected — that is, if the use is clearly in the interests of the individual, and consent cannot be obtained in a timely way, or it is being used for purposes related to the investigation of a breach of an agreement or a contravention of a federal or provincial law.

> **Example:** Fred Dogbone has put in an insurance claim to Global Giant Insurance for falling on Jane Lee's front step. Global Giant has collected information about Fred from other insurance companies through the Insurance Crime Prevention Bureau, and has discovered that he has made five such previous claims. They now wish to compare the details of these claims and use the information in them to deny the claim.

It is exceedingly unlikely that Fred, if asked, would agree to share the nature of his earlier claims or the responses of the earlier companies so that the company could build a case against his interest.

Disclosure without knowledge or consent

(3) For the purpose of clause 4.3 of Schedule 1, and despite the note that accompanies that clause, an organization may disclose personal information without the knowledge or consent of the individual only if the disclosure is

The paragraphs in subsection 7(3) set out the limited circumstances in which information may be disclosed without consent. The list is much longer than those for collection and use because there are fewer compelling reasons why an organization cannot seek consent when collecting and using the information. The list of permitted disclosures is limited and it is very likely that there are many information-sharing practices in Canada that will need to change as a result of this legislation.

(a) made to, in the Province of Quebec, an advocate or notary or, in any other province, a barrister or solicitor who is representing the organization;

Paragraph 7(3)(a) provides that information about an individual may be disclosed without the knowledge or consent of the individual to a notary or lawyer acting for the organization. This sort of disclosure may be impossible to foresee at the time of collection. The disclosure may be in the larger context of a legal action unrelated to the individual.

> **Example**: In the example just given above, it is highly likely that unless Fred accepts the first letter from Global Giant indicating they do not intend to honour his claim, there will be the possibility of litigation. Global can use this section to disclose the information about Fred to its external lawyers.

(b) for the purpose of collecting a debt owed by the individual to the organization;

Paragraph 7(3)(b) provides that personal information may be disclosed without the knowledge or consent of the individual for the purpose of collecting a debt owed by the individual to the organization.

Sometimes organizations collect their own debts, but more often this is done by collection agencies acting on behalf of the organization, and in some cases the debt is sold to a third party. Although in some of these circumstances consent of the individual may be implied, as in when the organization contracts out the debt-collecting function, in others it may not be, as in when the debt is sold.

> **Example**: Susan Smith has run up a huge phone bill and has left her apartment and her phone bill behind when she moved to another city. The phone company tracks her down and sends her a letter but receives no response. Several demand letters later the company, having lost patience, turns the debt over to Debts Unlimited for collection. That disclosure is permitted under this paragraph.

(c) required to comply with a subpoena or warrant issued or an order made by a court, person or body with jurisdiction to compel the production of information, or to comply with rules of court relating to the production of records;

Paragraph 7(3)(c) contains a list of circumstances where personal information may be disclosed without the knowledge or consent of the individual to comply with (1) a subpoena, warrant or order, issued by a Court, person or body with jurisdiction to compel production of information, or (2) the Rules of Court relating to the production of records.

Although the wording in the Act "an organization may disclose" suggests there is a discretion on the part of the organization to refuse to comply with such a warrant or order, the organization would usually be in the position of having to produce the information unless it had grounds, unrelated to this Act, to refuse to do so.

A warrant usually is quite specific about the data required, but a subpoena to produce documents in civil actions may be broadly worded and it is often possible to negotiate a more limited disclosure with this law. There is now a requirement to make these efforts to limit disclosure, so staff must be adequately trained to respond to these requests with the interests of the individual uppermost in their minds.

(c.1) made to a government institution or part of a government institution that has made a request for the information, identified its lawful authority to obtain the information and indicated that

Paragraph 7(3)(c.1) was added by Parliament to address the concerns of the federal law enforcement/national security communities. When it was introduced, the government stated that the amendment did not give any new powers to law enforcement but that it merely reflects the status quo.

There are three circumstances in this paragraph where personal information may be disclosed without the knowledge or consent of the individual.

The disclosure is made to a government institution or part of a government institution that

1. has requested the information, so the impetus for disclosure comes from the government institution;
2. has identified its lawful authority to obtain the information and that it has the statutory right to the information; and
3. has indicated as follows:

(i) it suspects that the information relates to national security, the defence of Canada or the conduct of international affairs,

(ii) the disclosure is requested for the purpose of enforcing any law of Canada, a province or a foreign jurisdiction, carrying out an investigation relating to the enforcement of any such law or gathering intelligence for the purpose of enforcing any such law, or

- It suspects the information relates to national security, the defence of Canada, or to the conduct of international affairs. Suspicion is the threshold test for national security matters; the higher standard of reasonable grounds to believe, which applies in law enforcement, is not a requirement with this Act.
- The disclosure is requested for the purpose of enforcing federal, provincial, or foreign law, or carrying out an investigation relating to the enforcement of those laws, or gathering intelligence for the purpose of enforcing those laws. This paragraph is aimed at "pre-warrant" activities in which private sector organizations cooperate with domestic law enforcement agencies who are collecting the information on a "casual" or "routine" basis and for which no warrant is required. Only information that is of a relatively innocuous nature will be collected by these means, since the collection of information in which the individual has a reasonable expectation of privacy would require the *Charter* protection of a warrant.[19] The reasonable expectation of privacy test enunciated by the Supreme Court of Canada in *Plant* was as follows:
  - the nature of the information;
  - the nature of the relationship between the party releasing the information and the party claiming confidentiality;
  - the place where the information was obtained; and
  - the seriousness of the crime being investigated.

The majority in the Court found that in balancing the societal interest in individual dignity and autonomy with effective law enforcement, the seriousness of the crime

---

[19] See *R. v. Plant*, [1993] S.C.R. 281, where the Court found that an individual did not have a reasonable expectation of privacy in his hydro consumption records — he was growing marijuana in greenhouses.

(iii) the disclosure is requested for the purpose of administering any law of Canada or a province;

outweighed the privacy interest. Note that foreign law enforcement agencies do not carry out investigations in Canada. The investigation of breaches of foreign laws is carried out by the RCMP or other domestic police forces, at the request of foreign law enforcement agencies.

- The disclosure is requested for administering any federal or provincial law. This paragraph would allow, not require, organizations to provide information to federal or provincial agencies who have a legal mandate to get the information for the purposes of administering statutory programs or activities.

Examples:

1. A hotel clerk is approached by a person claiming to be a CSIS agent, looking for information about an individual staying at the hotel. To the question, "Is Tom Terrorist registered in this hotel?" the clerk may consider responding by releasing the information since there is probably little expectation of privacy in the information, and it is not always necessary for CSIS to have a warrant to conduct inquiries.

   The clerk should ask to see the agent's identification, and may release the information as "pre-warrant information."

2. A hotel clerk is approached by Sergeant Renfrew of the Mounted Police who (1) asks whether an individual dressed in black casual attire carrying several duffel bags and a violin case has just checked into the hotel, and what his room number might be; and (2) asks to see all the billing and call records of the individuals in the adjoining rooms. The clerk would be justified in insisting on a warrant and should keep a record of the disclosure so the individual can exercise his right under clause 4.9 of the Schedule to

obtain information concerning disclosures of his personal information; except for the limited circumstances described in section 9 of the Act, this includes disclosures to law enforcement officials.

3. A representative of Human Resources Development Canada goes to a small trucking firm and asks for the names of all part-time employees who have worked at the company in the past year, as well as their social insurance numbers and when they worked. The stated reason is that HRDC wants to run a cross-check to see if these individuals are claiming employment insurance and not declaring their part-time earnings.

Release of this information is not mandatory, so the decision must be made by the organization as to whether or not it wants to comply. If it does comply, it should get the request in writing, ask HRDC to state its lawful authority to obtain the information, and should keep a record of all disclosures.

(c.2) made to the government institution mentioned in section 7 of the *Proceeds of Crime (Money Laundering) Act* as required by that section;

Paragraph 7(3)(c.2) was added through section 97 of the *Proceeds of Crime (Money Laundering) Act*,[20] introduced into Parliament in the spring of 1999 and passed in June 2000. It received Royal Assent on 29 June 2000 and will come into force on a date to be fixed by order of the Governor in Council.

Section 97, which amends this Act, will come into force on 1 January 2001, or on the date the *Money Laundering Act* comes into force, whichever is later. Since the *Money Laundering Act* is not expected to come into force until sometime in 2001, this provision will not be in force on 1 January 2001.

The government institution referred to in section 7 of the *Money Laundering Act* is the Financial Transaction and Reports Analysis Centre of Canada, established under that Act.

---

[20] S.C. 2000, c. 17 [*Money Laundering Act*].

Section 7 obliges banks, including authorized foreign banks, credit unions, caisses populaires, insurance companies, trust and loan companies, securities and investment dealers, foreign exchange dealers, lawyers, accountants, casinos, and some government departments and agencies to report suspicious transactions, in addition to regular transactions involving dollar amounts over certain prescribed limits.

Section 7 of the *Money Laundering Act* reads:

> In addition to the requirements referred to in section 9(1), every person or entity shall report to the Centre, in the prescribed form and manner, every financial transaction that occurs in the course of their activities and in respect of which there are reasonable grounds to suspect that the transaction is related to the commission of a money laundering offence.

Section 8 of that Act prohibits the maker of a suspicious transaction report from disclosing the contents of the report with the intent to prejudice a criminal investigation, whether or not the investigation has begun.

The Centre itself is not a law enforcement agency but it analyzes suspicious transactions and refers some cases to law enforcement. The Centre is subject to the federal *Privacy Act* but the application of the exemptions under that Act make it unlikely that an individual will get access to a suspicious transaction report and is not likely to be told that such a report even exists.

The amendment to subsection 7(3) of this Act, which added (c.2), allows organizations subject to the *Money Laundering Act* to make suspicious transaction reports to the Centre without the knowledge or consent of the individual. Although such disclosures could have been permitted under paragraph 7(3)(i) — "required by law" — for what appears to have been drafting reasons related to section 9, the separate paragraph approach seems more appropriate.

Example: An alert bank teller in a big city bank notices that a certain young man makes irregularly timed but frequent deposits of large sums of money (not large enough to trigger an automatic report under the Act) in small bills. The amounts deposited are always different, never on the same day of the week and the customer appears at times to be quite nervous.

After observing this for a number of weeks, the teller decides to raise the possibility with his supervisor that the customer may be laundering drug money. His supervisor writes a memo to her supervisor and after much correspondence back and forth between the branch and head office, the bank decides to file a suspicious transaction report to the Centre in the prescribed form.

The disclosure of this personal information is permitted under paragraph 7(3)(c.2) of this Act.

(d) made on the initiative of the organization to an investigative body, a government institution or a part of a government institution and the organization

  (i) has reasonable grounds to believe that the information relates to a breach of an agreement or a contravention of the laws of Canada, a province or a foreign jurisdiction that has been, is being or is about to be committed, or

  (ii) suspects that the information relates to national security, the defence of Canada or the conduct of international affairs;

Paragraph 7(3)(d) allows for the disclosure of personal information without the knowledge or consent of the individual, to be made on the initiative of the organization to an investigative body, a government institution, or a part of a government institution. It also establishes the tests for this disclosure: the organization must have reasonable grounds to believe that the information relates to (1) a breach of an agreement or a private contract, or (2) the contravention of the laws of Canada, a province, or a foreign jurisdiction (this is very broad, covering everything from copyright law to the highway traffic laws); or the organization suspects that (3) the information relates to national security, the defence of Canada, or the conduct of international affairs.

It is not necessary for the government to name its law enforcement agencies although there is a regulation-making power to do so. Disclosures may be made to law enforcement agencies simply through the language that permits disclosure to government institutions. Investigative bodies are specified by regulation and will include the private sector bodies that perform an investigative function either for associations or individual companies. (See discussion of regulations in chapter 5.)

Examples:

1. The Insurance Crime Prevention Bureau of the Insurance Council of Canada acts as an investigative body for its member property and casualty insurance companies. It is clear that this body performs a service for its members by accumulating all the members' claims and enabling them to detect multiple claims, which they may then research further to determine whether individuals are perpetrating insurance fraud.

   The provision of claims information to this body is a disclosure under this paragraph.

2. A small trucking firm is shipping coffee between Mexico and Vancouver, and the staff are starting to suspect that there are drugs in the coffee. The organization has to have "reasonable grounds" but this condition is satisfied when one of the cases is dropped and disgorges bags of white powder along with the coffee. At this point the company decides to call in the RCMP and discloses all the records it has, including cellular telephone numbers and records of conversations with the individuals with whom it has been doing business.

   At first, these records might be assumed to be business records, but since the small trucking company never checked thoroughly into the identity of the people with whom it was doing business, the information may well constitute personal information. The firm should document this disclosure and note the reasons it had for the decision.

3. The Prime Minister of France is visiting Quebec City. The operator of a small motel

outside of town begins to be suspicious when two strangers carrying foreign passports arrive in a rental van. They behave in a furtive manner and are using disposable cellular phones. Her cleaning staff reported that they have maps of the city spread out all over their room and refuse to let the room be cleaned. She becomes extremely suspicious when they slam the back of the rental truck shut as she comes by, and she decides to call the local police.

For the purposes of national security and international affairs, suspicion of a threat is sufficient for an inquiry. There appears to be sufficient justification for the release of this information, and from the point of view of the organization there is no requirement to document the reasons for the report, but it would be prudent to do so in case of civil action.

(e) made to a person who needs the information because of an emergency that threatens the life, health or security of an individual and, if the individual whom the information is about is alive, the organization informs that individual in writing without delay of the disclosure;

Paragraph 7(3)(e) provides for exigent circumstances where an individual's life, health, or security are in jeopardy. If it is possible to get the consent of the individual, this should be done, but if time presses this section allows disclosure. The organization must inform the individual of the disclosure in writing without delay.

Example: An employee of a telephone company is involved in a hostage taking outside of the workplace. He has a gun and is holding it to the head of a woman inside a home in the suburbs. The RCMP have asked the employer to get for them instantly all personnel records of the employee, as well as any information that fellow employees might have about his personal life. His Harvard Planner shows appointments with a psychiatrist, and the employer releases that name and phone number as well.

The test for an emergency has certainly been met. The organization needs to simply send a letter advising him of the fact of the release after the fact.

(f) for statistical, or scholarly study or research, purposes that cannot be achieved without disclosing the information, it is impracticable to obtain consent and the organization informs the Commissioner of the disclosure before the information is disclosed;

Paragraph 7(3)(f) permits the organization to disclose personal information for the purposes of scholarly study and research. It sets up three requirements:

1. It must be demonstrated that non-personally identifiable, or anonymous information will not suffice.
2. It must be impracticable to obtain consent, meaning practically impossible.
3. The organization must inform the Privacy Commissioner before the information is released.

This language tracks that used in paragraph 7(2)(c), the only difference being that this paragraph does not require that the information be disclosed in a manner that ensures its confidentiality. This provision allows disclosure for scholarly work, study, and publishing, and obviously it would be inappropriate to enforce its confidentiality. Efforts should be made to control further use of the information depending on the circumstances; if the information is medical information being used for research, certainly a caveat could be added to restrict publishing of the personal identifiers, for instance.

> **Example**: A team of medical researchers from a teaching hospital wants to do a long-term study of workers exposed to radiation. They approach all the nuclear facilities in Canada and ask for the records of their employees. In some cases it will be possible to get consent, but in other cases this may be almost impossible. The researchers want a full data set and decide to appeal to the organization to release the information under this paragraph in the event that the written consent and the telephone appeal fail to locate all the individuals. The organization performs the consent search under contract to the researchers and informs the Privacy Commissioner of the list of individuals it has failed to find, whose records they intend to release to the researchers without consent.

(g) made to an institution whose functions include the conservation of records of historic or archival importance, and the disclosure is made for the purpose of such conservation;

Paragraph 7(3)(g) allows an organization to donate its records to an archival or historical institution. Archival or historical organizations and museums are not within the scope of this legislation because they are not collecting data in the course of commercial activities. Some may be subject to provincial privacy laws, if they are creatures of a province or a municipality. Others, such as a small town historical society, are unlikely to be caught by any regulation. Records obtained from the private sector by the National Archives of Canada, as well as the national museums, are not covered by the *Privacy Act* either.

However, archivists adhere to codes of conduct with respect to the protection of personal information. When an organization is considering donating its records to a museum or historical organization, it would be a good idea to impose terms on the further use that can be made of the information. Such terms might include restrictions on access by researchers for a set period of time or restrictions on the publication of personal information that may be considered sensitive.

(h) made after the earlier of

(i) one hundred years after the record containing the information was created, and

(ii) twenty years after the death of the individual whom the information is about;

Paragraph 7(3)(h) allows an organization to disclose personal information without consent either one hundred years after the record was created or twenty years after the death of the individual, whichever is earlier. Note that this does not mean the information is not still personal information, as is the case in the federal *Privacy Act*, but the paragraph provides logical relief from obtaining consent. In the case of an individual who has been dead for only ten years, it will be necessary to find a provision in the rest of subsection 7(3), since clearly it will be impossible to obtain consent.

(h.1) of information that is publicly available and is specified by the regulations;

Paragraph 7(3)(h.1) simply permits the organization to release information that is publicly available and has been specified in the regulations. For instance, if a data miner has assembled individual profiles from many sources, including the white pages of the phone book, the postal code directory, and the land titles registry, he may be permitted by this paragraph to sell or rent all this information.

(h.2) made by an investigative body and the disclosure is reasonable for purposes related to investigating a breach of an agreement or a contravention of the laws of Canada or a province; or

Paragraph 7(3)(h.2) permits an investigative body to release information for purposes related to the investigation of a breach of an agreement or a contravention of the laws of Canada or a province. For instance, if the investigative body created by the Canadian Bankers Association is listed in the regulations, that body could release the reports concerning known or suspected perpetrators of fraud to other banks to minimize further losses or gather additional evidence while the investigation is ongoing.

(i)   required by law.

There is no discretion in the application of paragraph 7(3)(i); if a disclosure is required by law, the organization must comply.

> **Example**: The GST provisions of the *Excise Tax Act* empower the auditors of Canada Customs and Revenue to collect the personal information of patients, when they audit dentists, to ensure that the dentists are appropriately collecting GST for cosmetic treatment. This clause would therefore empower dentists to release the names and certain medical records of their patients.

Although the dentist is under a strict obligation to minimize disclosure, this paragraph does permit him to release whatever the organization represents as information they have a right to acquire. The government organizations, on the other hand, do not usually have to pass an equally stringent test for the collection of information — the language of the *Privacy Act*, for example, is "related directly to an operating program or activity." This is a lower threshold and puts the private sector organization in the unenviable position of being obliged to comply with government requests for personal information that their customers may consider excessive. Customers who become aware of the disclosure could complain to the Privacy Commissioner about the practice.

Use without consent

(4) Despite clause 4.5 of Schedule 1, an organization may use personal information for purposes other than those for which it was collected in any of the circumstances set out in subsection (2).

Subsection 7(4) addresses clause 4.5 of Schedule 1, which is Principle 5, "Limiting Use, Disclosure, and Retention," but in particular it addresses the new uses element of Principle 5. This principle states that an organization shall not use or disclose information for purposes other than those for which it was collected except with the consent of the individual or as required by law. The information may only be retained for as long as is necessary to fulfil those purposes.

This subsection expands the circumstances under which information may be used for a new purpose without consent, to include any of the circumstances listed in 7(2). It follows, then, that the organization may retain the information for as long as is necessary to fulfil those new purposes.

Subsection 7(4) appears to be somewhat redundant because the use for the new purpose without consent has been exempted by subsection 7(2), but the emphasis in 7(2) was on the restrictions of the consent clause 4.3, whereas in this subsection the emphasis is on clause 4.5. For greater clarity, this subsection reiterates that the information may be used for a new purpose according to any of the paragraphs in 7(2).

Disclosure without consent

(5) Despite clause 4.5 of Schedule 1, an organization may disclose personal information for purposes other than those for which it was collected in any of the circumstances set out in paragraphs (3)(a) to (h.2).

Subsection 7(5) simply does for new disclosures what 7(4) does for new uses. It refers to the list of allowable disclosures without knowledge or consent which is found in 7(3)(a) to (h.2). It does not include 7(3)(i) in that list because the "required by law" element is addressed in Principle 5 itself and subsection 7(5) adds the other circumstances.

Section 8: Access Procedures

Written request

8.(1) A request under clause 4.9 of Schedule 1 must be made in writing.

Section 8 refers to Principle 9 of the Schedule and sets out the procedures that must be followed in providing individuals access to information about themselves.

The request must be in writing. Under section 41 of the Act (Part 2) there is a provision for this to be done electronically in accordance with regulations.

Those regulations presumably would be made on the recommendation of the Minister of Industry.

Assistance

(2) An organization shall assist any individual who informs the organization that they need assistance in preparing a request to the organization.

The organization must assist the individual in preparing the request if asked. This provision is for the benefit of anyone who because of physical or mental disability would have difficulty formulating the request in writing, but it will also assist someone to prepare a precise request, who is unfamiliar with the organization or about his rights with respect to personal information.

Time limit

(3) An organization shall respond to a request with due diligence and in any case not later than thirty days after receipt of the request.

Extension of time limit

(4) An organization may extend the time limit

(a) for a maximum of thirty days if

  (i) meeting the time limit would unreasonably interfere with the activities of the organization, or

  (ii) the time required to undertake any consultations necessary to respond to the request would make the time limit impracticable to meet; or

(b) for the period that is necessary in order to be able to convert the personal information into an alternative format.

In either case, the organization shall, no later than thirty days after the date of the request, send a notice of extension to the individual, advising them of the new time limit, the reasons for extending the time limit and of their right to make a complaint to the Commissioner in respect of the extension.

The organization is obliged to answer a request for individual access promptly but no later than thirty days after receiving it unless the organization has extended the time limit. The limit may be extended for a further thirty days (for a total response period of sixty days) if meeting the original time would interfere with the activities of the organization or the organization needs time to carry out consultations.

The organization may also extend the period for any time necessary to convert the information into an alternative format (which is defined in section 2 as "a format that allows a person with a sensory disability to read or listen to the personal information") as required by section 10.

Where an organization does seek an extension of the thirty-day time limit, it must send a notice of the extension to the individual within the original thirty-day period, setting out the reason for the extension and of the individual's right to complain to the Privacy Commissioner about the extension.

Deemed refusal

(5) If the organization fails to respond within the time limit, the organization is deemed to have refused the request.

Failure on the part of the organization to respond within the time limits, including extensions, is a deemed refusal of access giving rise to a right to complain to the Privacy Commissioner. That complaint must be made within six months of the refusal or deemed refusal unless the Privacy Commissioner grants an extension (see subsection 11(3)).

Costs for responding

(6) An organization may respond to an individual's request at a cost to the individual only if

(a) the organization has informed the individual of the approximate cost; and

(b) the individual has advised the organization that the request is not being withdrawn.

Clause 4.9.4. of Schedule 1 provides that an organization must grant access at "minimal or no cost to the individual." This reflects the practice in public sector data protection laws of not charging individuals for access to their own information. Clearly, the emphasis is on providing access without placing a burden on individuals, so organizations would be well advised to document the rationale behind their fee requests.

Subsection 8(6) requires that where the organization charges a fee for responding to a request, it must first inform the individual of the approximate cost and the individual must agree to it by advising the organization that the request is not withdrawn. Since fees are likely to generate complaints, it would be advisable to give fee estimates in writing, and get the agreement with the individual for the fee estimate in writing, although the requirement is only to inform the individual of the cost, and to be advised by the individual that the request is not being withdrawn.

Reasons

(7) An organization that responds within the time limit and refuses a request shall inform the individual in writing of the refusal, setting out the reasons and any recourse that they may have under this Part.

Where an organization refuses a request for access to personal information, it must inform the individual in writing of the refusal, must give the reasons for the refusal, and must notify the individual of her right to complain to the Privacy Commissioner.

Retention of information

(8) Despite clause 4.5 of Schedule 1, an organization that has personal information that is the subject of a request shall retain the information for as long as is necessary to allow the individual to exhaust any recourse under this Part that they may have.

Although clause 4.5 of Schedule 1 requires that personal information shall only be retained for as long as is necessary to fulfil the purposes for which it was collected, subsection 8(8) of the Act requires an organization to retain personal information that is the subject of a request for as long as necessary for an individual to exhaust his recourses under the Act. If the organization knowingly contravenes this provision, it is guilty of an offence under section 28.

Section 9: Exceptions to the Right of Access

Principle 9 of Schedule 1 states:

> Upon request, an individual shall be informed of the existence, use, and disclosure of his or her personal information and shall be given access to that information. An individual shall be able to challenge the accuracy and completeness of the information and have it amended as appropriate.

Section 9 of the Act sets out the following circumstances where, despite the principle, an organization must not or should not provide access.

When access prohibited

9.(1) Despite clause 4.9 of Schedule 1, an organization shall not give an individual access to personal information if doing so would likely reveal personal information about a third party. However, if the information about the third party is severable from the record containing the information about the individual, the organization shall sever the information about the third party before giving the individual access.

Subsections 9(1) & (2):

- where providing access to the individual's personal information would be likely to reveal the personal information of another individual unless the two can be severed from one another, or the other individual consents, or the requesting individual needs the information because an individual's life, health, or security is threatened.

Limit

(2) Subsection (1) does not apply if the third party consents to the access or the individual needs the information because an individual's life, health or security is threatened.

An example of this limit might be when the subject individual is visiting the second at a private residence with an unlisted telephone number, and it is necessary to contact the subject individual and obtain the private location and telephone information of the second individual, because the subject individual has information or can materially assist in a life or death situation with a third individual.

Information related to paragraphs 7(3)(c), (c.1), or (d)

(2.1) An organization shall comply with subsection (2.2) if an individual requests that the organization

(a) inform the individual about

    (i)   any disclosure of information to a government institution or a part of a government institution under paragraph 7(3)(c), subparagraph 7(3)(c.1)(i) or (ii) or paragraph 7(3)(c.2) or (d), or

    (ii) the existence of any information that the organization has relating to a disclosure referred to in subparagraph (i), to a subpoena, warrant or order referred to in paragraph 7(3)(c) or to a request made by a government institution or a part of a government institution under subparagraph 7(3)(c.1)(i) or (ii); or

(b) give the individual access to the information referred to in subparagraph (a)(ii).

Notification and response

(2.2) An organization to which subsection (2.1) applies

(a) shall, in writing and without delay, notify the institution or part concerned of the request made by the individual; and

Subsections 9(2.1), (2.2), (2.3), & (2.4):

- where an individual requests information about any disclosures of personal information about the individual made to government institutions under paragraph 7(3)(c) (warrant or subpoena), subparagraphs 7(3)(c.1)(i) or (ii) (national security, law enforcement), paragraph 7(3)(c.2) (suspicious transaction reports), or in paragraph 7(3)(d) (made on the initiative of the government relating to law enforcement or national security; for instance, where information was disclosed to the RCMP);
- where an individual requests information about the existence of any information that the organization has about disclosures under the provisions listed above (except for paragraphs 7(3)(c.2) or 7(3)(d), where there is no request; e.g., Is there any record of a disclosure made to CSIS? Or of a suspicious transaction report made to the Centre?);
- where an individual requests access to information about him that would reveal requests made by law enforcement or national security agencies;

In all these circumstances, the organization must notify the government institution of the request and must not respond to the request until the government institution approves the release or the access, or thirty days have passed since the government institution was notified, whichever comes first. This means that the institution must act within the thirty-day period or risk the consequences of release or access.

(b) shall not respond to the request before the earlier of

    (i) the day on which it is notified under subsection (2.3), and

    (ii) thirty days after the day on which the institution or part was notified.

Objection

(2.3) Within thirty days after the day on which it is notified under subsection (2.2), the institution or part shall notify the organization whether or not the institution or part objects to the organization complying with the request. The institution or part may object only if the institution or part is of the opinion that compliance with the request could reasonably be expected to be injurious to

(a) national security, the defence of Canada or the conduct of international affairs; or

(a.1) the detection, prevention or deterrence of money laundering; or

(b) the enforcement of any law of Canada, a province or a foreign jurisdiction, an investigation relating to the enforcement of any such law or the gathering of intelligence for the purpose of enforcing any such law.

Once notified of the request, the onus is on the national security or law enforcement agency to object to the release or access if there are grounds for doing so.

The grounds for objection are that compliance with the request could reasonably be expected to be injurious to

- national security, the defence of Canada or the conduct of international affairs;
- the detection, prevention, or deterrence of money laundering; or
- the enforcement of any law of Canada, a province, or a foreign jurisdiction, an investigation relating to the enforcement of any of those laws or intelligence gathering for the purpose of enforcing any of those laws.

If the government institution objects to the release or the access, the organization must refuse to provide the individual with access to the information and must notify the Privacy Commissioner of the refusal. Furthermore, the organization must not let the individual know that it has contacted the government institution, or provide the response of the government institution, or reveal that the Privacy Commissioner has been notified.

> **Example:** In the example given above under paragraph 7(3)(c.2) on page **[79]** where the bank made a suspicious transaction report to the Centre, if the person about whom that report was made — our suspected Drug Dealer (DD) —asks the bank for access to all the per-

Prohibition

(2.4) Despite clause 4.9 of Schedule 1, if an organization is notified under subsection (2.3) that the institution or part objects to the organization complying with the request, the organization

(a) shall refuse the request to the extent that it relates to paragraph (2.1)(a) or to information referred to in subparagraph (2.1)(a)(ii);

(b) shall notify the Commissioner, in writing and without delay, of the refusal; and

(c) shall not disclose to the individual

   (i) any information that the organization has relating to a disclosure to a government institution or a part of a government institution under paragraph 7(3)(c), subparagraph 7(3)(c.1)(i) or (ii) or paragraph 7(3)(c.2) or (d) or to a request made by a government institution or a part of a government institution under either of those subparagraphs,

   (ii) that the organization notified an institution or part under paragraph (2.2)(a) or the Commissioner under paragraph (b), or

   (iii) that the institution or part objects.

sonal information the bank has about him and to whom it was disclosed, the procedures set out in 9(2.1) through (2.4) must be followed:

1. The bank must notify the Centre that DD has requested access to his personal information, which would include the report and all the surrounding evidence such as the memos back and forth to head office.

2. The bank cannot give DD access to his information until 30 days after it notified the Centre or until it hears back from the Centre, whichever comes first. This essentially means that the Centre has only thirty days to deal with the notice from the bank. If it takes longer than that, the bank can release the information to DD.

3. Within those thirty days the Centre must notify the bank either that there is no problem releasing the information to DD or that the Centre objects to the release to DD on the grounds that giving him access to the information could reasonably be expected to be injurious to the detection, prevention, or deterrence of money laundering.

4. If the Centre notifies the bank that it objects to the release within the thirty days, the bank must refuse DD access to any information it has about him that would reveal that the bank had formed a suspicion, considered whether to make a report (all those memos), made the report, the report itself, the notice by the bank to the Centre, and the Centre's response objecting to the release.

5. When the bank refuses all that information, it must notify the Privacy Commissioner that it has done so, but of course it can't reveal that to DD either.

When access may be refused

(3) Despite the note that accompanies clause 4.9 of Schedule 1, an organization is not required to give access to personal information only if

(a) the information is protected by solicitor-client privilege;

(b) to do so would reveal confidential commercial information;

(c) to do so could reasonably be expected to threaten the life or security of another individual;

(c.1) the information was collected under paragraph 7(1)(b); or

(d) the information was generated in the course of a formal dispute resolution process.

However, in the circumstances described in paragraph (b) or (c), if giving access to the information would reveal confidential commercial information or could reasonably be expected to threaten the life or security of another individual, as the case may be, and that information is severable from the record containing any other information for which access is requested, the organization shall give the individual access after severing.

The end result is that DD will never know that the suspicious transaction report was made, and other individuals will never know that CSIS or the RCMP or the OPP were asking questions about them. The question is — and the authors of this book have no answer — can this sort of provision survive a challenge under the *Canadian Charter of Rights and Freedoms?*

Subsections 9(3), (4), & (5):

This is the second instance when the Act has had to state that the note in a principle, in this case Principle 9, must be ignored.

This subsection contains a closed list of circumstances where an organization can, but not *must,* refuse to give access to personal information when requested by the individual.

Those circumstances are as follows:

(a) The information is protected by solicitor-client privilege, which includes information prepared in contemplation of litigation.

(b) Providing access would reveal commercial confidential information, provided the information could not reasonably be severed. One example would be the complete assessment of an individual's projected lifetime purchasing profile. An argument could be made by the company that this analysis is proprietary, that it is not actually the information of the individual but is the firm's analysis of trends and patterns, and that releasing it could reveal the company's patented data extrapolation process.

(c) Providing access could reasonably be expected to threaten the life or security of another person, provided that the information could not reasonably be severed.

(c.1) The information was collected under paragraph 7(1)(b). Once again, this applies if the sensitive information could not reasonably be severed.

(d) The information was generated in the course of a formal dispute resolution process.

Limit

(4) Subsection (3) does not apply if the individual needs the information because an individual's life, health or security is threatened.

Subsection (4) contains a general override to the above circumstances so that access must be provided if the individual needs the information because an individual's life, health, or security is threatened.

Notice

(5) If an organization decides not to give access to personal information in the circumstances set out in paragraph (3)(c.1), the organization shall, in writing, so notify the Commissioner, and shall include in the notification any information that the Commissioner may specify.

Subsection (5) provides that when access is refused on the grounds that the information was collected under paragraph 7(1)(b), because it would compromise the availability, and collection is reasonable for purposes related to breach of an agreement or contravention of a law, the organization must inform the Privacy Commissioner.

> **Example**: Joe Quickbuck has assembled a data mine with complex customer profiling software in place. Mary Monsterbucks, fed up with being the target of direct mail solicitations and phone calls, takes a collection of them and complains, asking how the companies got her name. They all point to Joe Quickbuck, who did the customer profiling for them and arranged for the actual solicitations. When told that she is showing up on all of these mailshots because of the profile Joe Quickbuck's company produces, she wants to see not just the raw information but the interpolation made by Joe's company of the information.
>
> Although Joe is prepared to release final conclusions — that is, Mary has an income of $150,000, has a certain kind of taste, likes red cars, dates frequently, and so on — he is unwilling to release actual worksheets that might show the software's processes in arriving at this decision. He has the discretion to protect this under paragraph 9(3)(b).

Section 10: Sensory Disability

10. An organization shall give access to personal information in an alternative format to an individual with a sensory disability who has a right of access to personal information under this Part and who requests that it be transmitted in the alternative format if

(a) a version of the information already exists in that format; or

(b) its conversion into that format is reasonable and necessary in order for the individual to be able to exercise rights under this Part.

Section 10 places an obligation on an organization to give access to personal information in an "alternative format" to an individual with an auditory or visual disability. The onus is on the individual to request access in an alternative format, and the organization must give access if the information or a version of it exists in the format; or conversion into the format is (a) reasonable and (b) necessary for the individual to have meaningful access to his information.

Thus, although it might be "necessary" for an individual with a visual impairment to have a thousand-page document in Braille so she could read it, requiring the organization to translate the document might not be "reasonable." The example is extreme for argument's sake only; in real life the circumstances are more likely to be less cut and dried.

The term "alternative format" is defined in section 2 as "with respect to personal information, means a format that allows a person with a sensory disability to read or listen to the personal information."

DIVISION 2: REMEDIES

Section 11: Filing of Complaints

Division 2 of the Act sets out the remedies available to an individual who has not been able to settle a complaint at the organizational level. It begins by providing for complaints to be made to the Commissioner in section 11, the powers of the Commissioner in section 12, the preparation by the Commissioner of a report on the complaint, and ends with the remedies available from the Federal Court in sections 14 through 17.

Contravention

11.(1) An individual may file with the Commissioner a written complaint against an organization for contravening a provision of Division 1 or for not following a recommendation set out in Schedule 1.

Subsection 11(1) provides that an individual has a right to file a complaint with the Commissioner against an organization for contravening any provision of Division 1, which is to say sections 5 through 10, or for the organization's failure to follow a recommendation found in Schedule 1.

It would make sense for the individual to begin the complaint process with the organization concerned, since it is obliged by the Act to have established mechanisms for dealing with complaints. It would be in the best interests of the organization to try to settle with the complainant and thus avoid having the Commissioner begin a formal investigation.

The Commissioner has the power under section 13(2) to decline to prepare a report if the complaint could be dealt with through other mechanisms, and he could exercise this by insisting that the individual first make an effort to settle with the organization before he proceeds with the investigation.

The right to complain about the failure of an organization to follow the recommendations in Schedule 1 attracted some criticism from business during the Act's passage through Parliament. Their argument was that a recommendation is merely that, a recommendation, and if an organization chooses not to follow it, should it have to justify that to the individual or to the Commissioner?

On the other hand, the recommendations flow from the obligations, explain how the obligations can and should be met, and generally prescribe fair information practices in action. In many cases, it would be unlikely that an organization could meet the obligation without adhering to the recommendation.

The complaint must be in writing. We assume that electronic means of communicating with the Commissioner's office will be recognized by a listing of this provision under Schedule 2 of the Act. This listing in Schedule 2 would presumably be done on the recommendation of the Minister of Industry, as soon as the Commissioner's Office is ready to receive complaints electronically.

A complainant might do well to begin the process by contacting the Commissioner's office:

Telephone: 1-613-995-8210
Toll free: 1-800-282-1376
Web site: www.privcom.gc.ca
e-mail: info@privcom.gc.ca

A caller might quickly learn whether the Commissioner has already investigated a similar matter or had the same complaint against the organization. Certainly staff should be able to assist in focusing, limiting, or expanding the scope of the complaint.

Commissioner may initiate complaint

(2) If the Commissioner is satisfied that there are reasonable grounds to investigate a matter under this Part, the Commissioner may initiate a complaint in respect of the matter.

Subsection 11(2) provides that if the Commissioner is satisfied that there are reasonable grounds to investigate any matter under the Act, he may initiate his own complaint. He might do this in circumstances where he has had a tip from a whistleblower (see section 27), or where in the course of an investigation on another matter he becomes aware of another questionable practice of an organization.

Time limit

(3) A complaint that results from the refusal to grant a request under section 8 must be filed within six months, or any longer period that the Commissioner allows, after the refusal or after the expiry of the time limit for responding to the request, as the case may be.

Subsection 11(3) provides that a complaint concerning refusal of access under section 8 must be filed within six months of the refusal to grant access or a deemed refusal for not responding within the time limits. The Commissioner may allow for a period longer than six months.

Notice

(4) The Commissioner shall give notice of a complaint to the organization against which the complaint was made.

Subsection 11(4) obliges the Commissioner to notify an organization that a complaint has been filed against it. If this is the first time the organization has heard of the problem and believes that it could be solved or that the complaint is unfounded, it should consider contacting the Commissioner about its intention to try to setttle the matter.

Section 12: Investigations of Complaints

Powers of Commissioner

12.(1) The Commissioner shall conduct an investigation in respect of a complaint and, for that purpose, may

(a) summon and enforce the appearance of persons before the Commissioner and compel them to give oral or written evidence on oath and to produce any records and things that the Commissioner considers necessary to investigate the complaint, in the same manner and to the same extent as a superior court of record;

Section 12 provides that the Commissioner must investigate any complaint he receives and sets out his powers in carrying out that investigation as follows:

a) In exercising the powers described here, the Commissioner may do so in the same manner and to the same extent as a superior court of record. Failure by any person to comply with the Commissioner's powers, when he exercises them under this paragraph, can lead to findings of contempt and conviction for offences such as perjury. It is not likely that the Commissioner will formally invoke all these powers in the normal investigation of complaints. Organizations would be well advised to cooperate with the Commissioner when he approaches them more informally so as to avoid creating the kind of atmosphere where the Commissioner would be left with no choice but to invoke his formal powers:

   i) to summon persons (individuals or corporations acting through individuals) to appear before him and to enforce their appearance;

   ii) to compel them to give evidence, orally or in writing, under oath. Anyone who lies to the Commissioner under oath could be charged with perjury under the *Criminal Code*;

   iii) to compel persons to produce "records" as defined in section 2 and also things that he considers necessary to investigate the complaint. "Things" could include the hard drive of a computer or a locked safe.

(b) administer oaths;

b) The Commissioner has the power to administer oaths to persons compelled to appear before him to give evidence.

(c) receive and accept any evidence and other information, whether on oath, by affidavit or otherwise, that the Commissioner sees fit, whether or not it is or would be admissible in a court of law;

(d) at any reasonable time, enter any premises, other than a dwelling-house, occupied by an organization on satisfying any security requirements of the organization relating to the premises;

c) The Commissioner has the power to receive and accept any evidence and other information, under oath or not, that he sees fit, regardless of whether that evidence would be admissible in a court. In other words, he is not bound by the rules of evidence so he can hear and accept hearsay evidence, for example.

d) The Commissioner has the right, at any reasonable time, to enter the premises occupied by an organization after satisfying any security requirements of the organization. The Commissioner is not authorized to enter a dwelling house for such purposes, which may limit his ability to investigate a business run out of someone's basement. His power to compel a person to appear and produce records and "things" could make up for this in some cases.

The term "dwelling house" is defined in the *Criminal Code* as meaning "the whole or any part of a building or structure that is kept or occupied as a permanent or temporary residence, and includes (a) a building within the curtilage of a dwelling house that is connected to it by a doorway or by a covered or enclosed passageway, and (b) a unit that is designed to be mobile and to be used as a permanent or temporary residence and that is being used as such residence."

Case law on the term is a bit thin. A motel is a dwelling house.[21] According to *Martin's Annual Criminal Code: 2000*, "[c]urtilage is not a term of normal usage in Canada, but has been extensively considered in the United States because of the Fourth Amendment protection against unreasonable search and seizure. In *United States* v. *Potts,* 297 F.2d 688 (6th Cir. 1961), curtilage was defined to include all buildings in close proximity to a dwelling, which are continually used for

---

21　See *R.* v. *Henderson,* [1975] 1 W.W.R. 360 (B.C. Prov. Ct.).

carrying on domestic employment; or such place as is necessary and convenient to a dwelling and is habitually used for family purposes."[22]

(e) converse in private with any person in any premises entered under paragraph (d) and otherwise carry out in those premises any inquiries that the Commissioner sees fit; and

e) The Commissioner has the power, once he has entered premises, to speak privately with any person in those premises or make any other inquiries he sees fit, such as looking at paper files or requiring access to computerized files.

(f) examine or obtain copies of or extracts from records found in any premises entered under paragraph (d) that contain any matter relevant to the investigation.

f) The Commissioner has the power to obtain copies of any records found on the premises that contain "any matter relevant to the investigation." This qualification would allow an organization to challenge "fishing expeditions," since anything sought by the Commissioner must be "relevant" to the actual investigation.

Dispute resolution mechanisms

(2) The Commissioner may attempt to resolve complaints by means of dispute resolution mechanisms such as mediation and conciliation

Although the Commissioner has considerable powers as listed above, subsection 12(2) provides that the Commissioner is empowered to seek resolution of any matter through mediation and other alternative dispute resolution mechanisms. Given the incentive of the organization to settle a matter without publicity and expense, and the growing use of ADR to settle disputes instead of costly court proceedings, this provision is key.

Delegation

(3) The Commissioner may delegate any of the powers set out in subsection (1) or (2).

Subsection 12(3) provides that the Commissioner may delegate any of the powers listed above. The power to delegate is not limited to the staff of the Commissioner's office — he can delegate to others such as contractors and consultants or to his provincial counterparts.

---

[22] *Martin's Annual Criminal Code: 2000* (Aurora, ON: Canada Law Book Inc., 2000) at 12.

Return of records

(4) The Commissioner or the delegate shall return to a person or an organization any record or thing that they produced under this section within ten days after they make a request to the Commissioner or the delegate, but nothing precludes the Commissioner or the delegate from again requiring that the record or thing be produced.

Subsection 12(4) obliges the Commissioner to return any record or thing seized under 12(1) within ten days of a request to do so, from the person or organization from whom the record was seized. The Commissioner can always ask for materials to be produced again.

Certificate of delegation

(5) Any person to whom powers set out in subsection (1) are delegated shall be given a certificate of the delegation and the delegate shall produce the certificate, on request, to the person in charge of any premises to be entered under paragraph (1)(d).

Subsection 12(5) provides that anyone who has a delegation from the Commissioner will have a certificate of the delegation which that person must produce at the request of the organization whose premises he wants to enter under 12(1)(d).

Section 13: Commissioner's Report

Section 13 deals with the duty of the Commissioner to prepare a report respecting a complaint, states to whom the report must be sent, and sets out the circumstances where he is not required to prepare a report.

Contents

13.(1) The Commissioner shall, within one year after the day on which a complaint is filed or is initiated by the Commissioner, prepare a report that contains

Subsection 13(1) says that the Commissioner has one year from when a complaint was filed with the Commissioner, or from when the Commissioner initiated his own complaint, to prepare a report containing the following:

(a) the Commissioner's findings and recommendations;

a) the Commissioner's findings and any recommendations he has to make. He could find, for example, that the complaint is well founded, and recommend that the organization change its practices or that it follow more closely some of the recommendations in Schedule 1;

(b) any settlement that was reached by the parties;

b) any settlement that was reached by the individual and the organization, or between the Commissioner and the organization. Settlement of reasonable complaints should be the norm, especially if the Commissioner's mediation powers are used effectively;

(c) if appropriate, a request that the organization give the Commissioner, within a specified time, notice of any action taken or proposed to be taken to implement the recommendations contained in the report or reasons why no such action has been or is proposed to be taken; and

(d) the recourse, if any, that is available under section 14.

c) where the Commissioner has recommended that the organization implement changes or take particular actions, the Commissioner may request that the organization give him notice of a specified time limit for the changes to take place or to report to him reasons why the organization hasn't done what the Commissioner recommended;

d) the recourse that is available, if any, to the complainant under section 14. If the complaint was about some matter that can be taken to the Federal Court, the Commissioner will inform the complainant of his rights and the time frame in which they must be exercised. However, if the complaint is about a recommendation in Schedule 1, for example, the Commissioner should inform the individual that his recourse under the Act has been exhausted.

Terms to Designate a Finding

Under the federal *Privacy Act* the Commissioner uses six terms to designate a finding. These were set out at length in the Commissioner's 1999–2000 Annual Report[23] and are reproduced here as follows:

Not Well-Founded

A finding of *not well-founded* acknowledges that the investigation uncovered no evidence to lead the Privacy Commissioner to conclude that the government institution violated the *Privacy Act* rights of the complainant. For example, such a finding would be made when

• In the case of a denial of access complaint, all information relevant to the access request had been processed or the exemptions cited by the government institution to refuse access were justified; or

• In the case of a complaint of improper disclosure, the Privacy Commissioner was satisfied based on the evidence gathered during investigation, along with representations by the government institution, that the disclosure of personal information met the requirements of section 8(2) of the *Privacy Act*.

---

[23] *Annual Report of the Privacy Commissioner of Canada, 1999–2000* (Ottawa: Minister of Public Works and Government Services Canada, 2000) at 101–3 (Cat. No. IP 30-1/2000 ISBN 0-662-64957-5).

Well-Founded

A finding of *well-founded* recognizes that the government institution failed to respect the *Privacy Act* rights of an individual, and that no corrective measures could mitigate the loss of privacy. In other words, while the government institution is at fault, the incident has already occurred and nothing can be done to correct the situation. This category of finding is usually rendered in situations where the institution improperly used or disclosed personal information or it failed to respond to an access request within the legislated time limits. It could also be used in a situation where the government institution refuses to grant access to personal information, despite the Commissioner's recommendation that it be released. The next step would be to seek a review by the Federal Court of Canada.

Well-Founded/Resolved

A finding of *well-founded/resolved* is rendered in situations where the allegations raised in the complaint were substantiated by the investigation, but the government institution readily agreed to take corrective measures to rectify the problem. Such a finding would be made when, for example a department

- Agrees to release to the complainant information that had been originally exempted; or

- Undertakes to improve a policy or practice to ensure compliance with the *Privacy Act*.

Resolved

The *resolved* category recognizes the need for a finding that is consistent with the ombudsman's role to provide flexibility in complaint resolution. Prior to 1994, the Office struggled with complaints where "well-founded" appeared too harsh to fit what essentially had been miscommunication or misunderstanding.

Examples of *resolved* complaints:

- A misunderstanding or miscommunication has occurred between the complainant and the government institution about what information was sought. Both parties agree to a mutually satisfactory solution.

- The individual has claimed that specific information is missing. The government institution maintains that it has disclosed the records in question, but readily agrees to send the information again.

- The government institution has the right to exempt specific information, but is persuaded by the investigator to exercise the discretion to release it.

- The investigation has identified inconsistent processing of large volumes of information for an applicant, and the government institution is persuaded to release more information to make the disclosure consistent.

In all instances, the Privacy Commissioner's Office assists in negotiating a solution that satisfies all parties, a full and thorough investigation is conducted, and a formal finding is provided to complainants. With a resolved finding, the complainant still maintains the right to pursue the matter in Federal Court.

There are two other categories used under the *Privacy Act* that are not applicable under this Act. They are "Settled During the Course of the Investigation" and "Discontinued." Because of the requirement to issue a report under 13(1), except in the circumstances set out in 13(2), neither category will be available for use under this Act, although a report could simply state that a complaint had been settled or that it had been dropped by the complainant.

Where no report

(2) The Commissioner is not required to prepare a report if the Commissioner is satisfied that

Subsection 13(2) deals with the situation where, after a preliminary investigation, the Commissioner concludes that a report does not have to be prepared for any of the reasons set out below. Where there is no report to be made, the matter ends with the Commissioner's notice that he won't prepare the report. Any matter can, of course, be reopened with a fresh complaint.

The Commissioner does not have to prepare a report in certain circumstances:

(a) the complainant ought first to exhaust grievance or review procedures otherwise reasonably available;

a) The complainant ought to exhaust other remedies available to him. For example, in the case of a complaint against a bank, the Commissioner might suggest that the individual complain to the bank ombudsman first.

(b) the complaint could more appropriately be dealt with, initially or completely, by means of a procedure provided for under the laws of Canada, other than this Part, or the laws of a province;

b) The complaint could more appropriately be dealt with in its beginning stages, if not completely, by other procedures under federal or provincial laws. For example, the complaint may lie within the jurisdiction of the Information and Privacy Commissioner of British Columbia and that is where the individual will be referred.

(c) the length of time that has elapsed between the date when the subject-matter of the complaint arose and the date when the complaint was filed is such that a report would not serve a useful purpose; or

c) The complaint is stale-dated because too much time has elapsed between the matter complained of and the time the complaint was filed with the Commissioner. The Commissioner must decide whether a report would serve a useful purpose and if it wouldn't, he is not required to prepare it.

(d) the complaint is trivial, frivolous or vexatious or is made in bad faith.

If a report is not to be prepared, the Commissioner shall inform the complainant and the organization and give reasons.

d) The complaint is trivial, frivolous, or vexatious or is made in bad faith. This is a very useful provision because without it, the Commissioner would probably have to undertake a full-scale investigation on a case before he could safely determine that it was frivolous, which would be a waste of expensive resources. This provision should offer some comfort to organizations that might be concerned about being harassed by groundless complaints, particularly by disgruntled employees.

Report to parties

(3) The report shall be sent to the complainant and the organization without delay.

Section 14: Review by the Federal Court

Application

14.(1) A complainant may, after receiving the Commissioner's report, apply to the Court for a hearing in respect of any matter in respect of which the complaint was made, or that is referred to in the Commissioner's report, and that is referred to in clause 4.1.3, 4.2, 4.3.3, 4.4, 4.6, 4.7 or 4.8 of Schedule 1, in clause 4.3, 4.5 or 4.9 of that Schedule as modified or clarified by Division 1, in subsection 5(3) or 8(6) or (7) or in section 10.

Once the complainant has received the Privacy Commissioner's report, he may apply to the Federal Court to review:

a) any matter complained of, or

b) any matter referred to in the Commissioner's report *and*

c) that is referred to in one or more of the following:

- Clause 4.1.3 of Schedule 1, whether an organization has failed to provide a comparable level of protection while the information is being processed by a third party;
- Clause 4.2 of Schedule 1, whether the organization has properly identified and documented the purposes for which information is being collected, used, and disclosed, at or before the time of collection;

- Clause 4.3.3 of Schedule 1, whether an organization has refused to provide a person with a service because the person would not provide more information than was necessary to fulfil the legitimate purposes;
- Clause 4.4 of Schedule 1, whether an organization has collected more information than is necessary for the purposes;
- Clause 4.6 of Schedule 1, whether information is as accurate, up to date, and complete as necessary;
- Clause 4.7 of Schedule 1, whether the organization has taken the necessary steps to safeguard the information;
- Clause 4.8 of Schedule 1, whether an organization has documented its information practices and made specific information about its policies and practices relating to the management of personal information readily available to individuals;
- Clause 4.3 of Schedule 1, as modified or clarified in subsections 7(1), (2), and (3) of the Act, including whether information was collected, used, or disclosed without the consent of the individual in circumstances not authorized by the Act under section 7;
- Clause 4.5 of Schedule 1, as modified or clarified in subsections 7(4) and (5) or 8(8) of the Act, whether personal information was used or disclosed for purposes other than those for which it was collected without the consent of the individual in circumstances not authorized by the Act; or whether the information was retained for as long as necessary for a complainant to exhaust his remedies under the Act;
- Clause 4.9 of Schedule 1, as modified or clarified in sections 8 and 9 of the Act, whether an individual was wrongfully denied access to information about himself, or whether a request to correct information or add an annotation to a file was denied;
- Subsection 5(3) of the Act, whether the information was collected, used, or disclosed

for purposes that a reasonable person would consider appropriate in the circumstances;

- Subsection 8(6) of the Act, read in conjunction with clause 4.9.4, whether an individual was charged too much for access to information about himself or was not notified of the cost in advance;
- Subsection 8(7) of the Act, whether the organization responded within the time limits, or did not provide reasons for its refusal to provide access;
- Section 10, whether an organization failed to grant access in an alternative format.

Time of application

(2) The application must be made within forty-five days after the report is sent or within any further time that the Court may, either before or after the expiry of those forty-five days, allow.

For greater certainty

(3) For greater certainty, subsections (1) and (2) apply in the same manner to complaints referred to in subsection 11(2) as to complaints referred to in subsection 11(1).

The Privacy Commissioner may also apply to the Federal Court in respect of any of the matters listed above. In both cases, the application to the Federal Court must be made within forty-five days after the Commissioner's report referred to in section 13 is sent. The Court may grant an extension of time as long as it is applied for within the initial forty-five-day period.

See commentary under subsection 11(2).

Section 15: Commissioner's Application for Review

Commissioner may apply or appear

15. The Commissioner may, in respect of a complaint that the Commissioner did not initiate,

(a) apply to the Court, within the time limited by section 14, for a hearing in respect of any matter described in that section, if the Commissioner has the consent of the complainant;

(b) appear before the Court on behalf of any complainant who has applied for a hearing under section 14; or

(c) with leave of the Court, appear as a party to any hearing applied for under section 14.

In addition to the Privacy Commissioner's right to apply for review by the Federal Court for complaints he himself has initiated, he may also apply for a hearing in respect of a complaint initiated by an individual if he has that individual's consent.

The Privacy Commissioner may also appear at a hearing on behalf of any complainant who has applied to the Court and may appear as a party in such a proceeding, with permission of the Court.

Because of the ombudsman-like role of the Privacy Commissioner and the fact that he does not make binding decisions, he has a great deal of latitude in his ability to assist and advise a complainant who wishes to take a case to Court.

Section 16: Remedies

16. The Court may, in addition to any other remedies it may give,

In addition to any of the powers of the Court to grant remedies, the Act has specifically expanded the power of the Court by giving it the power to

(a) order an organization to correct its practices in order to comply with sections 5 to 10;

a) order an organization to correct its practices with respect to personal information to comply with sections 5 through 10 of the Act. For example, the Court may agree with a complainant that a particular collection practice was unreasonable, using the test in subsection 5(3), and may order the organization to cease the practice;

(b) order an organization to publish a notice of any action taken or proposed to be taken to correct its practices, whether or not ordered to correct them under paragraph (a); and

b) order an organization to publish a notice of an action taken by the organization or which the organization proposes to take to correct its practices, whether or not it was ordered to do so. Let us imagine that a cable TV company is asking for the Social Insurance Number to be provided before they will rent a cable Internet modem. The complainant was successful in arguing that this was a demand for information not necessary to provide the service (4.3.3), and the Court ordered the company to destroy all the SINs in its files, and publish a notice in the paper that it was doing so;

(c) award damages to the complainant, including damages for any humiliation that the complainant has suffered.

c) award damages to the complainant, including damages for humiliation that the individual may have suffered. Most damages for humiliation are likely to be no more than nominal, but in some cases it may be the only relief that the individual gets since actual damages in these cases are rare.

Section 17: Summary Hearings by Federal Court

Summary hearings

17.(1) An application made under section 14 or 15 shall be heard and determined without delay and in a summary way unless the Court considers it inappropriate to do so.

Section 17 provides that applications for review made by the individual or the Privacy Commissioner are to be heard in an expedited manner unless the Court considers the expedited process to be inappropriate. The term "determination without delay" that is used in the Act has been interpreted to mean that the application should be moved to the hearing stage as quickly as possible.[24]

The rules of the Court allow for case management of files, which means that a judge can give directions necessary for more just, more expeditious, and less expensive determinations of proceedings. Case management can also fix dates for subsequent steps in the proceedings and can plan dispute resolution and pre-trial conferences. An individual can act for himself if he wishes, but corporations, partnerships, and unincorporated associations must act through a lawyer.

The cost to file an application is $50, and the registry is open from 9 to 5 weekdays except holidays. The Court has offices and registries in most cities (see Appendix 4), and registrars are very helpful.

The Trial Division of the Court can sit anywhere in Canada, and in special circumstances can hold hearings by means of teleconferences and video conferences.

Precautions

(2) In any proceedings arising from an application made under section 14 or 15, the Court shall take every reasonable precaution, including, when appropriate, receiving representations ex parte and conducting hearings in camera, to avoid the disclosure by the Court or any person of any information or other material that the organization would be authorized to refuse to disclose if it were requested under clause 4.9 of Schedule 1.

Subsection 17(2) provides that the Court must take all the appropriate measures necessary including closed hearings and one-sided representations to avoid the disclosure of any information or other material that the organization would be authorized to refuse to disclose to an individual under section 9.

Closed hearings and one-sided representations are extraordinary measures taken only in exceptional circumstances and always at the discretion of the Court.

---

[24]   See *David Bull Laboratories (Canada) Inc.* v. *Pharmacia Inc.*, [1995] 1 F.C. 588 (C.A.).

DIVISION 3: AUDITS

Section 18: Audits

To ensure compliance

18.(1) The Commissioner may, on reasonable notice and at any reasonable time, audit the personal information management practices of an organization if the Commissioner has reasonable grounds to believe that the organization is contravening a provision of Division 1 or is not following a recommendation set out in Schedule 1, and for that purpose may

(a) summon and enforce the appearance of persons before the Commissioner and compel them to give oral or written evidence on oath and to produce any records and things that the Commissioner considers necessary for the audit, in the same manner and to the same extent as a superior court of record;

(b) administer oaths;

(c) receive and accept any evidence and other information, whether on oath, by affidavit or otherwise, that the Commissioner sees fit, whether or not it is or would be admissible in a court of law;

(d) at any reasonable time, enter any premises, other than a dwelling-house, occupied by the organization on satisfying any security requirements of the organization relating to the premises;

(e) converse in private with any person in any premises entered under paragraph (d) and otherwise carry out in those premises any inquiries that the Commissioner sees fit; and

(f) examine or obtain copies of or extracts from records found in any premises entered under paragraph (d) that contain any matter relevant to the audit.

Under subsection 18(1) the Commissioner has a discretionary power to audit the personal information management practices of an organization according to certain conditions:

- reasonable notice must be given to the organization;
- the audit must take place at a reasonable time, that, is during normal business hours;
- the Commissioner must have reasonable grounds to believe that the organization is contravening a provision of Division 1, that is, sections 5 to 10, or that it is not following a recommendation set out in Schedule 1.

In conducting audits, the Commissioner has the same array of powers as he has in respect of investigations that are outlined above under section 12.

In addition, the provisions under subsections 18(2), (3), and (4) respecting delegation and return of records mirror the provisions of subsection 12(3), (4), and (5), which were also discussed above.

The role of the audit has been somewhat misunderstood. It is not an informal site visit, nor is it a policing action given that the Commissioner lacks binding powers.

Audits are not likely to be undertaken with respect to isolated incidents — the Commissioner would likely initiate a complaint for that. With limited resources at his disposal — and an audit would almost certainly require the expertise for which the Commissioner would have to contract out — it is not likely that many audits will take place except in cases where an organization has serious or systemic problems with the way it is managing its personal information.

Organizations that have put in place policies and procedures to ensure basic compliance with Schedule 1 are very unlikely to be the subject of one of the Commissioner's audits.

Organizations should recognize that the powers of the Commissioner include the power under subsection 20(2) to make public any information relating to the personal information management practices of an organization if the Commissioner considers it is in the public interest to do so. The Commissioner can also include an audit report in his annual report under section 25.

Delegation

(2) The Commissioner may delegate any of the powers set out in subsection (1).

Return of records

(3) The Commissioner or the delegate shall return to a person or an organization any record or thing they produced under this section within ten days after they make a request to the Commissioner or the delegate, but nothing precludes the Commissioner or the delegate from again requiring that the record or thing be produced.

These powers to publicize sloppy personal information practices should encourage organizations to ensure that their practices are compliant. All organizations should consider the possibility of carrying out periodic internal or external audits of their own. This is perhaps something the Commissioner should promote as well.

Audits can perform a useful function for an organization by educating employees; rationalizing the collection, use, disclosure, and retention of personal information; and identifying problem areas. All this can lead to significant cost savings and increased customer confidence.

Certificate of delegation

(4) Any person to whom powers set out in subsection (1) are delegated shall be given a certificate of the delegation and the delegate shall produce the certificate, on request, to the person in charge of any premises to be entered under paragraph (1)(d).

Section 19: Audit Reports

Report of findings and recommendations

19.(1) After an audit, the Commissioner shall provide the audited organization with a report that contains the findings of the audit and any recommendations that the Commissioner considers appropriate.

Reports may be included in annual reports

(2) The report may be included in a report made under section 25.

Subsection 19(1) obliges the Commissioner to provide the organization with a report of the results of the audit containing

- the findings of the audit, that is, what the Commissioner discovered about the organization's personal information management practices;
- any recommendations that the Commissioner considers appropriate. These are likely to be extensive; otherwise the Commissioner would not have undertaken the audit. Although these recommendations cannot be forced on the organization, it would be wise for an organization to take the recommendations seriously and improve its practices.

As stated in the discussion under section 18 above, subsection 19(2) allows the Commissioner to include an audit report in his annual report to Parliament.

DIVISON 4: GENERAL

Section 20: Confidentiality

20.(1) Subject to subsections (2) to (5), 13(3) and 19(1), the Commissioner or any person acting on behalf or under the direction of the Commissioner shall not disclose any information that comes to their knowledge as a result of the performance or exercise of any of the Commissioner's duties or powers under this Part.

Subsection 20(1) establishes a general rule that the Commissioner or any person acting on his behalf or under his direction shall not disclose any information they learn in the performance of their duties under the Act.

That rule is subject to the following limited exceptions:

1. disclosure of some information under subsections 20(2) to (5), which are discussed below. They mirror section 64 of the *Privacy Act*;
2. reports made to the complainant and the organization under subsection 13(3); and

3. audit reports made to the organization under section 19. As mentioned above, subsection 19(2) also allows those reports to be included in annual reports to Parliament.

Public interest

(2) The Commissioner may make public any information relating to the personal information management practices of an organization if the Commissioner considers that it is in the public interest to do so.

Subsection 20(2) is the first exception in section 20 to the confidentiality rule. It provides that the Commissioner may make public any information relating to the personal information management practices of an organization if he considers it to be in the public interest to do so. The competing interests here are society's interest in the general protection of privacy and the interest of the organization in protecting its reputation.

In the context of the Act, the interest in privacy which is at risk through the actions of the organization is likely to weigh heavier in the balance than a corporate interest, particularly in light of the purpose clause in section 3. But, clearly, potential damage to the economic interests of the organization will be a factor the Commissioner will have to take into account when considering whether to publicize.

Disclosure of necessary information

(3) The Commissioner may disclose, or may authorize any person acting on behalf or under the direction of the Commissioner to disclose, information that in the Commissioner's opinion is necessary to

(a) conduct an investigation or audit under this Part; or

(b) establish the grounds for findings and recommendations contained in any report under this Part.

Subsection 20(3) is the second exception to the confidentiality rule and it authorizes the Commissioner to disclose — and he may authorize anyone acting on his behalf or under his direction to disclose — any information that the Commissioner considers necessary to conduct an audit or establish the grounds for findings and recommendations contained in an investigation report, an audit report, or an annual report.

For example, this would allow the Commissioner to contact clients of an organization to establish certain facts relevant to an audit. To do so he might have to disclose some information; certainly he would disclose the fact of the audit, and the nature of his inquiries would likely reveal other information as well.

Disclosure in the course of proceedings

(4) The Commissioner may disclose, or may authorize any person acting on behalf or under the direction of the Commissioner to disclose, information in the course of

(a) a prosecution for an offence under section 28;

(b) a prosecution for an offence under section 132 of the *Criminal Code* (perjury) in respect of a statement made under this Part;

(c) a hearing before the Court under this Part; or

(d) an appeal from a decision of the Court.

Subsection 20(4) is the third exception, and it allows the Commissioner and anyone acting on his behalf or under his direction to disclose information in the course of

a) a prosecution for an offence under section 28 of the Act;

b) a prosecution for perjury under section 132 of the *Criminal Code* in respect of statements made to the Commissioner under oath;

c) a hearing before the Federal Court under the Act, or

d) an appeal from a decision of the Federal Court. Appeals can be taken to the Appeal Division of the Federal Court and, with leave, to the Supreme Court of Canada.

Disclosure of offence authorized

(5) The Commissioner may disclose to the Attorney General of Canada or of a province, as the case may be, information relating to the commission of an offence against any law of Canada or a province on the part of an officer or employee of an organization if, in the Commissioner's opinion, there is evidence of an offence.

Subsection 20(5) is the final exception to the confidentiality rule, and it allows the Commissioner to disclose to the Attorney General of Canada or of a province, information relating to the commission of an offence under federal or provincial law, on the part of an officer or employee of an organization, if the Commissioner has sufficient evidence of an offence.

Section 21: Competent Witness

Not competent witness

21. The Commissioner or person acting on behalf or under the direction of the Commissioner is not a competent witness in respect of any matter that comes to their knowledge as a result of the performance or exercise of any of the Commissioner's duties or powers under this Part in any proceeding other than

Other than in respect of the proceedings listed in subsection 20(4) above, neither the Commissioner nor anyone acting on his behalf or under his direction, is a competent witness in respect of any matter that comes to their attention during the performance of their duties under the Act. That means no court could successfully summon them to appear.

(a) a prosecution for an offence under section 28;

(b) a prosecution for an offence under section 132 of the *Criminal Code* (perjury) in respect of a statement made under this Part;

(c) a hearing before the Court under this Part; or

(d) an appeal from a decision of the Court.

This provision in section 21 should go some way towards allaying the fears of organizations that the Commissioner will somehow be able to blow the whistle on them in respect of unrelated matters — other than criminal offences referred to in subsection 20(5).

In a recent case under the *Access to Information Act*, the Federal Court found that the compellability of the Information Commissioner is subject to similar provisions of that Act which place the full discretion of disclosure with the Commissioner. The Court had no jurisdiction to subpoena the Commissioner or anyone acting on his behalf.[25]

Section 22: Protection of the Commissioner

22.(1) No criminal or civil proceedings lie against the Commissioner, or against any person acting on behalf or under the direction of the Commissioner, for anything done, reported or said in good faith as a result of the performance or exercise or purported performance or exercise of any duty or power of the Commissioner under this Part.

Subsection 22(1) protects the Commissioner and persons acting on his behalf or under his direction from criminal and civil proceedings, in respect of things said, done, or reported in good faith in carrying out or purporting to carry out their duties under the Act. Even if the Commissioner were ultimately to be found to have been outside his jurisdiction, as long as he believed he was within his jurisdiction and was acting in good faith, he is protected by this section.

Libel or slander

(2) For the purposes of any law relating to libel or slander,

(a) anything said, any information supplied or any record or thing produced in good faith in the course of an investigation or audit carried out by or on behalf of the Commissioner under this Part is privileged; and

Subsection 22(2) provides:

a) Anything said, any information supplied or any record or thing produced in good faith during the course of an investigation or audit carried out by or on behalf of the Commissioner is privileged for the purposes of libel and slander laws. Again we find the "good faith" test.

This section is broad enough to protect persons other than the Commissioner and his staff so, for example, if there is a defamatory state-

---

[25] *Sheldon Blank & Gateway Industries Ltd.* v. *Minister of the Environment* (22 November 1999), No. T-1111-98 (F.C.T.D.).

ment in a record produced by an organization during the course of an investigation, regardless of whether the Commissioner's formal powers have been invoked, the person defamed has no cause of action against the organization or against the Commissioner should he repeat the statement in a public report, as long as all parties acted in good faith.

(b) any report made in good faith by the Commissioner under this Part and any fair and accurate account of the report made in good faith for the purpose of news reporting is privileged.

b) Any report made in good faith by the Commissioner under the Act, whether it is an investigation, audit, or annual report, is privileged, as is any accurate and good faith news reporting of that report. This allows the Commissioner to express himself freely in his reports as long as he acts in good faith. That freedom is carried through to the news media in its reporting of the Commissioner's activities.

Section 23: Consultation with Provinces

23.(1) If the Commissioner considers it appropriate to do so, or on the request of an interested person, the Commissioner may, in order to ensure that personal information is protected in as consistent a manner as possible, consult with any person who, under provincial legislation that is substantially similar to this Part, has powers and duties similar to those of the Commissioner.

Subsection 23(1) is designed to encourage and promote federal, provincial, and territorial cooperation and harmonization to ensure the greatest possible consistency in privacy protection across the country. It encourages the Commissioner to work with his provincial and territorial counterparts, the various privacy commissioners and ombudsmen, who oversee privacy legislation that is substantially similar to the Act.

It is interesting that the consultation referred to can be undertaken at the request of an interested person, which leaves some scope for privacy advocates, businesses, and associations to try to influence federal, provincial, and territorial cooperation on privacy issues.

Agreements

(2) The Commissioner may enter into agreements with any person with whom the Commissioner may consult under subsection (1)

Subsection 23(2) contains more specific language about the sort of cooperation that might take place. It allows the Commissioner to enter into agreements with his counterparts to

(a) to coordinate the activities of their offices and the office of the Commissioner, including to provide for mechanisms for the handling of any complaint in which they are mutually interested;

a) coordinate the activities of their offices including providing for procedures to handle complaints in which they have a mutual interest. The Commissioner will have ongoing responsibility for interprovincial and international transactions and he will need to be able to cooperate with his provincial counterparts to carry out that mandate. This section will allow for him to enter into formal arrangements to do that.

(b) to undertake and publish research related to the protection of personal information; and

b) undertake and publish research on the protection of personal information. This will allow for the pooling of resources to carry out research projects.

(c) to develop model contracts for the protection of personal information that is collected, used or disclosed interprovincially or internationally.

c) develop model contracts for the protection of personal information that is collected, used, or disclosed interprovincially or internationally. This power will be particularly useful with respect to international transfers of personal information.

The reality of the situation is that it is not possible for the Commissioner to oversee international transactions unless he can influence organizations in Canada, and some of these organizations may be under provincial jurisdiction right up until the time the international disclosure is made. It will be useful for the Commissioner to be able to work with his provincial counterparts to convince those organizations to use contractual means to protect personal information they are sending outside of Canada.

Section 24: Promoting the Purposes of the Part

24. The Commissioner shall

(a) develop and conduct information programs to foster public understanding, and recognition of the purposes, of this Part;

Section 24 requires the Commissioner to carry out a number of activities designed to promote the purposes of Part 1 of the Act. Aside from a general duty to promote those purposes, there are specific activities that the Commissioner must engage in:

(b) undertake and publish research that is related to the protection of personal information, including any such research that is requested by the Minister of Industry;

(c) encourage organizations to develop detailed policies and practices, including organizational codes of practice, to comply with sections 5 to 10; and

(d) promote, by any means that the Commissioner considers appropriate, the purposes of this Part.

- Develop and conduct public education programs to foster public understanding and recognition of the purposes. This activity may take many forms including publishing educational material, public appearances, and advertising. It will require a lot of effort over the next three to five years to educate not only the general public but especially business on the implications for them of this new law. This is a new mandate for the Commissioner.
- Undertake and publish research related to the protection of personal information. As noted above, he can do this in cooperation with his provincial counterparts. He must also undertake any research requested by the Minister of Industry.
- Encourage organizations to develop detailed policies and practices, which could include company codes, to comply with sections 5 to 10.

Section 25: Annual Reports to Parliament

Annual report

25.(1) The Commissioner shall, as soon as practicable after the end of each calendar year, submit to Parliament a report concerning the application of this Part, the extent to which the provinces have enacted legislation that is substantially similar to this Part and the application of any such legislation.

The Commissioner must submit annual reports to Parliament. The report is due as soon as practicable after the end of the calendar year and must deal with

- the application of Part 1 of the Act,
- the extent to which the provinces have enacted substantially similar legislation, and
- the application of the provincial legislation.

Consultation

(2) Before preparing the report, the Commissioner shall consult with those persons in the provinces who, in the Commissioner's opinion, are in a position to assist the Commissioner in reporting respecting personal information that is collected, used or disclosed interprovincially or internationally.

Before he prepares his report, the Commissioner must consult anyone in the provinces, not just his counterparts, who can help him in respect of personal information that is collected, used, or disclosed across borders.

Section 26: Regulations

26.(1) The Governor in Council may make regulations

(a) specifying, by name or by class, what is a government institution or part of a government institution for the purposes of any provision of this Part;

(a.01) specifying, by name or by class, what is an investigative body for the purposes of paragraph 7(3)(d) or (h.2);

(a.1) specifying information or classes of information for the purpose of paragraph 7(1)(d), (2)(c.1) or (3)(h.1); and

(b) for carrying out the purposes and provisions of this Part.

Orders

(2) The Governor in Council may, by order,

(a) provide that this Part is binding on any agent of Her Majesty in right of Canada to which the *Privacy Act* does not apply; and

Section 26 is the regulation and order-making power. It allows the Governor in Council (on the recommendation of the Minister of Industry) to make:

1. Regulations

a) specifying government institutions or parts thereof, by name or by class, for the purposes of any section in part 1 of the Act. Government institutions are referred to in sections 7(3), and 9.

b) specifying investigative bodies, by name or by class, for the purposes of paragraph 7(3)(d) or (h.2). These are private sector bodies that perform investigative functions. (See discussion of regulations in chapter 5.)

c) specifying publicly available information, or classes of publicly available information, for the purposes of paragraphs 7(1)(d), 7(2)(c.1), or 7(3)(h.1). (See discussion of regulations in chapter 5.)

d) generally for carrying out the purposes and provisions of Part 1 of the Act. Although this may appear to be a broad power, these sorts of basket clauses have been rather narrowly interpreted by the courts.

2. Orders

a) providing that Part 1 of the Act is binding on any agent of Her Majesty in right of Canada to which the *Privacy Act* does not apply. Without this specific power, although the Act might apply to these agents because they are federal works, undertakings or businesses, such as the CBC, they would not be bound by it because that requires specific reference to binding the Crown.

(b) if satisfied that legislation of a province that is substantially similar to this Part applies to an organization, a class of organizations, an activity or a class of activities, exempt the organization, activity or class from the application of this Part in respect of the collection, use or disclosure of personal information that occurs within that province.

b) Providing that the Governor in Council may exempt any organization or class of organization, or any activity or class of activity from the application of Part 1 of the Act in respect of collection, use, or disclosure of personal information that occurs within a province, where the Governor in Council is satisfied that the province has legislation substantially similar to the Act that applies to that organization or activity.

This paragraph has to be read in conjunction with paragraph 4(1)(a) and subsection 30(1). The Act will apply to all organizations that collect use or disclose personal information in the course of commercial activities. By virtue of subsection 30(1), the exercise by Parliament of this general branch of the trade and commerce power is delayed for a three-year period following coming into force.

At that point, in 2004, the Act will apply to intraprovincial collection, use, and disclosure of personal information by all organizations in the course of commercial activities unless the Governor in Council passes an exemption order.

For example, any organization that is an "entreprise" for the purposes of the Quebec private sector legislation will be exempt by Order from the application of the federal law for intraprovincial collection, uses, and disclosures of personal information. Such an order will carve out federal works, undertakings, and businesses as still subject to Part 1 of the Act, even for intraprovincial transactions.

Interprovincial and international collections, uses, and disclosures will always fall under this Act after 2004.

There has been a lot of discussion as to what "substantially similar" means. It is not defined and although the term is used in a few other federal statutes, it has not been judicially interpreted. The only public statement made by the government is that a substantially similar law would have to address all the principles of the CSA Code, have an effective independent oversight regime, and provide redress for the individual.

Section 27: Whistleblowing

27.(1) Any person who has reasonable grounds to believe that a person has contravened or intends to contravene a provision of Division 1, may notify the Commissioner of the particulars of the matter and may request that their identity be kept confidential with respect to the notification.

Section 27 was added on the recommendation of the Industry Committee. It affords protection to persons who having reasonable grounds to believe that a person intends to contravene or has contravened sections 5 to 10, notify the Commissioner and request confidentiality.

Confidentiality

(2) The Commissioner shall keep confidential the identity of a person who has notified the Commissioner under subsection (1) and to whom an assurance of confidentiality has been provided by the Commissioner.

Subsection 27(2) requires the Commissioner to keep the identity of the person confidential if the Commissioner has provided an assurance of confidentiality.

Section 27.1: Discipline of Employees

Prohibition

27.1(1) No employer shall dismiss, suspend, demote, discipline, harass or otherwise disadvantage an employee, or deny an employee a benefit of employment, by reason that

(a) the employee, acting in good faith and on the basis of reasonable belief, has disclosed to the Commissioner that the employer or any other person has contravened or intends to contravene a provision of Division 1;

(b) the employee, acting in good faith and on the basis of reasonable belief, has refused or stated an intention of refusing to do anything that is a contravention of a provision of Division 1;

Where the whistleblower is an employee, including a contractor, the employer is prohibited from dismissing, suspending, demoting, disciplining, harassing, or otherwise disadvantaging that employee or denying a benefit because the employee, acting in good faith and on the basis of reasonable belief,

- has disclosed to the Commissioner that the employer or someone else has contravened or intends to contravene sections 5 to 10;
- has refused or stated an intention to refuse to do anything in contravention of sections 5 to 10; or
- has done or stated an intention to do anything that is required to be done so that sections 5 to 10 are not contravened.

(c) the employee, acting in good faith and on the basis of reasonable belief, has done or stated an intention of doing anything that is required to be done in order that a provision of Division 1 not be contravened; or

(d) the employer believes that the employee will do anything referred to in paragraph (a), (b) or (c).

Saving

(2) Nothing in this section impairs any right of an employee either at law or under an employment contract or collective agreement.

Definitions

(3) In this section, "employee" includes an independent contractor and "employer" has a corresponding meaning.

The employer may not discipline any employee even if he believes the employee is about to do any of the things listed above.

Section 27.1 allows the employee to blow the whistle on his employer or anyone else, protects him from having to contravene the Act, and allows him to take steps to see that the Act is not contravened, all without fear of reprisal.

Subsection 27.1(2) makes it clear that the section is not intended to interfere with any other rights an employee has under the law, a contract, or an agreement.

Section 28: Offence and Punishment

28. Every person who knowingly contravenes subsection 8(8) or 27.1(1) or who obstructs the Commissioner or the Commissioner's delegate in the investigation of a complaint or in conducting an audit is guilty of

(a) an offence punishable on summary conviction and liable to a fine not exceeding $10,000; or

(b) an indictable offence and liable to a fine not exceeding $100,000.

Section 28 provides that it is an offence (on summary conviction, fine up to $10,000, or on indictment, fine up to $100,000) for any person

- who knowingly contravenes subsection 8(8) — failure to retain information that is the subject of a request for as long as is necessary to allow an individual to exhaust his recourses under the Act;
- who knowingly contravenes subsection 27.1(1) — dismiss, suspend, demote, discipline, harass, or otherwise disadvantage an employee who is a whistleblower;
- who obstructs the Commissioner or the Commissioner's delegate in the investigation of a complaint or in conducting an audit.

Section 29: Review of Part by Parliamentary Committee

29.(1) The administration of this Part shall, every five years after this Part comes into force, be reviewed by the committee of the House of Commons, or of both Houses of Parliament, that may be designated or established by Parliament for that purpose.

Section 29 provides that the administration of Part 1 of the Act is subject to a review by Parliament every five years. The first five-year review should take place in 2006.

The review is to be carried out by a House Committee or a joint House and Senate Committee, either specially established for the purpose or by an existing committee designated for the task.

Review and report

(2) The committee shall undertake a review of the provisions and operation of this Part and shall, within a year after the review is undertaken or within any further period that the House of Commons may authorize, submit a report to Parliament that includes a statement of any changes to this Part or its administration that the committee recommends.

The committee must undertake the review and must report to Parliament within one year of beginning the review. That one-year period may be extended by authority of the House of Commons.

The report must include a statement of any changes to Part 1 or its administration that the Committee recommends.

DIVISION 5: TRANSITIONAL PROVISIONS

Section 30: Transitional and Coming into Force

Part 6 of the law consists of section 72, which is the provision for the coming into force of the various parts of the Act, or any provision of any of those Parts, by Order of the Governor in Council. This will occur on the recommendation of the Minister of Industry for Parts 1 and 2, and the Minister of Justice for Parts 3 to 5.

By Order of the Governor in Council dated 26 April 2000, SI/2000-29, Parts 2 to 4 came into force on 1 May 2000. Part 1 came into force on 1 January 2001. No date was set for the coming into force of Part 5.

Application

30.(1) This Part does not apply to any organization in respect of personal information that it collects, uses or discloses within a province whose legislature has the power to regulate the collection, use or disclosure of the information, unless the organization does it in connection with the operation of a federal work, undertaking or business or the organization discloses the information outside the province for consideration.

Expiry date

(2) Subsection (1) ceases to have effect three years after the day on which this section comes into force.

Expiry date

(2.1) Subsection (1.1) ceases to have effect one year after the day on which this section comes into force.

Application

(1.1) This Part does not apply to any organization in respect of personal health information that it collects, uses or discloses.

According to section 30 of the Act, when Part 1 came into force on 1 January 2001, it applied immediately to

1) federal works, undertakings, and businesses that collect, use, or disclose personal information in the course of commercial activities, including employee records of those organizations; and

2) any disclosure of personal information by an organization in the course of commercial activities, for consideration, outside the province where the organization is located.

However, in that first year the Act will not apply to "personal health information," as defined in section 2, which is collected, used, or disclosed by any of the organizations described in (1) and (2) above. This delay in application for personal health information is only for one year, so that on 1 January 2002, it will cease to have effect, and the Act will cover personal health information.

The third stage of application occurs on 1 January 2004, when the law will apply to all organizations that collect, use, or disclose personal information in the course of commercial activities, including organizations under the jurisdiction of the provinces.

CHAPTER 4

PARTS 2 TO 5: MOVING FEDERAL LEGISLATION OUT OF THE "AGE OF PAPER"

A. Introduction

The central purpose of Parts 2 to 5 of the *Personal Information Protection and Electronic Documents Act* is to remove "paper bias" in federal legislation by allowing for the creation of electronic alternatives for doing business with government agencies, facilitating the use of electronic documents in judicial proceedings, and giving legal recognition to electronic versions of official Parliamentary publications.

On 22 September 1998, Prime Minister Chretien announced the Canadian Electronic Commerce Strategy or "E-Comm" strategy. The stated goal of the E-Comm strategy was to make Canada a "world leader in Electronic Commerce by the year 2000."[1] The *Personal Information Protection and Electronic Documents Act* was a major component of the initiative. The Act, which went through the House as Bill C-6, was originally developed as two separate bills. The first, which is now Part 1 of the Act, addressed the protection of data, and the second was concerned with electronic documents (Parts 2 to 5 of the current Act).

Both the privacy and electronic document bills were vital to the success of the E-Comm strategy. While the first would provide for the protection of personal data to increase public comfort and confidence in electronic transactions, the second would remove many of the legal barriers to the development of electronic commerce and, it was hoped, would enable the federal government to "lead by example" by providing the public with

---

[1] Prime Minister Chretien announced the E-Comm strategy in an address to the participants of SoftWorld '98 in St. John's, Newfoundland, on 22 September 1998.

electronic means of communicating and transacting with federal agencies. Since both bills were central to the implementation and success of this strategy, both bills were merged into a single piece of legislation just prior to their introduction into the House of Commons in October 1999.

Part 2, entitled "Electronic Documents," provides for the use of electronic alternatives where federal law previously only contemplated the use of paper to communicate or record information. Part 3 makes several amendments to the *Canada Evidence Act* to clarify how the courts assess the reliability of electronic documents used as evidence in judicial proceedings. Finally, Parts 4 and 5 amend other federal statutes to facilitate the use and legal recognition of electronic documents.

B. Part 2: Electronic Documents

The stated purpose of Part 2 is to provide for the use of electronic alternatives "where federal laws contemplate the use of paper to record or communicate information and transactions."[2] The intention is to remove "paper bias" and to put electronic and paper media on equal footing. It became apparent during the development of the E-Comm strategy that there may be legal barriers to the federal government realizing the full potential of the Internet as a tool for communicating with, and providing services to, the public.

In 1996, the Department of Justice established the Electronic Commerce Secretariat, which began a review of federal legislation for language that suggested a bias towards paper. The Department reviewed over 600 federal statutes and found 330 contained language that indicated information must be provided or received in paper form *only*, or language that was uncertain as to whether or not electronic alternatives would be acceptable.[3] The purpose of Part 2 is to adapt federal legislation to make it compatible with the electronic environment by removing paper-only requirements wherever possible.

Part 2 is non-prescriptive in nature. It allows individual agencies to "opt in" to the initiative and begin using electronic means of doing business when they feel it is appropriate to do so and when they have the required technology in place. Individual departments and agencies are also given the power to make regulations concerning when, and by what means, their agency will provide electronic services.

---

[2]   *Personal Information Protection and Electronic Documents Act*, S.C. 2000, c. 5, [*PIPEDA*] s. 32.

[3]   Department of Justice Backgrounder, "Adjusting the legal framework for electronic commerce," <http://canada.justice.gc.ca/en/news/nr/1998/attback1.html>, accessed 04/11/ 2000, 5:25 p.m.

A key component of Part 2 is the introduction of the concept of the "secure electronic signature" as a technological means of ensuring the reliability and integrity of electronic documents.

1) Filing Documents and Making Payments by Electronic Means

Section 33 is a general enabling section that allows federal departments, agencies, bodies, corporations, and so on to use electronic means to create, collect, receive, store, transfer, distribute, publish or otherwise deal with documents or information whenever a federal law does not specify the manner of doing so.

Section 34 provides that payments to be made to the federal government may be made in an electronic form specified by the Receiver General. Michael Power[4] wrote that this section was included in the Act to avoid possible uncertainty that may arise as a result of subsection 8(1) of the *Patent Act*,[5] which provides that "subject to the regulations, any document, information or fee that is authorized or required to be submitted to the Commissioner under this Act may be submitted in an electronic form or any other form in a manner specified by the Commissioner." One of the basic rules of statutory interpretation provides that omissions and inconsistencies in legislation are intentional. The drafters of Bill C-6 were concerned that if the bill were silent as to payments to the government, it could be interpreted that Parliament did not intend Bill C-6 and subsection 8(1) of the *Patent Act* to operate in the same way. Section 34 deals with payments *to* the government only, as the *Financial Administration Act*[6] already permits the government to make payments in an electronic manner.

Subsections 35(1), (2), and (3) permit the "responsible authority"[7] for each federal department or agency to make regulations concerning electronic versions of federal forms, methods of filing, and submitting information to its particular department or agency. Subsection 35(4) expands the current powers under federal law to issue, prescribe, or establish a form or manner of filing electronic documents, or a manner of submitting information in electronic form. This section deliberately makes a distinction between "federal law" and an "Act of Parliament." Federal law is a broader term including statutes, regulations, and other legislative instruments. The term "responsible authority" is used instead of "Minister" or some similar term because the Minister is not always the person or body

---

[4]   M. Power, "Bill C-6: Federal Legislation in the Age of the Internet," (1999) 26 Man. L.J. 235 at para. 23.

[5]   R.S.C. 1985, c. P-4.

[6]   R.S.C. 1985, c. F-11, s. 35.

[7]   *PIPEDA*, 31(1).

responsible for making regulations in every department or agency. If it is not clear who the responsible authority is in a particular department or agency, subsection 31(2) provides that the Governor in Council may designate a person or body as a responsible authority for the purposes of Part 2.

2) Electronic Alternatives

Sections 38 to 47 are a series of equivalency provisions that enable electronic documents to satisfy statutory document requirements.

There are many references to "notarial acts" in federal legislation. Section 38 provides that a document that is recognized as a notarial act in Quebec is deemed to include an electronic version of the document as long as the electronic version is recognized as a notarial act under Quebec law and the relevant federal law or the provision is listed in Schedule 2 or 3.

Section 38 is the first section to refer to Schedules 2 and 3. Statutes must be listed in Schedule 2 and regulations in Schedule 3 before the ability to utilize an electronic alternative arises. The Schedules were included as a mechanism to prevent the ability to use an electronic alternative to "automatically" apply a particular provision. This structure recognizes that there may be a valid reason for some provisions to continue to require paper only. Power identified two reasons why paper bias may be required under some provisions.[8] First, international or interprovincial obligations may require paper records. Second, a particular area of government may not be ready to accept electronic alternatives, since the use of electronic alternatives requires redesign of business processes that often involves the expenditure of great time and resources.

Sections 38 to 47 require the same basic, general structure before an electronic version will satisfy a particular legislative document's purpose. First, the statute or regulation must be listed in the appropriate Schedule and, second, the appropriate regulations must be complied with. Subsection 50(1) empowers the responsible authority in each department or agency to make regulations for its own acts and regulations with respect to sections 40 to 47.

Section 41 provides that a requirement that a document be "in writing" may be satisfied by an electronic alternative if the above general requirements are satisfied. Similarly, section 43 provides that, in most cases,[9] a requirement for a "signature" may be fulfilled by an electronic signature provided the general requirements are met. Section 47 provides that a requirement under federal law for one or more "copies" of a docu-

---

[8]   Power, above note 4 at para. 34.

[9]   Subject to ss. 44 to 46.

ment to be submitted can be fulfilled by the submission of electronic documents as long as the basic, general requirements are met.

Section 40 provides that a requirement under federal law for a person to provide another person with a document or information, can usually[10] be satisfied by the provision of the document in electronic form if

a) the federal law or provision is listed in Schedule 2 or 3;
b) both persons have agreed to use the electronic format; and
c) the document or information will be under the control of the person receiving it and will be readable to them so as to be usable for subsequent reference.

3) Secure Electronic Signatures

A number of provisions in Part 2 refer to "secure electronic signatures." The first reference is in section 36 which provides that a provision of federal law that requires that a certificate or other document be signed by a specified government official[11] may be satisfied by an electronic version as long as the electronic document is signed with the relevant official's "secure electronic signature." Section 39 provides that a secure electronic signature can also substitute for a person's seal under certain specified conditions.

Under section 42, a requirement in federal law for a document to be an "original" can be satisfied by an electronic document if, in addition to the provision being listed in the appropriate Schedule and compliance with the regulations, the electronic document contains a secure electronic signature that was added when the document was first generated in its final form and that can be used to verify that the electronic document has not been altered since the signature was added.

Additionally, sections 42, 44, 45, and 46 provide that through the use of secure electronic signatures, electronic documents can satisfy legislative requirements for "original documents," "statements made under oath," a declaration of the truth, and witnessed signatures.

The secure electronic signature is intended to be a means of ensuring the integrity and reliability of electronic documents. A secure electronic signature differs from the electronic signatures familiar to most people, such as a scanned handwritten signature or a person's name and title printed at the bottom of an e-mail message, in that a secure electronic signature cannot be tampered with and thus provides a means of verifying, with great certainty, the source of the document and whether or not it has

---

[10] Subject to certain provisions referred to in ss. 41 to 47.

[11] Power, above note 4, gives the example of Fish Inspection certificates under s. 14(1) of the *Fish Inspection Act*, R.S.C. 1985, c. F-12.

been tampered with. Subsection 48(2) provides that an electronic signature will only qualify for designation as a secure electronic signature if

a) it is unique to the individual using it;
b) the technology used to attach the secure electronic signature is under that person's sole control;
c) the process can be used to identify the person using the technology or process; and
d) the electronic signature can be linked to the document in such a way that it can be used to determine whether the electronic document has been changed since the signature was attached to it.

Section 48 of the Act provides that only the Governor in Council can designate a technology a "secure electronic signature." At the time the legislation was drafted, the only technology that the government felt satisfied these criteria was "public key cryptography."[12] The term "secure electronic signature" was used in recognition of the fact that in the future other technologies would certainly be developed to meet these requirements.

4) Public Key Cryptography

Public key cryptography encrypts information by using two mathematically related keys: one is private, and the other is public. The private key is personal and cannot be determined using the public key. Basically, public key cryptography works like this: An individual who wants to send a message uses the public key of the recipient to encrypt the message and then the recipient will use her private key to decrypt the message.[13] Therefore, the sender can be certain that only the intended recipient is able to read the message.

This same technology is used to make a secure electronic signature. The sender generates a unique numeric summary of the message (called a "hash summary"), encrypts this summary using his private "digital signature key" and attaches it to the end of the message. The result is known as a "digital signature." The recipient then uses the sender's public key to decrypt the digital signature to access the summary. She then passes the message through the same mathematical summary to produce a hash summary. If the digital signature can be decrypted and the summaries are identical, then the recipient is assured of both the sender's identity and the integrity of the message. The recipient will know that the message has not

---

12 Power, above note 4 at para. 28.

13 Interdepartmental PKI Task Force, *Supporting Electronic Government: The Government of Canada Public Key Infrastructure* (Ottawa: Treasury Board Secretariat, October 1998) at 5.

been altered since the moment it was digitally signed.[14] Although the process appears complicated, the user would not have to undertake these various steps because the software application would do it automatically.

In December 1995, the Treasury Board approved the development and implementation of a Government of Canada Public Key Infrastructure (PKI). The goal of the PKI is to implement public key cryptography on a large scale to federal government agencies and departments that wish to participate.[15]

5) Retention of Documents

Section 37 addresses potential problems related to the retention of electronic documents. This section provides that a requirement under a federal law to retain a document for a specified period of time can be satisfied, with respect to an electronic document, by the retention of the electronic document provided that

a) the electronic document is retained for the specified period of time in the format in which it was made, sent, or received or in a format that does not change the information in the document;
b) the information contained in the document must be readable by a person who is entitled to have access to that document; and
c) if the electronic document was sent or received (e.g. e-mail), any information that identifies the origin and destination of the electronic document and the date and time when it was sent or received also must be retained.

The retention and storage of electronic documents was the subject of great concern for the Association of Canadian Archivists (ACA). The association presented its concerns to the Standing Committee on Industry hearings on Bill C-54. Bill C-54 was the predecessor bill to Bill C-6, which was identical in content to Bill C-54 as it was amended by the Standing Committee on Industry in the spring of 1999.[16]

The ACA expressed two main concerns that may not have been adequately addressed in the final version of the bill. First, it expressed concern over the use of data encryption and secure electronic signatures, lobbying for a requirement that all encryption be removed before data are archived. The archivists were concerned that if this requirement were not added, electronic documents would have no archival value. In their submissions to the Standing Committee, they stressed that if the documents cannot be decoded they cannot be used: "[G]iven the depth and complexity of the

---

[14] *Ibid.*

[15] *Ibid.* at 3.

[16] Parliamentary Research Branch, *Bill C-6: Personal Information Protection and Electronic Documents Act* by J. Craig (Ottawa: Library of Parliament, 15 October 1999).

encryption, there will be no retrospective 'recovery' unless it is planned and budgeted for at the time it is implemented — meaning now."[17] It was stressed that documents must not only be unencrypted, but the procedure must be done in such a way that would preserve evidence of their former state (previously encrypted) to provide evidence of a once-secure transaction.

Second, the ACA was concerned about the permissive structure of the legislation, describing it as "de facto a general, enabling piece of legislation to allow each federal department and agency to undertake its own initiatives for secure PKI signatures and document encryption."[18] The archivists were concerned that such an approach would result in a "multitude of different systems, procedure, and policies" and they feared for the long term implications, suggesting that "central direction and careful planning" were needed to preserve the legal, economical, archival, and historical value of the documents.

Subsection 37(b) appears to address the association's concerns regarding long-term readability of electronic information; however, the legislation still in large part allows individual departments to develop their own systems and policy. Time will tell if this permissive structure will lead to problems down the road as predicted by the Association of Canadian Archivists.

6) Regulations and Orders

Regulation-making powers are divided between the Governor in Council and the responsible authorities. Section 50 enables the responsible authority to make regulations specific to its own department or agency, while the Cabinet retains central control over the designation of secure electronic signature technology.

Section 48 enables the Governor in Council to designate technologies or processes that meet specified requirements for the purpose of defining a secure electronic signature.

Section 49 allows each responsible authority to amend Schedule 2 or 3, in certain circumstances, by adding or striking out a reference to a provision. Section 51 provides that the striking out of a reference in Schedule 2 or 3 will not affect the validity of anything done while the provision was listed in that Schedule. The provision of this power recognizes that departments may need to go offline to replace or upgrade technology.[19]

Section 50 is a general enabling provision that enables each responsible authority, for the purposes of sections 41 to 47, to make regulations respecting the application of those sections to its statutes or regulations.

---

[17]   Association of Canadian Archivists, *Brief to Parliament on Bill C-54: Personal Information Protection and Electronic Documents Act*, February 1999, at 5.

[18]   *Ibid.*

[19]   Power, above note 4 at para. 44.

Subsection 50(2) provides an outline of the types of provision contemplated in subsection 50(1). These regulations include

a) the technology or processes that must be used to make or send the electronic document;
b) the format of the electronic document;
c) the designation of a place where electronic document can be made or sent;
d) the time and circumstances when an electronic document is considered sent or retrieved and the place where it is considered sent or received; and
e) the technology used to make or verify an electronic signature.

Where the responsible authority does not wish to make regulations, but is required to under sections 40 to 47, subsection 50(3) sets out minimum rules that may be enacted. These basic rules provide that both parties must agree to the electronic format and that the document must be under the control of the recipient and be in a readable form.

C. Part 3: Amendments to the *Canada Evidence Act*

Part 3 contains a number of detailed amendments to the *Canada Evidence Act*[20] to permit the use of electronic documents as evidence in court and to provide for their reliable authentication. The goal is to allow people to create and rely on computer-generated records in court proceedings, rather than requiring them to produce paper originals. The amendments attempt to update the law to accommodate technology and be as neutral as possible to media so that people can choose to use paper or any form of technology without prejudice to their rights.

Part 3 contains essentially two types of amendments. The first strives to make various document-related provisions of the *Canada Evidence Act* media-neutral and the second incorporates the provisions of the *Uniform Electronic Evidence Act (UEEA)* developed by the Uniform Law Conference of Canada.[21]

The amendments in Part 3 cover four main areas: the authentication of electronic documents, satisfaction of the best evidence rule, evidentiary presumptions with respect to electronic signature, and the ability of the courts to recognize various standards of electronic record keeping.

---

[20]   R.S.C. 1985, c. C-5.

[21]   Uniform Law Conference of Canada, *Uniform Electronic Evidence Act: Consultation Paper* (Ottawa: March 1997).

1) Media-Neutral Documents

The first category of amendments replaces the word "printed" with the word "published" in sections 19, 20(c), 21(b) and (c), and 22(1)(b) of the *Canada Evidence Act* in reference to legislative instruments produced by the Queen's Printer (of either Canada or a province) to permit electronic versions of statutes, imperial documents, regulations, orders, notices, and proclamations to be admitted into evidence.[22] Section 57 does essentially the same thing with respect to notices, advertisements, and documents found in the *Canada Gazette*, providing that something published in an electronic version of the *Canada Gazette* is admissible as proof of the original and its contents, in the absence of evidence to the contrary.

2) *Uniform Electronic Evidence Act*

Section 56 adds a number of new sections after section 31 of the *Canada Evidence Act*. These new sections have been adopted from the work of the Uniform Law Conference of Canada (ULCC). The ULCC is an organization devoted to harmonizing the Canadian statute law where such consistency would be beneficial.[23] It does so largely by preparing uniform statutes that it recommends for enactment by the various governments across Canada. In 1993, the ULCC began its work on electronic evidence, which eventually led to the *Uniform Electronic Evidence Act*, which has been incorporated into Bill C-6 through section 56, adding sections 31.1 to 31.8 to the *Canada Evidence Act*.

In a *UEEA* consultation paper released in March 1997, the ULCC articulated the need for provisions dealing with electronic evidence. It found that "most electronic records are in practice being admitted in litigation. However, courts have struggled with the traditional rules of evidence, with inconsistent results. The common term 'reliability' has caused confusion among the principles of authentication, best evidence, hearsay and weight."[24]

The ULCC was also troubled by the fact that "many records managers and their legal advisors have not been confident that modern information systems, especially electronic imaging with paper originals destroyed, will produce records suitable for use in court."[25]

---

[22] *PIPEDA*, ss. 52 to 55.

[23] Above note 21.

[24] *Ibid.* at 2.

[25] *Ibid.*

3) Authentication

Section 31.1 provides that the party wishing to introduce an electronic record as evidence has the burden of proving its authenticity. This section codifies the common law on authentication which applies equally to paper records. The party needs only to bring evidence that the record is the type of record which he or she claims it to be (e.g., an invoice or a message).

4) Best Evidence Rule

Section 31.2 addresses the issue of the best evidence rule as it relates to electronic documents. Briefly, the best evidence rule requires that a party produce the best evidence available, which in most cases is the original record. This concept is problematic in relation to electronic records because in many cases, there is no "original" in the usual sense of the word. The purpose of the best evidence rule is to try to ensure the integrity of the record, since alterations in the document are more likely detectable on the original. Since it is often difficult, if not impossible, to provide direct evidence of the integrity of the electronic record itself, *system* reliability is substituted for record reliability. Paragraph 31.2(1)(a) provides that a party can satisfy the best evidence rule with evidence of the integrity of the *system* that generated the electronic document.

Under subsection 31.2(2), if a party has relied upon a printout of an electronic document, the integrity of the computer system will not be an issue. If the particular document "lives its life on paper," and that paper is presented as evidence, it will satisfy the best evidence rule, in absence of evidence to the contrary. The printout is to be treated as a paper record and will be considered the original for the purposes of the best evidence rule.

5) Presumption of Integrity

Section 31.3 sets out three presumptions regarding the integrity of electronic documents. If any of these three conditions are met, the integrity of the computer system (and consequently that of the document itself) will be presumed in the absence of evidence to the contrary.

First, subsection 31.3(a) provides that an electronic document-keeping system will be presumed to have generated a reliable electronic document if the system was working properly or, if it was not working properly, the problems with the system had no effect on the integrity of the document. In an annotated version of the *UEEA*, the ULCC provided that "the integrity of most electronic records is not disputed; they are admitted in evidence routinely. This Act does not intend to make the process more difficult, or to provide grounds for frivolous but possibly expensive attacks on otherwise acceptable records. It does intend to point out the basic criteria on which an electronic record can be judged."[26]

Second, subsection 31.3(b) provides that a record obtained in the course of litigation from an adverse party will be presumed reliable.

Third, subsection 31.3(c) creates a presumption of reliability of business records of a third party. If a litigant wishes to rely upon a record obtained by a third party, the record will be presumed reliable if the proponent of the record did *not* have control over the system that generated it. If the proponent did in fact have control over the document system, integrity can be established under subsection (a). This qualification was included to prevent parties from contracting out their records management and then claiming that their records are actually someone else's.[27]

Section 31.4 provides that the Governor in Council may make regulations establishing evidentiary presumptions related to electronic documents signed with secure electronic signatures. Power stated that secure electronic signatures were dealt with in this manner simply because "it is difficult to place presumptions in a statute about a technology that is unknown at the time of enactment of the statute."[28] This section contemplates the enactment of regulations related to the linkage of a person to a particular signature and the integrity of the document signed with a secure electronic signature.

6) Electronic Record Keeping

Section 31.5 provides that a court, in determining the admissibility of evidence, may take into consideration evidence of industry or practice standards in record keeping. This section makes adherence to a system of recognized record-keeping standards, or even adherence to one's own record-keeping standards, a relevant consideration.

Affidavit evidence can be used in place of oral evidence for the purposes of subsection 32.2(2) and the presumptions in sections 31.3 and 31.5.[29] Subsection 31.6(2) provides that an affidavit deponent can be cross-examined and subsection (b) provides that other deponents can be cross-examined with permission from the court. The intention of this subsection is to provide the opportunity for the opponent of the evidence to

---

[26] Uniform Law Conference of Canada, *Uniform Electronic Evidence Act*, accessed at <http:www.law.ualberta.ca/alri/ulc/current/eeeact.htm>, 4/13/2000 at 12:54 p.m. at s. 5(a).

[27] *Ibid.* at s. 5(c).

[28] Power, above note 4 at para. 59.

[29] *PIPEDA*, s. 31.6(1).

cross-examine the record keeper, or some other person relevant to the production and integrity of the document.[30]

D. Part 4: Amendments to the *Statutory Instruments Act*

Part 4 amends the *Statutory Instruments Act* to acknowledge that notices, acts, and regulations published in an electronic version of the *Canada Gazette* have the same legal force as their paper equivalents. This Part sets the groundwork for the development of an "official" online *Canada Gazette;* however, in the event of a discrepancy between the electronic and paper versions of a document, the original paper statute, regulations, or notice prevails.

E. Part 5: Amendments to the *Statute Revision Act*

The purpose of the *Statute Revision Act* is to provide for the continuing revision and consolidation of federal statutes and regulations to be conducted by the Statute Revision Commission. The Commission prepared Consolidated Regulations in 1978, the Revised Statutes in 1985, and developed a looseleaf edition of the Statutes, which was discontinued in 1993, before the Commission ceased operations in the early 1990s.[31] Since 1995, the Department of Justice has maintained a database of consolidated regulations and statutes on its Web site. In fact, the federal legislation is the most popular part of the Department of Justice Web site.[32] This database is updated three times a year, but it is unofficial, meaning that its material cannot be used for any purpose under the *Canada Evidence Act*. The amendments in Part 5 of the *PIPEDA* are intended to facilitate the production of an official online consolidation of the federal statutes and regulations.

Section 60 of the *PIPEDA* changes the name of the *Statute Revision Act* to the *Legislation Revision and Consolidation Act (LRCA)* to more accurately reflect its purposes. The amendments in Part 5 of the *PIPEDA* divide the duties of revision and consolidation between the Commission and the Minister of Justice. Consolidation involves the amalgamation of amendments to a particular piece of legislation into a single up-to-date document. Revision, on the other hand, involves more than consolidation in that it may also involve reorganizing, renumbering, or even rewriting

---

[30]   *UEEA*, above note 21, s. 8(2).

[31]   Power, above note 4 at para. 65.

[32]   *Ibid.*

portions of the legislation. Section 62 provides that the Commission shall be responsible for the revision of the statutes and regulations.

Section 68 of the *PIPEDA* adds a new section 21 to the *LRCA*, which permits the Queen's Printer to publish the Revised Regulations in electronic form and provides that a copy of a revised regulation in electronic form is sufficient as evidence of the regulation and its contents, unless the contrary is shown.

Section 71 of the *PIPEDA* adds a completely new Part III to the *LRCA*, entitled "Consolidated Statutes and Regulations of Canada." Section 26 of this new Part authorizes the Minister of Justice to maintain consolidations of both the regulations and statutes. Section 28 provides that the Minister may publish and distribute the consolidated regulations and statutes in an electronic form that the Minister considers appropriate. Section 31 provides that in the event of an inconsistency between a consolidated statute or regulation published by the Minister and the original statute or regulation, the original will prevail to the extent of the inconsistency. The Minister is also given authority to enter into agreements for the production and sale of consolidated regulations and statutes.[33]

As is the case with Parts 3 and 4, Part 5 comes into force on the recommendation of the Minister of Justice.[34] Presumably this is not to happen until technology is in place to ensure the integrity of online versions of statutes and regulations.

In summary, Parts 2 to 5 of the *Personal Information Protection and Electronic Documents Act* have been enacted to help modernize the federal government's provision of services by moving federal legislation out of the "age of paper." This modernization is to take place gradually, with government departments and agencies participating when they have the technology and resources in place. Amendments to the *Canada Evidence Act, Statutory Instruments Act,* and *Statute Revision Act* give legal significance to electronic records and Parliamentary documents. The Government of Canada, through this Act, has attempted to lay the groundwork not only for its electronic commerce strategy but for a paperless society.

---

[33] See new s. 32 of the *Canada Evidence Act.*

[34] *PIPEDA,* s. 72(b).

CHAPTER 5

CRITICAL PRIVACY ISSUES

A. Introduction

This book was written before the coming into force of the *Personal Information Protection and Electronic Documents Act*, when the debate about the effective implementation of the legislation had barely begun. Very few companies have started to get ready for the coming into force, although those that have done so are certainly the largest and most important from a consumer protection point of view. It is likely that in the year following the coming into force of the Act, there will be a decided maturing of the debate on privacy in Canada.

There are several privacy issues that we expect will evolve and which we will treat more extensively in the next edition of this text. In this chapter, we will sketch out some of the debate on a few of the current privacy issues and position the protections that this legislation affords within that discussion.

B. Definition of Personal Information and the Concept of Anonymity

The definition of personal information that was used in the CSA Code was based on the one used in the federal *Privacy Act*,[1] but the recitals of examples — such as age, race, name, address, phone number — were removed. Even when cloaked with the customary caveat, "Without restricting the generality of the foregoing," it had been the experience of those who had worked with the federal *Privacy Act* that inevitably people look to the list for the element at play and claim that it is not included if it does not appear on the list. The Ontario Information and Privacy Commissioner had sent detailed advice in response to the discussion of the Uniform Law Conference of Canada draft law, suggesting that an even longer

---

[1] R.S.C. 1985, c. P-21.

list of recitals than the one that appears in the Ontario Act[2] be included because her office had experienced some difficulty with certain data elements. However, the drafting team decided to keep it simple.

When the legislation was being discussed in the Industry Committee, the B.C. Civil Liberties Association suggested that the definition be amended to specifically include bodily tissues and fluids. They had had a case under British Columbia law where urine samples were held not to be subject to the legislation because they were not considered to be recorded information. The response of the drafting team to this problem, which they considered to be a serious one, was to delete "recorded in any form" from the definition. The resulting definition is as broad as any you could find and encompasses oral information that is not recorded.

The breadth of this definition is unusual in a data protection statute and some find the concept alarming. It will probably prove difficult to investigate, but it would be a serious oversight to leave it out. For example, if an organization is not allowed to collect certain types of information, such as medical conditions or sexual preference, but it is the practice of the organization to exchange the information among decision makers orally, the data protection statute is ineffective and leaves the affected individuals without recourse. The concept, of course, leads to philosophical discussion about whether knowing a fact constitutes a collection and use of personal information, and whether the agents of the state can enter into your head and audit. Nevertheless, the telling of secrets is a concept that everyone understands, and this legislation will enable individuals to complain when it happens.

Since the Internet has entered into the phase of electronic commerce, the term "personally identifiable information," or PII, has gained currency. It is not as clear a concept as it might be. Presumably, the intent is to describe information about an identifiable individual. Always when we say this, the next question should be: "Identifiable to whom?" If one company does not know or retain the name and address of a group of customers, but assigns a number, and their partners hold the information necessary to identify the people, is the company holding *personal* information, *personally identifiable* information, or *anonymous* information? What is the threshold of work necessary to identify the individuals, beyond which the information is no longer considered to be personal information? Or should we consider all information that pertains to an individual *personal*, regardless of whether we can name the individual? It is the position of the Canadian Medical Association that this is the case, and that anonymous medical records are still personal information.

Latanya Sweeney of Carnegie Mellon University has done pioneering work on these issues, particularly with respect to re-identifying data that

---

2   *Freedom of Information and Protection of Privacy Act*, R.S.O. 1990, c. F.31, as amended, s. 2.

were alleged to be anonymous. She has demonstrated that she can take a large sample of "anonymized" medical data and re-identify the individuals simply by matching with publicly available databases, such as the tax rolls and drivers' licences.[3] This research has caused a re-examination in data protection circles about when it is safe to call information "anonymous."

Zero Knowledge Systems (ZKS) is a software company headquartered in Montreal, Canada, which develops consumer software that, when loaded onto the user's computer, enables her to choose five pseudonyms and completely protect her identity. It hides her IP address, encrypting traffic from her machine and routing it through a network of Internet service providers, each one removing an envelope of encryption as it passes it to the next address. The final server in the chain sees the destination, but cannot link it to the sender. The software has a facility for managing cookies and can be programmed to question any release of identifying information, in case a user forgets and tries to send a message with her name and address in it while using her pseudonym. The software is recognized as being the strongest privacy solution on the Internet today, but ZKS avoids using the word "anonymous" to describe it.

The company has published a technical white paper describing all the known flaws in the system that would enable an attacker to identify the individual. One of the simplest ways to compromise one's anonymity is simply to link the pseudonym once with the real identity. At that point, potentially years of hitherto "anonymous" transactions precipitate out as personal information, linked to the individual, and because of the strength and nature of the cryptography employed, they are impossible to repudiate.

Given the enormous quantity of publicly available personal information today, the ubiquity of computing power, and the growing desire of organizations to capitalize on this information and make better decisions concerning the individual — a practice somewhat euphemistically called "customer relationship management," or CRM — is it really possible to talk about depersonalized data? Not according to Zero Knowledge, whose comment today is that it is more honest to speak of the scale of the attack that would be required to relink the information to the individual concerned. Cryptographers do not consider cryptographic systems as unbreakable, but rather speak about the scale of the attack necessary to defeat it. In the same way, one should be cautious in describing information as anonymous, but must talk instead about the scale of attack necessary to identify the individual.

The impact of this in terms of this legislation is that great caution must be exercised in the treatment of personal data that is supposed to be "anonymized." It is best to treat information that relates to an individual or is

---

[3]   L. Sweeney, *Foundations of Privacy Protection from a Computer Science Perspective* (Pittsburgh, PA: Carnegie Mellon University, 2000).

derived from an individual's transaction profile as personal, especially if only the name has been removed.

C. Publicly Available Information

This data protection bill appears long after data-mining practices have been established, and after computerization and scanning technologies have made the collection of vast amounts of information available on public registries not only easily accessible, but cheaply available from a multitude of resellers. The data business is well known to insiders in the direct marketing or credit reporting industry, but not to consumers. Few understand what information is assumed from their postal code, for instance, or how they are profiled. The core of these data used to profile is gathered from public registries or government records, such as motor vehicle licence records, land tax registries, and various licences, from fishing and hunting to airplane pilots. Data protection statutes have dealt with the problem of how to grapple with these data in several ways,[4] but most duck it by allowing information that has been released under statutory authority to be reused without consent. Canada's statute does not. Instead, it says that information may be collected, used, and disclosed without consent if specified by the regulations. The regulations were tabled for public comment on 7 October 2000 and are listed below. They cover publicly available information and the investigative bodies referred to in paragraphs 7(3)(d) and (h.2).

D. Regulations

The regulations specifying publicly available information and investigative bodies for the purposes of section 7 were pre-published by Industry Canada on 7 October 2000 and were open for comment for a thirty-day period. Since major changes would result in having to consult again, it seems likely that the regulations will go forward in that form to be in place on 1 January 2001 when the first phase of the Act comes into force.

Copies of the submissions on behalf of the Insurance Crime Prevention Bureau of the Insurance Council of Canada (otherwise known as the Insurance Bureau of Canada) and the Bank Crime Prevention and Investigative Office of the Canadian Bankers Association, which will be listed as investigative bodies, are available on the Industry Canada site at <http://e-com.ic.gc.ca/english/privacy/632d1.html#privup>.

What follows is the entire text of the regulations as pre-published, including the Regulatory Impact Analysis Statements for both regulations.

---

4   For an interesting discussion of the problem, see the Hong Kong Data Commissioner's Web site at <http://www.pco.org.hk>, the 1999 Annual Data Commissioners' Conference.

Canada Gazette, Part I
Volume 134, Number 41
OTTAWA, SATURDAY, OCTOBER 7, 2000

Regulations Specifying Investigative Bodies

Statutory Authority

*Personal Information Protection and
Electronic Documents Act*

Sponsoring Department
Department of Industry

REGULATORY IMPACT ANALYSIS STATEMENT

Description

Part 1 of the *Personal Information Protection and Electronic Documents Act* (the *Act*) establishes rules to govern the collection, use and disclosure of personal information by organizations in the course of commercial activity. The legislation requires an organization, which is disclosing personal information, to obtain the individual's consent in most circumstances. An exception to this rule is found in paragraphs 7(3)(*d*) and (*h*.2) of Part 1 of the *Act* which permit the disclosure of personal information to and by a private investigative body, without the knowledge or consent of the individual, if the investigative body is specified by the Regulations. The purpose of these Regulations is to name the investigative bodies for the purposes of paragraph 7(3)(*d*) or (*h*.2) of Part 1 of the *Act*.

Increasingly, many fraud investigations are initially launched by private sector organizations (e.g., a bank or insurance company) by way of an independent, non-governmental investigative body. Should the investigative body's preliminary investigation reveal grounds for suspecting that a fraud has been committed or a law contravened, the organization will then turn the findings over to a police or other enforcement agency for further action. Paragraph 7(3)(*d*) allows an organization to disclose personal information, without the consent of the individual, to the appropriate private sector investigative body in order to conduct the preliminary investigation. The disclosure is circumscribed as it must be a reasonable disclosure related to investigations of breaches of agreements or contraventions of the law. Paragraph 7(3)(*h*.2) allows an investigative body to disclose personal information back to the client organization on whose behalf it is conducting the investigation.

Paragraph 7(3)(*h*.2) completes the exception provided in paragraph 7(1)(*b*) for collection without consent for the purposes of the prevention of fraud by extending it to disclosure. Collection alone would be of limited use to those combatting fraud, unless the information could be disclosed to the parties that need the information. However, without paragraph 7(3)(*h*.2), the flow of information could only go in one direction — from the organization to the investigative body. The investigative body would be unable to disclose the results of its investigation back to the client organization without consent.

The ability to exchange personal information between private organizations without consent for investigative purposes is the only exception granted to these organizations by the Regulations. Organizations and investigative bodies which exchange personal information will remain responsible for compliance with all other requirements of the *Act* for this information, and will be subject to oversight by the Privacy Commissioner of Canada and the ability of individuals to seek redress in the Federal Court of Canada.

During the preparation of these Regulations, Industry Canada developed a set of criteria that would be used in the assessment of candidates for investigative bodies. These criteria were intended to cover privacy concerns associated with allowing organizations to disclose personal information without consent for investigative purposes. All of the criteria would not necessarily be applicable to each investigative body. The criteria were based on the following considerations:

- The specific contraventions of law or breaches of agreements against which the investigative activities are directed;
- The specific personal data elements which are disclosed by other organizations to the body; the specific personal data elements which flow back to the organizations from the body; the uses and disclosures made of the information by the body; whether audit trails are maintained; the length of time the information is kept; and the security standards and practices in place for retention and disposal of the information;
- Whether the operational structure of the body or process is fully documented and formalized and the authority, responsibility and accountability centres are identified;
- Whether there are specific legal regime, licensing requirement, regulation or oversight mechanisms to which it is subject and whether sanctions or penalties for non-compliance exist;
- The privacy protection policies and procedures, such as a privacy code, followed by the body. The extent to which the policies and procedures comply with Part 1 of the *Act*;
- The extent to which the investigative body is independent from the association of members or client organizations that it serves;
- The extent to which all alternative methods of complying with the *Act*, such as contract or consent, have been exhausted; and
- The amount of information provided to individuals about the existence and operation of the body and about how to make a complaint or seek redress.

Part 1 of the *Act* will be implemented in two stages. On January 1, 2001, it will apply to the personal information of the customers and employees of the federally regulated private sector, including telephone and transportation companies, broadcasters and banks. It will also apply to organizations that sell personal information across provincial borders, e.g., companies selling or renting mailing lists. On January 1, 2004, the *Act* will apply to all personal information collected, used or disclosed in the course of commercial activity. Due to the phased introduction of the legislation and the fact that it is new to the private sector, it is expected that additions to the list of investigative bodies in the Regulations may be necessary. For this reason, the Department will continue to consider applications on a case-by-case basis in the future.

Of the organizations which submitted information to Industry Canada describing their internal structure and investigative process, those listed satisfied the criteria on the basis of the documentation submitted. Copies of their submissions may be obtained by contacting Industry Canada or by visiting the Electronic Commerce Web site at: http://e-com.ic.gc.ca/english/privacy/632d1.html#privup.

Alternatives

The legislative framework in Part 1 of the *Act* requires that an investigative body, for the purposes of paragraph 7(3)(*d*) or (*h*.2) of the *Act*, be specified by the Regulations. There are no alternatives to deal with the collection, use and disclosure of this information without consent.

BENEFITS AND COSTS

Benefits

Insurance fraud is estimated to cost the property and casualty insurance industry $1.3 billion annually. Credit and debit card fraud, robbery, and counterfeit payments are estimated to cost the banking industry $250 million annually (additional losses related to cyber crime and other fraud would add to this figure). If the legislation did not allow information sharing between organizations and their private investigative bodies, the detection and prevention of fraud would be more difficult. This would add to the cost of insurance borne by law abiding policyholders and bank customers through increased premiums, service charges and fees.

Costs

The Regulations should not impose significant additional costs on the organizations to which it applies as it merely permits the continuation of existing information sharing relationships between organizations and their investigative bodies.

The Regulations will have no impact on Department resources.

Consultation

Bill C-54 (the precursor to Bill C-6) was introduced on October 1, 1998, and received extensive hearings before the Standing Committee on Industry and the Standing Senate Committee on Social Affairs, Science and Technology. Representatives of the insurance and banking industries, among others, appeared before the Standing Committee on Industry and raised the issue of the viability of private sector investigative activities under the proposed legislation. As a result, the bill was amended to provide for disclosure without consent to and by investigative bodies that were specified in the Regulations.

Subsequent to the Royal Assent of the Bill on April 13, 2000, Industry Canada had discussions with interested parties, including representatives of the insurance, credit reporting, telephone, banking, information technology, direct marketing, real estate, cable television, retail sale, as well as private investigators, Internet service providers, the Chamber of Commerce and the manufacturers and exporters associations. Consumer and privacy organiza-

tions, the provincial and territorial privacy commissioners and the members of the federal-provincial-territorial discussion group on privacy legislation were included in these discussions. Consultations were also undertaken with the federal Privacy Commissioner.

Compliance and Enforcement

Individuals may make complaints about the practices of an organization to the Privacy Commissioner of Canada who will investigate the matter and deliver a report to the parties. The Commissioner may make recommendations to an organization concerning its practices and whether they are considered to comply with Part 1 of the *Act* but the Commissioner does not have the power to issue binding orders on the organization. The individual or the Privacy Commissioner, or both acting together, may take unresolved complaints to the Federal Court of Canada which has the power to order an organization to change a practice and to pay damages to the individual.

Contact

Mr. Richard Simpson, Director General, Electronic Commerce
Branch, Industry Canada, 300 Slater Street, Room D2090, Ottawa,
Ontario K1A 0C8, (613) 990-4292 (Telephone), (613) 941-0178 (Facsimile), simpson.richard@ic.gc.ca (Electronic mail).

PROPOSED REGULATORY TEXT

Notice Is Hereby Given That The Governor In Council, Pursuant To Paragraph 26(1)(A.01) Of The *Personal Information Protection And Electronic Documents Act* (<Reference A> A S.C. 2000, C. 5), Proposes To Make The Annexed Regulations Specifying Investigative Bodies.

Interested Persons May Make Representations With Respect To The Proposed Regulations Within 30 Days After The Date Of

Publication Of This Notice. All Such Representations Must Cite The Canada Gazette, Part I, And The Date Of Publication Of This Notice, And Be Addressed To Mr. Richard Simpson, Director General, Electronic Commerce Branch, Industry Canada, 300 Slater Street, Room D2090, Ottawa, Ontario, K1A 0C8.

Ottawa, October 4, 2000.
Marc O'Sullivan
Assistant Clerk Of The Privy Council

REGULATIONS SPECIFYING INVESTIGATIVE BODIES

INVESTIGATIVE BODIES

1. The Following Investigative Bodies Are Specified, By Name Or By Class, For The Purposes Of Paragraphs 7(3)(D) And (H.2) Of The *Personal Information Protection And Electronic Documents Act*:

(a) The Insurance Crime Prevention Bureau, A Division Of The Insurance Council Of Canada; And

(b) the Bank Crime Prevention and Investigation Office of the Canadian Bankers Association.

COMING INTO FORCE

2. These Regulations come into force on January 1, 2001.

Regulations Specifying Publicly Available Information

Statutory Authority

Personal Information Protection and Electronic Documents Act

Sponsoring Department
Department of Industry

REGULATORY IMPACT ANALYSIS STATEMENT

Description

Part 1 of the *Personal Information Protection and Electronic Documents Act* (the *Act*) establishes rules to govern the collection, use and disclosure of personal information by organizations in the course of commercial activity. The legislation requires an organization, which is collecting, using or disclosing personal information, to obtain the individual's consent in most circumstances. Exceptions to this rule are found in paragraphs 7(1)(*d*), (2)(*c*.1)or (3)(*h*.1) of the *Act* which permit the collection, use and disclosure of personal information, without the knowledge or consent of the individual, if the information is publicly available and is specified by the Regulations. The purpose of this regulation is to specify what information and classes of information is publicly available information for the purposes of paragraphs 7(1)(*d*), (2)(*c*.1) and (3)(*h*.1) of the *Act*.

The basic premise underlying this regulation is that the collection, use and disclosure of publicly available personal information for commercial purposes should be subject to the same fair information practices as are required by the *Act* for all other personal information. As a rule, individuals are able to decide for themselves with whom they will share personal information and under what circumstances. However, some personal information enters into the public sphere through a variety of channels, often without the knowledge or consent of the individual. Examples include personal information that appears in telephone or other directories, public registries maintained by governments, public court records or that is published in the media. This personal information is made public for a specific and primary purpose, e.g., individuals allow their name, address and telephone number to appear in the telephone or other directories to enable others to contact them for personal reasons, to enable potential clients to reach them in their professional capacity or to enable others to verify their title, membership or professional qualifications. Some government registries such as land titles, personal property, municipal property tax rolls, are open to the public to promote longstanding public policy purposes. Public access is permitted to some court records to facilitate transparency in the justice system, while other personal information is placed in publications to publicize specific information about the individual (e.g., birth and marriage announcements).

Privacy concerns arise because more information is sometimes collected in public registries (many of which were created in an era when privacy concerns were not fully considered) than is required for the fulfilment of the primary purpose. Other concerns relate to the manner in which the information is made publicly available, e.g., whether there are any controls or limitations placed on who may collect and use it and how (increasingly access is possible to an electronic record rather than to the traditional hard copy. Internet access is more common as well). The fact that individuals have continuing expectations of privacy for some publicly available personal information is seldom addressed. Another privacy issue is the growing use that commercial organizations make of this information for purposes that often have nothing to do with the primary

purpose for which the information was made public, i.e., to contact individuals and offer them products or services. There is also an increasing tendency to collect and use publicly available information to create comprehensive personal profiles of the individual, including their consumption habits, lifestyles and personal histories for a variety of other purposes, including employment decisions. Many, if not most, of these secondary uses are presently carried out without the knowledge or consent of the individual. A final issue is that, with few rules to govern publicly available personal information, organizations have little incentive to consider obtaining consent from the individual.

The proposed Regulations will permit one exception from fair information practices by allowing commercial organizations to collect, use and disclose certain personal information without consent. The Regulations are based on a recognition that some personal information is publicly available for a legitimate primary purpose, often with the individual's tacit agreement (e.g., the telephone directory and announcements). In these circumstances, it is reasonable to allow organizations to collect, use and disclose this information without adding the requirement to obtain consent. To require an organization to obtain consent to use this information for its primary purpose would not contribute to the protection of the individual's privacy, would add to the organization's costs and could frustrate some public policy purpose. However, it is also reasonable to insist that any purpose other than the primary one should be subject to the consent requirement. This approach is consistent with Principle 2 of Schedule 1 of the *Act* (paragraph 4.2.4) which states that a new purpose requires consent unless required by law. Using the criteria of consistency with the primary purpose or tacit consent as the basis for the regulation of publicly available personal information strikes the appropriate balance between the individual's right of privacy and the business need for information. Organizations will remain responsible for compliance with all other requirements of the *Act* for this information, including the appropriate purpose requirement in Clause 5(3) and will be subject to oversight by the Privacy Commissioner of Canada and the ability of individuals to seek redress in the Federal Court of Canada.

Part 1 of the *Act* will be implemented in two stages. On January 1, 2001, it will apply to the personal information of the customers and employees of the federally regulated private sector, including telephone and transportation companies, broadcasters, and banks. It will also apply to organizations that sell personal information across provincial borders, e.g., companies selling or renting mailing lists. On January 1, 2004, the *Act* will apply to all personal information collected, used or disclosed in the course of commercial activity. Due to the phased introduction of the legislation and the fact that it is new to the private sector, it is expected that additions or amendments to the regulation may be necessary. For this reason, the Department will continue to consider suggestions on a case by case basis in the future.

Alternatives

The legislative framework in Part 1 of the *Act* requires that publicly available information be specified by the Regulations. There are no alternatives to deal with the collection, use and disclosure of this information without consent.

BENEFITS AND COSTS

Benefits

The total growth of electronic commerce on the Internet is expected to increase from $195 billion (CAN) in 1999 to $2.8 trillion (CAN) in 2003. By developing the proper framework, Canada could capture a market share of $94 billion

(CAN) in 2003, leading to new business opportunities and job creation to the benefit of all Canadians. By enacting the *Personal Information Protection and Electronic Documents Act* and these Regulations, the Government is putting in place one of the essential foundations of electronic commerce which will promote its acceptance and growth. The effect of the *Act* and Regulations will be to build trust in electronic commerce by providing individuals with assurance of protection for their personal information. The Regulations will also create a level playing field for business with clear, predictable rules for all. It will work to encourage on-line connectedness of Canadians — to each other, to business and to the federal government. Consumers and business will be able to conduct their on-line transactions with the confidence that privacy protection measures are in place and that they will be overseen by the Privacy Commissioner.

The legislation and the Regulations have been designed to be light and flexible for businesses to implement. Its principles are taken from the CSA International's Model Code for the Protection of Personal Information, developed and recognized by both businesses and consumers as a standard for privacy protection. Organizations will incur some implementation costs but the benefits of increased sales through the growth of electronic commerce transactions will more than compensate.

The Regulations will have no impact on the Department's resources.

Consultation

Consultations leading to this legislation began in October 1994 with the establishment of the Information Highway Advisory Council, which released a discussion paper entitled *Privacy and the Canadian Information Highway.* In 1998, the Government issued a discussion paper entitled *The Protection of Personal Information: Building Canada's Information Economy and*

Society. Bill C-54 (the precursor to Bill C-6) was introduced on October 1, 1998, and received extensive hearings before the Standing Committee on Industry. The bill was subsequently re-introduced as Bill C-6 and received extensive public hearings before the Standing Senate Committee on Social Affairs, Science and Technology.

Subsequent to the Bill's receiving Royal Assent on April 13, 2000, Industry Canada had discussions with interested parties, including representatives of the insurance, credit reporting, telephone, banking, information technology, direct marketing, real estate, cable television, retail sale, as well as private investigators, Internet service providers, Chamber of Commerce and the manufacturers and exporters associations. Consumer and privacy organizations, the provincial and territorial privacy commissioners, the members of the federal-provincial-territorial discussion group on privacy legislation and the Treasury Board of Canada were included in these discussions. Consultations were also undertaken with the federal Privacy Commissioner.

Compliance and Enforcement

Individuals may make complaints about the practices of an organization to the Privacy Commissioner of Canada who will investigate the matter and deliver a report to the parties. The Commissioner may make recommendations to an organization concerning its practices and whether they are considered to comply with Part 1 of the *Act* but the Commissioner does not have the power to issue binding orders on the organization. The individual or the Privacy Commissioner, or both acting together, may take unresolved complaints to the Federal Court of Canada which has the power to order an organization to change a practice and to pay damages to the individual.

Contact

Mr. Richard Simpson, Director General, Electronic Commerce Branch, Industry Canada, 300 Slater Street, Room D2090, Ottawa, Ontario K1A 0C8, (613) 990-4292 (Telephone), (613) 941-0178 (Facsimile), simpson.richard@ic.gc.ca (Electronic mail).

PROPOSED REGULATORY TEXT

Notice is hereby given that the Governor in Council, pursuant to paragraph 26(1)(a.01) of the Personal Information Protection and Electronic Documents Act, proposes to make the annexed Regulations Specifying Publicly Available Information.

Interested persons may make representations with respect to the proposed Regulations within 30 days after the date of publication of this notice. All such representations must cite the Canada Gazette, Part I, and the date of publication of this notice, and be addressed to Mr. Richard Simpson, Director General, Electronic Commerce Branch, Industry Canada, 300 Slater Street, Room D2090, Ottawa, Ontario, K1A 0C8.

Ottawa, October 4, 2000.

Marc O'Sullivan
Assistant Clerk of the Privy Council

REGULATIONS SPECIFYING PUBLICLY AVAILABLE INFORMATION

INFORMATION

1. The following information and classes of information are specified for the purposes of paragraphs 7(1)(*d*), (2)(*c*.1) and (3)(*h*.1) of the *Personal Information Protection and Electronic Documents Act*:

(a) personal information consisting of the name, address and telephone number of a subscriber that appears in a telephone directory that is available to the public, where the subscriber can refuse to have the personal information appear in the directory;

(b) personal information including the name, title, address and telephone number of an individual that appears in a professional or business directory that is available to the public, where the collection, use and disclosure of the personal information relate directly to the purpose for which the information appears in the directory;

(c) personal information that appears in a registry collected under a statutory authority and to which a right of public access is required by law, where the collection, use and disclosure of the personal information relate directly to the purpose for which the information appears in the registry;

(d) personal information that appears in a court record to which public access is permitted, where the collection, use and disclosure of the personal information relate directly to the purpose for which the information appears in the record; and

(e) personal information that appears in a publication, including a magazine, book or newspaper, that is available to the public, where the individual has provided the information.

2. These Regulations come into force on January 1, 2001.

E. Comments on Investigative Bodies

The Act makes no allowances for private or commercial investigative bodies to disclose personal information without the knowledge and consent of the individual. They may collect it and use it only if it relates to the breach of an agreement or the contravention of a law under paragraphs 7(1)(b) and 7(2)(a), but there is no parallel exemption for disclosure. This allows organizations to maintain a close watch for fraud and other such unlawful activities, but prevents them from sharing the information with the wide world or their business partners. They may share it with law enforcement under 7(3)(d). Obviously, this constrains the actions of private investigators significantly. If there were no such constraint, in other words if there were an exemption for the general category of private investigation, anybody who called themselves a private investigator would be exempted from obtaining consent for the collection, use, and disclosure of personal information.

The compromise reached in the House of Commons Industry Committee was to include a power whereby some private sector investigative bodies could be listed in the regulations. This does not exempt them from the coverage of the bill; it merely allows organizations to disclose information to them under paragraph 7(3)(d), and it permits them to share information among themselves under 7(3)(h.2). The two organizations that have applied to be included in the regulations as of the closure of the public comment period are good examples.

The Insurance Crime Prevention Bureau maintains a database of insurance claims that may be queried by insurance companies as they prepare to write a policy. In the event that an individual has, for example, already claimed for five house fires, the database will contain the information and enable the agent to put the individual at a much higher risk. It will also enable investigative and law enforcement action, if necessary. This system maintains the data in one secured area, avoids the promiscuous sharing of information among agents, yet allows companies to protect themselves from undue risk and fraud.

The banks have a similar investigative body, the Bank Crime Prevention and Investigative Office of the Canadian Bankers Association. This organization allows the banks to share in a secure manner information about a range of suspected illegal activity, some of which they are by law responsible to control and investigate.

F.   Comments on Publicly Available Information

The issue of publicly available information is a difficult one; it demonstrates one of those rare instances where it can truly be said that technology has caused the problem. The draft regulations attempt to limit secondary or commercial collections, uses, and disclosures of publicly available information by specifying that personal information from public registries, professional directories, and court records may only be collected, used, or disclosed for purposes directly related to the purposes for which the information appeared in the public registry, directory, and so forth. Although this is a laudable aim, one has to ask whether in some of these cases it will even be possible to determine what was the primary purpose of publication.

Take court records as an example. Why are they public? The obvious answer is that the transparency of the legal system is a long-held democratic principle that allows justice not only to be done, but to be seen to be done. The press plays a very large role in ensuring that this happens, as do various public authorities. Since the press isn't constrained by the law in collecting, using, and disclosing personal information for journalistic purposes, and public authorities are not subject to the law, one has to ask, what is the purpose of this paragraph of the regulation? What are the legitimate commercial uses of court records that needed to be addressed and that would meet the purposes test in the regulation?

The answer is probably that, particularly as court records become available on the Internet, it becomes easy to mine them for personal information, for purposes that have nothing to do with the court case in question. The privacy scholar Oscar Gandy, author of *The Panoptic Sort*,[5] mentioned

---

[5]   Oscar Gandy, *The Panoptic Sort: A Political Economy of Personal Information* (Boulder, CO: Westview Press, 1993).

in a speech at the Computers, Freedom, and Privacy Conference of 1995 his favourite example of egregious direct marketing lists at that time: families suffering from the separation of a member, whether through death, runaway children, or marital breakup. Clearly, access to court records would be necessary to put this list together, and its use for marketing has little to do with the purpose of an open court system.

The limitation on secondary uses of personal information in public registries, on the other hand, is less problematic and long overdue. Made public in an age when it was necessary to physically go somewhere to look up information on a case-by-case basis, these registries can now be downloaded in bulk and are being sold by various levels of government. Constraints on these uses of registry information are vital, and the trustees of these data banks are now going to be forced to ask for individual consent to secondary commercial uses of this information, thus putting the onus where it belongs.

If the regulation goes forward as anticipated, before organizations collect, use, or disclose publicly available information, they will need to satisfy themselves of the following:

- If using information from a telephone directory, they have taken only the name, address, and telephone number, and the individual had the right to refuse to have his or her name appear in the directory.
- If using a business or professional directory, it is available to the public, and the collection, use, or disclosure is directly related to the purpose for which the information appeared in the directory. Information from these sources is not restricted to name, address, and telephone number; it can include such elements as field of expertise, professional qualifications, and so forth.
- If using information from a public registry, the information was collected under a statutory authority and access to the registry by the public is *required*, as opposed to merely allowed, by law; and the collection, use, or disclosure by the organization relates directly to the purpose, presumably the statutory purpose, for which the information appears in the registry.
- If using information from court records, public access to the record is permitted, bearing in mind that some court records are not accessible to the public; and the collection, use, or disclosure of the information by the organization relate directly to the purpose for which the information appears in the record. The problems associated with making this determination are discussed above.
- If using information that appears in a magazine, book, newspaper and so forth, it is available to the public and the individual has provided the information. That sort of information might be found in birth and death notices, advertisements, notices of various sorts, and

information provided by individuals in interviews. It would appear not to cover any information that may have been provided by another person *even with the knowledge of the individual.*

This provision appears to open up the possibility of all kinds of collection of information if the individual has provided it. It is well to remember that the reasonable person test of subsection 5(3) applies to the collection, use, and disclosure of all elements of information. This will act as a constraint on automated sifting of public records, because the information must still be directly relevant to the purpose that the organization has stated for the collection, which must pass the reasonable person test.

G. Organizations and Their Affiliates

One of the issues that has occasioned a large number of questions during the parliamentary process has been what is meant by an organization. The answer is quite simple, for the definition is clear enough. The problem is that organizations generally want to share information with their business partners and affiliates and do not always want to either ask for consent, or clarify to whom they are giving the information. In some cases, information flows within one main computer system, and it will be necessary to control this process now that the Act is in force. It would be prudent for companies to err on the side of caution and ask consent for the sharing of all information among specified entities, because consumers cannot be assumed to understand how the business is structured.

Another issue of some concern is whether the personal information is protected in cases of the sale of a business or in bankruptcy. The short answer is that contractual obligations do not survive bankruptcy. But the intent of the Act is that data protection responsibilities migrate with personal information, ideally from one responsible keeper to another. The first high profile case of an Internet company's customer list going on the block for sale is Toysmart.[6] In that case, the U.S. Federal Trade Commission filed a complaint against Toysmart.com, a failed Internet retailer of children's toys, seeking injunctive and declaratory relief to prevent the sale of confidential customer information collected on the company Web site as part of the assets of the bankrupt company. Subsequently, the company agreed to settle these charges and issued an order in Bankruptcy court spe-

---

6   *FTC* v. *Toysmart.com, LLC, and Toysmart.com, Inc.*, Civil Action No. 00-11341-RGS (District of Massachusetts, 2000). Following the settlement of this complaint, the FTC filed an amended complaint with the U.S. District Court in Massachusetts alleging that Toysmart collected personal information from children in violation of the *Children's Online Privacy Protection Act* (COPPA) of 1998. See <http://www.ftc.gov/opa/2000/07/toysmart2.htm>.

cifically prohibiting the sale of customer information except under very limited circumstances. What is clear is that if the Federal Trade Commission had not intervened, the information would have been sold.

H. Scholarly, Historical, and Market Research

Another common theme during the debates was the impact that the legislation would have on research. Although there can be no question that data protection legislation will indeed have an impact, it is doubtful that legitimate research will be prevented. If this proves to be the case, the mandatory Parliamentary review will give an opportunity to researchers to seek amendments to the legislation. In the meantime, the debate has been somewhat clouded by the various different types of research and the varying jurisdictions under which the collections of information fall.

If we divide the various types of scholarly research into historical (including biographical), medical, and statistical and economic, we have covered the major areas. There is also market and opinion research, and genealogical research, which is most often done by individuals researching their own families. The exemptions from the obligation to obtain individual consent that apply to research activities are as follows: none for collection; and 7(2)(c) for use for statistical or scholarly research. Disclosures are covered by paragraph 7(3)(f) for statistical or scholarly research, 7(3)(g) to archival institutions, and 7(3)(h), which permits disclosure without consent after a hundred years of the creation of the record or twenty years after the death of the individual.

These exemptions are intended to accommodate use and disclosure for legitimate scholarly research. Organizations engaged in such research do not have an exemption for collection, because if they are associated with a research organization, a university, or a historical association or archives, they are not covered by the Act, because they are not engaged in commercial activity. This is something that the historians of Canada, who became quite concerned about the impact of the Act, tended to forget because of their experiences in Quebec, where they are covered by the Quebec legislation. Similarly, there were a number of genealogists who were concerned, but in fact they are exempt from the bill by virtue of paragraph 4(2)(b), for collections for personal or domestic purposes. Those researching for the purposes of publishing a book are exempt under the exemption for creative expression, 4(2)(c).

Market research is not covered by these exemptions from obtaining consent, but this merely means that market researchers have to obtain consent for the collection. There is a tendency in organizations to look for an exemption from consent under section 7 and panic if they do not find one that applies to them. In fact, consent in many cases will not be difficult to obtain. The obligation is just a rude shock to organizations that have simply been appropriating the information over the years.

The medical research issue should be covered under scholarly research, but it is more complicated because of the nature of the medical sector in Canada. We will deal with it separately under the discussion of medical issues because it became such a furious debate in the House of Commons that the application of this bill to medical information was delayed one year, to give the health sector an additional year to prepare. Since the bill would not have applied to them in the first year unless they were selling data across borders, there must be more sale of personal medical information than the average person on the street would have thought.

I. Medical Information

The issue of the coverage of medical information and organizations in the health sector blazed to prominence towards the end of the hearings of the Industry Committee. In one session, the Industry Committee heard from the Canadian Medical Association, the Canadian Dental Association, the Canadian Health Coalition, the Canadian Institute for Health Information, the Canadian Pharmacists' Association, and the Ontario Ministry of Health. The first half of this list felt the bill was too weak, and the second half felt it was too strong, some in fact making somewhat extravagant claims that it would grind medical care and research across Canada to a halt.

Medical information is well recognized as some of the most sensitive information that individuals have, and it is information that they want protected. It is not being protected at the moment in any comprehensive way by any provincial legislation outside of the province of Quebec, and it is squarely within the powers of the provinces to do so, particularly with respect to doctors, dentists, and hospitals and clinics. It is not a simple matter for the federal government to protect medical data, except insofar as it is held by organizations engaged in commercial activity. It is here that the rhetoric has risen during the past two years as the legislation has progressed: Are organizations in the health sector engaged in commercial activity? The provincial debates over the privatization of health care have unfortunately fanned the flames over this issue.

It is reasonably clear that a provincially funded public hospital providing health care is not covered by the Act because it is not, for the most part, engaged in commercial activity. But is the ambulance that delivers the patient to the hospital engaged in commercial activity? A private hospital is engaged in commercial activity, or at least the owners probably hope it is. So is a laboratory, a private clinic, and a private nursing home. Nevertheless, the lines are quite blurry because all these organizations can be delivering services that might be funded at least partially by provincial health insurance schemes. It is very likely that we will see litigation of some of these cases, partly because consumers feel strongly about medical data and will be inclined to seek protection and redress in this area. Furthermore, it is not clear that this sector has in place sufficient protections for personal information, and most do not provide routine access for patients to their files.

There are other organizations implicated in this debate, which get information other than directly from the patient, and which will be obliged to seek consent. The deputy Ministers of health ministries in all provinces except Quebec, as well as Health Canada, set up an organization to gather health and hospital data and perform various analyzes of these data, to ensure optimal health outcomes for patients and best use of resources. This organization, the Canadian Institute for Health Information (CIHI), which is classified as a non-governmental organization, not for profit, operates in part on a cost-recovery basis and has a great deal of patient data. It will likely be a key player in the Health Infoway. The year the Act was passed, it received $85 million from Health Canada to work on the electronic health record, among other things. CIHI is not currently covered by any data protection law. Although it is situated in Ontario, the only medical facilities covered by the Ontario public sector bill are mental health facilities, and it is of course itself a statistical centre, not a health-care provider. There are differing legal opinions as to whether CIHI is covered by the Act, but there is no doubt that advocates of medical privacy will select the legislation with the highest standards to attempt a challenge to current practices. At the moment, that would be the Act.

What has come to the fore in this debate is a fundamental question: Does an individual, participating in a national health-care scheme, have the right to say no to giving his information for research and statistical studies? Can a government simply expropriate the medical files in the interests of the greater public good, namely medical research and statistical studies of the effectiveness of health-care dollars? Researchers and bureaucrats alike expressed loathing for the very idea of seeking the patients' consent, for good reasons such as burdening the patient at a time of crisis, overloading an already straining health-care delivery system, and spoiling useful data sets by allowing people to opt out. There were other less compelling reasons, such as the difficulty of explaining what was happening to the data (informed consent), the cost, and the fact that in a complex health-care and research environment, often the user of the information was several steps removed from the patient.

Industry Canada, throughout this debate, maintained that what was sauce for the goose was sauce for the gander. If the banks and the direct marketers could seek consent, either directly from the individual or through their intermediaries, whoever those might be, surely the medical sector could also clean up its data-handling practices. The Minister of

Industry appeared before the Senate and argued unsuccessfully that this bill would not affect the medical sector until 2004, but the Senate amended the bill and allowed an extra year after the coming into force of phase one of the Act for medical information.

Other potential organizations implicated would include international life and health insurers, employers holding employee medical records in federal works such as telecommunications carriers, broadcasters, and inter-provincial transportation companies. The exemption would not likely assist these organizations, since the only part of the records that would not be covered until 2002 would be the medical information; the rest of the employee file would be covered in January 2001.

In the meantime, Ontario is preparing health privacy legislation. Three other provinces have health privacy laws.[7]

The next question will be: Will the Governor in Council find that legislation to be substantially similar and exempt it from the coverage of the federal Act? Another important issue is that the information must remain within the province for this exemption to apply; so how much of this information crosses borders?

---

[7]   Manitoba: *The Personal Health Information Act*, c. P33-5, assented to June 1997; Saskatchewan: *The Health Information Protection Act*, c. H-0.021, assented to May 1999 (not in force); Alberta: *The Health Information Act*, c. H-4.8, assented to December 1999 (expected to be proclaimed in force, January 31, 2001).

CHAPTER 6

FREQUENTLY ASKED QUESTIONS

A. Scope and Application

Q *What organizations and activities are covered by the Act in the first three years following coming into force?*

On 1 January 2001 the Act will cover

1. federal works, undertakings, and businesses, including the employee records in those organizations. Examples: telecommunications companies, radio and television broadcasters, airlines, railways, shipping companies, interprovincial truck and bus companies; and

2. any disclosure by an organization of personal information across provincial or national borders, for consideration. That means the information itself is sold, leased, or bartered. Examples: direct marketers who have rented a list, companies that sell their customer data across borders, charities that trade their lists across borders, credit reporting organizations.

Note that "personal health information" as defined in section 2 will not be covered in the first year, that is, until 1 January 2002.

Q *What organizations and activities are covered after 1 January 2004?*

As well as everything that was covered before that date, the Act will begin to apply to organizations that are under provincial jurisdiction (anything that isn't a federal work), if they are engaged in commercial activities and collect, use, or disclose personal information within the province. However, if the organization carries on business in a province that has substantially similar legislation such as Quebec, and as is anticipated in Ontario and British Columbia, and has been exempted by order of the Governor in Council, this Act will not apply to it for those intraprovincial collections, uses, and disclosures. But it will apply to all interprovincial and international collections, uses, and disclosures on a broader basis than in the first three years and would include intracorporate transfers.

Q *After 1 January 2004, assuming that a province has not passed substantially similar legislation, will employee records in organizations under provincial jurisdiction be covered?*

No. Information about employees collected, used, or disclosed by the employer within the scope of the employer/employee relationship is not collected, used, or disclosed in the course of commercial activities, so it is beyond the scope of the Act as being under exclusive provincial jurisdiction. Employee information would only ever be covered if the employer used or disclosed it in a commercial way. For example, if the employer traded the information to another company for marketing purposes, that would be a commercial activity and would be subject to the Act.

Q *Will federal works, undertakings, or businesses in Quebec be exempted from the application of the Act when the order exempting organizations in Quebec covered by the Quebec law is passed?*

No. Federal works, undertakings, and businesses will continue to be covered by the Act. This may mean that organizations, such as banks, that collect information about customers, may be subject to dual regulation, under this Act and under the Quebec law. In the event that there is actual conflict between the two, the federal law would prevail to the extent of the inconsistency.

Q *My company in Ontario sends its personal information to Quebec for processing and we pay for that. Is that disclosure for "consideration" within the meaning of section 30 and are we covered by the Act on 1 January 2001?*

No, this activity isn't covered. The consideration is for the processing, not the information. You would need to "sell" the information to be covered.

Q *My company is federally incorporated. Am I a "federal work"?*

You aren't a federal work unless you are engaged in a business that is federally regulated such as telecommunications or interprovincial transportation and you are subject to the *Canada Labour Code*. The mere fact of federal incorporation doesn't make you a federal work.

Q *Our association is unincorporated. Are we an organization under the Act?*

Yes, if you are engaged in a commercial activity, you are an organization. The definition is intended to be broad and inclusive.

Q *Our company is a federal work and our employee records contain some personal health information. We understand that this information isn't covered until 2002. How should we treat that information between 1 January 2001 and 1 January 2002?*

Legally, the information isn't covered by the Act during that one-year period but why not treat it as though it were covered? A year isn't very long and you might as well design your information management systems for the long term. If a person asks for her own personal health information, it would likely require more time to process the actual request if you decide to cut out the health information on the ground that there is no legal obligation to provide it.

Q *Our organization engages in commercial activities but we are an agent of the Ontario government. Are we covered by this Act?*

No. The Act doesn't bind agents of the provincial crown. If that had been the aim of the Act, it would have to be specified.

Q *My company operates out of Quebec. Will this Act apply to me?*

Assuming that you are not a federal work, for the most part the Act will not apply to you because Quebec has a substantially similar law that applies to you. However, if you collect, use, or disclose personal information interprovincially or internationally, it will apply to those activities. Since the two laws are similar, it should not be difficult for you to comply with both. All you would need to do to comply is follow the one that sets the higher standard in a given area. For example, the Quebec law requires express consent for disclosure unless an exception applies. Your dealings with your customers should probably follow that rule for all transactions to avoid confusion.

Q *Will this Act stop junk mail? Will it stop spam?*

An individual will be able to complain about the use of her name and address and her e-mail address by an organization sending junk mail. In practice, it may be difficult to track down where the organization obtained the information. Consumers have other remedies available to them, including putting their names on do not call/do not mail lists.

Q *Are oral disclosures of personal information covered by this Act?*

Yes. The definition of personal information is not limited to information that is recorded. In practice it may be difficult to enforce.

B. Collections, Uses, and Disclosures

Q *Can a large company share its customer information with its affiliates for marketing? Can a teleco share its customer information with its ISP affiliate?*

Yes, in both cases, if it has the consent of the customer. Without consent, this would be a disclosure to a third party, which isn't permitted under the Act. Companies will need to review their consent forms to ensure that they have what is necessary to continue this business.

Q *What do I need to do when I hire a collection agency to collect my debts as a small business?*

Assuming the debt is owed by a person, say a customer, and not one owed by a company, the best thing to do would be to at least notify the person in your last demand letter that you are turning the debt over to the collection agency. This might work to get the debt paid but if it doesn't, you can go ahead and disclose the personal information necessary to collect the debt without the consent of the person. This is a permissible disclosure under paragraph 7(3)(b).

Q *Can an individual hire a private detective to do a background check on (1) a prospective tenant, (2) a prospective son-in-law, or (3) a prospective employee such as a babysitter?*

In all these examples, the consent of the person would be required. In examples (1) and (3), consent would be easy to obtain. Example (2) is somewhat more problematic and in the absence of consent, the check might not be possible. Most of these activities take place within a province so may ultimately be covered by provincial laws.

Q *An elderly customer of a bank is seen regularly coming to the bank with a young relative, always to withdraw money. Bank staff are concerned that the customer is the victim of elder abuse and either unknowingly, because of gradually encroaching dementia, or due to intimidation by the young man, is not defending her own interests. Can the bank contact the daughter who lives in another city with the details of the case?*

This is a very difficult question and raises a problem that banks may often encounter. Without consent the banks may be faced with a problem that can't be solved. The Act does not permit the disclosure of this information without consent so perhaps the solution is for the banks to get consent from all its customers to disclose some information in case of an urgent situation like this. The consent would need to be limited and specific.

Q *Can a hospital use its patient address information to fundraise?*

Assuming we are talking about a public hospital, the answer is yes. Hospitals do not collect, use, or disclose personal information in the course of a commercial activity. Is fundraising a commercial activity? The better view would seem to be that it isn't. However, if the hospital sold or rented the list to a third party, even to a charity, it would be caught because that would be a commercial activity. Most provinces and territories have data protection legislation for the public sector that covers this particular activity.

C. Access

Q *If I want access to information about me that is held by a company, can they send it to me with a bill for the costs?*

The Act says that access must be provided at "minimal or no cost" (Schedule 1, clause 4.9.4). The company must also inform you that they will be charging you for access so if you don't want to pay, you can cancel your request. If the amount seems to be more than minimal, you should question the charges; but if the company doesn't budge, you may complain to the Privacy Commissioner.

Q *If I request access to my personal information, what does the company have to do?*

Assuming that there are no exceptions that apply to the information, the company has to tell you about all the information they have concerning you, how it is being used, and to whom it is being or has been disclosed. They should tell you the source of information collected from third parties but they aren't obliged to do so.

If it isn't possible for the company to tell you exactly to whom the information has been disclosed, it is obliged to give you a list of organizations to which it might have disclosed the information.

They must also provide you with access to the information unless there is authority under section 9 of the Act to withhold it.

Q *What if I find information that is wrong when the company shows it to me?*

You can challenge the company on wrong information and if you can demonstrate that it is wrong, the company has to amend it. That means it may be corrected, deleted, or information may be added to it if it was incomplete. The general rule is that a person can change factual information that is clearly wrong, such as a date or an address. With respect to more subjective information, such as a version of an event, the standard practice is for an organization to attach the person's version of what happened to the file, since it may not want to rewrite its own internal history of the event.

If it was disclosed to third parties, the company must send them the amended information, "where appropriate." It would be appropriate if the organization is still using the information, or if it had made a decision based on the information in practice. This will likely be based on customer demand.

Q *What if a company refuses to amend wrong information?*

If you haven't been able to convince the company that the information is wrong, the company has to record your challenge as unresolved and may have to notify third parties to whom the information was disclosed. You can also complain to the Privacy Commissioner if you believe the information should be amended or that third parties should be notified.

D. Complaints

Q *Should an individual complain to the organization before going to the Privacy Commissioner when he encounters a problem about personal information practices?*

Yes. Principle 10 of Schedule 1 obliges organizations to put in place procedures to receive complaints, and Principle 8 requires them to make information about these procedures easily available. Individuals should avail themselves of this remedy before complaining to the Privacy Commissioner. In fact, the Commissioner can insist that an individual exhaust these remedies before he undertakes a more thorough investigation.

Q *My company holds a lot of personal information about our customers. How should we prepare ourselves to handle complaints from our customers about our practices?*

The first thing you need to do is appoint a person in the company to be responsible for compliance with the Act. You should make that person's name or position readily available to your customers.

You need to put in place accessible and simple procedures to deal with privacy complaints. For example, your correspondence with your customers should contain a notice about how and to whom complaints should be addressed. A good starting point would be a phone number that gets through to a live person. Don't leave your customer, who may already be peeved, in an endless telephone holding pattern or in a blind alley of "press 8 for complaints about X . . ."

Take all privacy complaints seriously and investigate them. If the complaint is justified, address the problem. Remember, a satisfied customer won't complain to the Privacy Commissioner and you can avoid an investigation by that office.

E.   Lawful Investigations

Q *If an insurance company wants to be able to investigate the claims of its customers, what does it have to do?*

It should get the consent of the individual to carry out that investigation. That consent can be obtained at the time the claim is filed. If for some reason the company has reasonable grounds to believe that the claim is false or that the individual has previously filed false claims, and if it is a member of the Insurance Crime Prevention Bureau (ICPB), it might consider disclosing the claim details to the ICPB under paragraph 7(3)(d). [The assumption here is that the ICPB is listed as an "investigative body" in the regulations.] The ICPB collects the information under 7(1)(b) and then once it has run the check, it discloses the results of the investigation back to the company under 7(3)(h.2). All that can take place without the knowledge or consent of the individual.

Q *If the local police wish to obtain information about a customer, what must happen?*

If the police have an investigation under way and they can obtain a warrant, they should do so. The organization would be obliged to comply with the warrant and the disclosure would be permitted under paragraph 7(3)(c).

If the investigation is in a preliminary stage, the police may not be able to obtain a warrant. In that case the police can ask the organization to voluntarily provide the information. The organization can only comply with that request if the police can identify their lawful authority to get the information, which essentially means that it is information in which the individual does not have a reasonable expectation of privacy under section 8 of the *Charter*. Because this is a difficult area of the law, an organization should always ask the police to produce evidence in writing of their lawful authority to obtain the information and that the information is necessary to enforce a law, carry out an investigation, or gather intelligence for the purpose of enforcing a law.

Q *If a company discovers that a customer has committed a crime, what is it allowed to do?*

It can disclose any relevant personal information to the police under paragraph 7(3)(d).

Q *If an industry association wishes to share information about customers who do not pay their bills, what must it do?*

Unless the industry has an "investigative body" such as the ICPB, it can't share the information with its members. If it wants to set up such a body, it should contact Industry Canada to begin exploring the department's criteria for listing a body in the regulations.

Q *Will this Act have any implications for exchanges of personal information between the public and private sectors?*

Yes. Organizations in the private sector will be able to disclose personal information to public bodies, such as government departments or ministries, with consent but also without knowledge or consent under subparagraph 7(3)(c.1)(iii) where the government department or ministry has requested the information, identified its authority to obtain the information, and the disclosure is for the purpose of administering a law.

Government departments and ministries may well run into problems when they want to disclose personal information to the private sector unless they have the consent of the individual. The private sector organization receiving the personal information can only use it in compliance with the Act.

F.   Commissioner's Powers and Operations

Q *How will the Commissioner deal with annoying or repetitious requests?*

If the requests are "trivial, frivolous or vexatious or made in bad faith," the Commissioner, after doing a preliminary investigation and determining that the request falls into the trivial, frivolous category, may refuse to prepare a report as authorized by subsection 13(2) of the Act.

The result is that the complaint essentially ends there, and the complainant cannot ask the Federal Court to review the matter.

Q *If the Commissioner discovers evidence of criminal activity in the course of an investigation or an audit, what can he do about it?*

Under subsection 20(5) the Commissioner may disclose to the Attorney General of Canada or a province information relating to the commission of an offence against federal or provincial law, on the part of an officer or an employee of an organization. The Commissioner may only do so if he has enough evidence to form an opinion that the offence has been committed.

Q *What prevents a company from being maliciously attacked by a disgruntled employee?*

Nothing can prevent this sort of thing, but if the Privacy Commissioner concludes that complaints to him are not being made in good faith, he can decline to make a report on them and the complaint can't be taken any further. For example, an individual may make frivolous and vexatious requests to an organization and then complain to the Privacy Commissioner when the organization refuses to answer them. The Privacy Commissioner may see that as a "bad faith" complaint.

G. Federal Court

Q *In section 14 when it says that the Federal Court can review a complaint arising from a breach of clause 4.2 in Schedule 1, does that include breaches of any of the other obligations under clause 4.2, such as 4.2.4?*

No. The list in section 14 is limited to the clauses specifically enumerated, so the reference to clause 4.2. does not include 4.2.1 through 4.2.6.

Q *Can the recommendations in the Schedule be reviewed by the Federal Court?*

No. The recommendations can be the subject of a complaint to the Privacy Commissioner if an organization is not following them. The Privacy Commissioner can also audit an organization for failure to follow a recommendation. However, because they are not obligations and can't be enforced, they can't be reviewed by the Federal Court.

It would, however, be reasonable for a court to take notice of the organization's response to the recommendations, particularly because many of the recommendations are best practice approaches to fulfilling the obligations.

Q *As an individual, may I represent myself at the Federal Court?*

Yes. The rules allow for an individual to represent himself. Companies must act through a lawyer.

H. Research

1) Medical Research and Information

Q *Will this Act impede medical research?*

It should not. Most medical research takes place with patient or subject consent so the Act shouldn't present any problems. In some cases where the research needs to reach back into old health records, the Act allows for disclosure of those records without consent under limited circumstances. The personal information must be essential to the research, consent must be practically impossible to obtain, and the disclosing organization must notify the Privacy Commissioner in advance.

Q *Is health or medical information treated any differently from other personal information under the Act?*

No, the Act doesn't create different categories of personal information. Although we all realize that medical information is sensitive, all sorts of information can be sensitive depending on the context. The Act does recognize that medical information is usually sensitive and that the form of consent required for its collection, use, or disclosure should be appropriate to its sensitivity. That goes for the physical safeguards that should be afforded it as well.

Q *What can a genetic testing laboratory do with my personal information?*

Assuming that the laboratory is a commercial one, it can only use your information for the purposes for which you have consented.

Q *What kind of consent does a medical laboratory have to get from the patients who go there for lab tests?*

For most things that a lab does with your information, such as sending the test results back to your doctor, it has your implied consent. For anything beyond what a reasonable person would imagine that a lab does with personal information, it would need express consent from you.

2) Genealogical Research

Q *How does the Act treat genealogical research?*

Anyone doing her own genealogical research on her family is not subject to the Act because the collection and use of the personal information is for personal purposes; see paragraph 4(2)(b).

Anyone doing this type of research without being paid for it is not subject to the Act because they aren't collecting or using the information in the course of a commercial activity.

Anyone who is being paid to do this type of research will be covered by the Act, unless they are collecting, using, and disclosing it for journalistic, artistic, or literary purposes, in which case the activity is exempt under paragraph 4(2)(c).

3) The Standard

Q *What role do the notes in clauses 4.3 and 4.9 play in the Act?*

Legally, the notes have no effect in the Act. Subsection 2(2) says that references to clauses 4.3 or 4.9 do not include references to the note that accompanies the clause, and in subsection 7(1), 7(2), 7(3), and 9(3) the Act says "Despite the note . . . "

The notes were included in the CSA Code to provide examples of the exceptions to the general rule of obtaining consent and of giving access to information. These exceptions have been enumerated in the Act in sections 7 and 9, so there is no further need for the notes.

Q *Why can the "shoulds" be audited when they are not obligations?*

It is unlikely that a failure to follow a recommendation in itself would trigger an audit. The power to audit the recommendations simply allows the Privacy Commissioner to take the recommendations into account and to comment and report on them when he completes the audit. In some circumstances he may recommend that a company follow the recommendations in Schedule 1.

Q *If a company has developed and published its own CSA-based code, does it help the company or does it increase its liability before the Federal Court?*

It can probably only help it. A tailored code would demonstrate to the Federal Court that the company had made a genuine effort to comply with the Act and that it probably had complied at least with the requirement to develop policies and procedures. Since there is no obligation to develop tailored codes, the failure to do so cannot be held against the company.

I. Technology-Related Issues

Q *Will this Act be able to deal with the collection of personal information by foreign Web sites?*

If the organization has a presence in Canada, it will fall under the jurisdiction of the Privacy Commissioner and the Federal Court. If it doesn't have a Canadian presence, although the collection may take place in Canada, the law may be difficult to enforce. If the Web site is in a member state of the European Union, the Privacy Commissioner will have some influence through his European counterparts and may be able to facilitate the transfer of the complaint to the foreign jurisdiction. However, if the Web site is in a jurisdiction with no privacy laws, the individual may be out of luck. Individuals should be cautious about providing personal information over the Internet to sites they do not know.

Q *Are Java applets caught by the law?*

Any collection, use, or disclosure of personal information is caught by the law, regardless of the mechanism that is used to perform the action. The CSA Standard was developed with a view to technology neutrality so that any new technology would be covered by it.

Increasingly, the collection, use, and disclosure of personal information will be done by "entities," and it may be done remotely. The immediate discussion in the year 2000 has centred on Internet Web sites, but there are other mechanisms in place in the technology architecture which will have far-reaching effects on the rights and autonomy of the individual.

Q *How does this law provide notice and choice?*

Notice and choice are expressions that have achieved currency during the discussions between the European Union and the United States concerning whether the "Safe Harbor" practices championed by the federal Department of Commerce and U.S. industry groups meet the adequacy test of the European Union. They are relative newcomers in data protection parlance, and may provide rather thin rights compared to their older cousins "transparency" and "consent."

In the terms of this law, the knowledge and consent of the individual are required for the collection, use, and disclosure of personal information. That means before you collect information, you *must* ensure the individual has given a meaningful consent, has understood the purpose of the collection, and has available the means to find out exactly what your data practices are. This latter requirement is detailed in the openness principle. The two combine to meet any notice requirements. As for choice, the ability to withhold information subject to consent provides choice, and the law goes further by providing in clause 4.3.3 that an organization may not deny a product or service if an individual refuses to consent to the collection, use, or disclosure of personal information beyond that required to fulfil the explicitly specified and legitimate purposes. There are many Web sites, ad servers, and browsers that would not pass this test yet would comply with choice by simply offering the individual a "take it or leave it" option.

Most of us have seen the signs in the airport stating "No one must submit to a scan and an x-ray of their baggage if they do not wish to board a plane." Most of us consider this tolerable in a free and democratic society, where there is terrorism and planes do get hijacked and bombed. However, it is another matter to have to submit to surveillance on the Internet, which is fast becoming the public square, marketplace, library, and university of the entire globe. We deserve more than notice and choice here — we deserve control.

Q *Will P3P be compliant with the law?*

There has been considerable debate about the Platform for Privacy Preferences, or P3P, ever since its inception in 1996. Some privacy advocates greeted its formal release in June 2000 by labelling it "Pretty Poor Privacy." P3P is a protocol for exchange of information between a Web site and an individual user's browser, permitting a user to specify how much information he wants to share with a Web site. The Web sites that collect more information than the user's preferences then explain that fact and offer the user a chance to drop his privacy demands or not go to the Web site. To the extent that an individual can understand the impact of making choices about how much privacy he wants in his Web experience, it may be useful. Privacy advocates complain that P3P should not be considered a substitute for a law or a complete set of fair information practices.

In the terms of this legislation, all P3P achieves is knowledge and consent, and only in the barest terms. A Web site using P3P probably violates clause 4.3.3 of the Schedule, a mandatory provision of the law, every time it turns a user away. In terms of the other requirements of the Schedule, it has little to offer except a level of accountability, and some openness.

PERSONAL INFORMATION PROTECTION AND ELECTRONIC DOCUMENTS ACT

Second Session, Thirty-sixth Parliament, 48–49 Elizabeth II, 1999–2000, Statutes of Canada 2000, Chapter 5

An Act to support and promote electronic commerce by protecting personal information that is collected, used or disclosed in certain circumstances, by providing for the use of electronic means to communicate or record information or transactions and by amending the Canada Evidence Act, the Statutory Instruments Act and the Statute Revision Act

[Assented to 13th April, 2000]

Her Majesty, by and with the advice and consent of the Senate and House of Commons of Canada, enacts as follows:

SHORT TITLE

Short title

1. This Act may be cited as the *Personal Information Protection and Electronic Documents Act.*

PART 1

PROTECTION OF PERSONAL INFORMATION IN THE PRIVATE SECTOR

Interpretation

Definitions

2. (1) The definitions in this subsection apply in this Part.

"alternative format"

"alternative format", with respect to personal information, means a format that allows a person with a sensory disability to read or listen to the personal information.

"commercial activity"

"commercial activity" means any particular transaction, act or conduct or any regular course of conduct that is of a commercial character, including the selling, bartering or leasing of donor, membership or other fundraising lists.

"Commissioner"

"Commissioner" means the Privacy Commissioner appointed under section 53 of the *Privacy Act*.

"Court"

"Court" means the Federal Court—Trial Division.

"federal work, undertaking or business"

"federal work, undertaking or business" means any work, undertaking or business that is within the legislative authority of Parliament. It includes

(a) a work, undertaking or business that is operated or carried on for or in connection with navigation and shipping, whether inland or maritime, including the operation of ships and transportation by ship anywhere in Canada;

(b) a railway, canal, telegraph or other work or undertaking that connects a province with another province, or that extends beyond the limits of a province;

(c) a line of ships that connects a province with another province, or that extends beyond the limits of a province;

(d) a ferry between a province and another province or between a province and a country other than Canada;

(e) aerodromes, aircraft or a line of air transportation;

(f) a radio broadcasting station;

(g) a bank;

(h) a work that, although wholly situated within a province, is before or after its execution declared by Parliament to be for the general advantage of Canada or for the advantage of two or more provinces;

(i) a work, undertaking or business outside the exclusive legislative authority of the legislatures of the provinces; and

(j) a work, undertaking or business to which federal laws, within the meaning of section 2 of the *Oceans Act*, apply under section 20 of that Act and any regulations made under paragraph 26(1)(k) of that Act.

"organization"

"organization" includes an association, a partnership, a person and a trade union.

"personal health information"

"personal health information", with respect to an individual, whether living or deceased, means

(a) information concerning the physical or mental health of the individual;

(b) information concerning any health service provided to the individual;

(c) information concerning the donation by the individual of any body part or any bodily substance of the individual or information derived from the testing or examination of a body part or bodily substance of the individual;

(d) information that is collected in the course of providing health services to the individual; or

(e) information that is collected incidentally to the provision of health services to the individual.

"personal information"

"personal information" means information about an identifiable individual, but does not include the name, title or business address or telephone number of an employee of an organization.

"record"

"record" includes any correspondence, memorandum, book, plan, map, drawing, diagram, pictorial or graphic work, photograph, film, microform, sound recording, videotape, machine-readable record and any other documentary material, regardless of physical form or characteristics, and any copy of any of those things.

Notes in Schedule 1

(2) In this Part, a reference to clause 4.3 or 4.9 of Schedule 1 does not include a reference to the note that accompanies that clause.

Purpose

Purpose

3. The purpose of this Part is to establish, in an era in which technology increasingly facilitates the circulation and exchange of information, rules to govern the collection, use and disclosure of personal information in a manner that recognizes the right of privacy of individuals with respect to their personal information and the need of organizations to collect, use or disclose personal information for purposes that a reasonable person would consider appropriate in the circumstances.

Application

Application

4. (1) This Part applies to every organization in respect of personal information that

(a) the organization collects, uses or discloses in the course of commercial activities; or

(b) is about an employee of the organization and that the organization collects, uses or discloses in connection with the operation of a federal work, undertaking or business.

Limit

(2) This Part does not apply to

(a) any government institution to which the *Privacy Act* applies;

(b) any individual in respect of personal information that the individual collects, uses or discloses for personal or domestic purposes and does not collect, use or disclose for any other purpose; or

(c) any organization in respect of personal information that the organization collects, uses or discloses for journalistic, artistic or literary purposes and does not collect, use or disclose for any other purpose.

Other Acts

(3) Every provision of this Part applies despite any provision, enacted after this subsection comes into force, of any other Act of Parliament, unless the other Act expressly declares that that provision operates despite the provision of this Part.

DIVISION 1

PROTECTION OF PERSONAL INFORMATION

Compliance with obligations

5. (1) Subject to sections 6 to 9, every organization shall comply with the obligations set out in Schedule 1.

Meaning of "should"

(2) The word "should", when used in Schedule 1, indicates a recommendation and does not impose an obligation.

Appropriate purposes

(3) An organization may collect, use or disclose personal information only for purposes that a reasonable person would consider are appropriate in the circumstances.

Effect of designation of individual

6. The designation of an individual under clause 4.1 of Schedule 1 does not relieve the organization of the obligation to comply with the obligations set out in that Schedule.

Collection without knowledge or consent

7. (1) For the purpose of clause 4.3 of Schedule 1, and despite the note that accompanies that clause, an organization may collect personal information without the knowledge or consent of the individual only if

(a) the collection is clearly in the interests of the individual and consent cannot be obtained in a timely way;

(b) it is reasonable to expect that the collection with the knowledge or consent of the individual would compromise the availability or the accuracy of the information and the collection is reasonable for purposes related to investigating a breach of an agreement or a contravention of the laws of Canada or a province;

(c) the collection is solely for journalistic, artistic or literary purposes; or

(d) the information is publicly available and is specified by the regulations.

Use without knowledge or consent

(2) For the purpose of clause 4.3 of Schedule 1, and despite the note that accompanies that clause, an organization may, without the knowledge or consent of the individual, use personal information only if

(a) in the course of its activities, the organization becomes aware of information that it has reasonable grounds to believe could be useful in the investigation of a contravention of the laws of Canada, a province or a foreign jurisdiction that has been, is being or is about to be committed, and the information is used for the purpose of investigating that contravention;

(b) it is used for the purpose of acting in respect of an emergency that threatens the life, health or security of an individual;

(c) it is used for statistical, or scholarly study or research, purposes that cannot be achieved without using the information, the information is used in a manner that will ensure its confidentiality, it is impracticable to obtain consent and the organization informs the Commissioner of the use before the information is used;

(c.1) it is publicly available and is specified by the regulations; or by that section;

(d) it was collected under paragraph (1)(a) or (b).

Disclosure without knowledge or consent

(3) For the purpose of clause 4.3 of Schedule 1, and despite the note that accompanies that clause, an organization may disclose personal information without the knowledge or consent of the individual only if the disclosure is

(a) made to, in the Province of Quebec, an advocate or notary or, in any other province, a barrister or solicitor who is representing the organization;

(b) for the purpose of collecting a debt owed by the individual to the organization;

(c) required to comply with a subpoena or warrant issued or an order made by a court, person or body with jurisdiction to compel the production of information, or to comply with rules of court relating to the production of records;

(c.1) made to a government institution or part of a government institution that has made a request for the information, identified its lawful authority to obtain the information and indicated that

(i) it suspects that the information relates to national security, the defence of Canada or the conduct of international affairs,

(ii) the disclosure is requested for the purpose of enforcing any law of Canada, a province or a foreign jurisdiction, carrying out an investigation relating to the enforcement of any such law or gathering intelligence for the purpose of enforcing any such law, or

(iii) the disclosure is requested for the purpose of administering any law of Canada or a province;

(c.2) made to the government institution mentioned in section 7 of the *Proceeds of Crime (Money Laundering) Act* as required by that section;

(d) made on the initiative of the organization to an investigative body, a government institution or a part of a government institution and the organization

(i) has reasonable grounds to believe that the information relates to a breach of an agreement or a contravention of the laws of Canada, a province or a foreign jurisdiction that has been, is being or is about to be committed, or

(ii) suspects that the information relates to national security, the defence of Canada or the conduct of international affairs;

(e) made to a person who needs the information because of an emergency that threatens the life, health or security of an individual and, if the individual whom the information is about is alive, the organization informs that individual in writing without delay of the disclosure;

(f) for statistical, or scholarly study or research, purposes that cannot be achieved without disclosing the information, it is impracticable to obtain consent and the organization informs the Commissioner of the disclosure before the information is disclosed;

(g) made to an institution whose functions include the conservation of records of historic or archival importance, and the disclosure is made for the purpose of such conservation;

(h) made after the earlier of

(i) one hundred years after the record containing the information was created, and

(ii) twenty years after the death of the individual whom the information is about;

(h.1) of information that is publicly available and is specified by the regulations;

(h.2) made by an investigative body and the disclosure is reasonable for purposes related to investigating a breach of an agreement or a contravention of the laws of Canada or a province; or

(i) required by law.

Use without consent

(4) Despite clause 4.5 of Schedule 1, an organization may use personal information for purposes other than those for which it was collected in any of the circumstances set out in subsection (2).

Disclosure without consent

(5) Despite clause 4.5 of Schedule 1, an organization may disclose personal information for purposes other than those for which it was collected in any of the circumstances set out in paragraphs (3)(a) to (h.2).

Written request

8. (1) A request under clause 4.9 of Schedule 1 must be made in writing.

Assistance

(2) An organization shall assist any individual who informs the organization that they need assistance in preparing a request to the organization.

Time limit

(3) An organization shall respond to a request with due diligence and in any case not later than thirty days after receipt of the request.

Extension of time limit

(4) An organization may extend the time limit

   (a) for a maximum of thirty days if

      (i) meeting the time limit would unreasonably interfere with the activities of the organization, or

      (ii) the time required to undertake any consultations necessary to respond to the request would make the time limit impracticable to meet; or

   (b) for the period that is necessary in order to be able to convert the personal information into an alternative format.

In either case, the organization shall, no later than thirty days after the date of the request, send a notice of extension to the individual, advising them of the new time limit, the reasons for extending the time limit and of their right to make a complaint to the Commissioner in respect of the extension.

Deemed refusal

(5) If the organization fails to respond within the time limit, the organization is deemed to have refused the request.

Costs for responding

(6) An organization may respond to an individual's request at a cost to the individual only if

   (a) the organization has informed the individual of the approximate cost; and

   (b) the individual has advised the organization that the request is not being withdrawn.

Reasons

(7) An organization that responds within the time limit and refuses a request shall inform the individual in writing of the refusal, setting out the reasons and any recourse that they may have under this Part.

Retention of information

(8) Despite clause 4.5 of Schedule 1, an organization that has personal information that is the subject of a request shall retain the information for as long as is necessary to allow the individual to exhaust any recourse under this Part that they may have.

When access prohibited

9. (1) Despite clause 4.9 of Schedule 1, an organization shall not give an individual access to personal information if doing so would likely reveal personal information about a third party. However, if the information about the third party is severable from the record containing the information about the individual, the organization shall sever the information about the third party before giving the individual access.

Limit

(2) Subsection (1) does not apply if the third party consents to the access or the individual needs the information because an individual's life, health or security is threatened.

Information related to paragraphs 7(3)(c), (c.1) or (d)

(2.1) An organization shall comply with subsection (2.2) if an individual requests that the organization

   (a) inform the individual about

   (i) any disclosure of information to a government institution or a part of a government institution under paragraph 7(3)(c), subparagraph 7(3)(c.1)(i) or (ii) or paragraph 7(3)(c.2) or (d), or

   (ii) the existence of any information that the organization has relating to a disclosure referred to in subparagraph (i), to a subpoena, warrant or order referred to in paragraph 7(3)(c) or to a request made by a government institution or a part of a government institution under subparagraph 7(3)(c.1)(i) or (ii); or

   (b) give the individual access to the information referred to in subparagraph (a)(ii).

Notification and response

(2.2) An organization to which subsection (2.1) applies

   (a) shall, in writing and without delay, notify the institution or part concerned of the request made by the individual; and

(b) shall not respond to the request before the earlier of

(i) the day on which it is notified under subsection (2.3), and

(ii) thirty days after the day on which the institution or part was notified.

Objection

(2.3) Within thirty days after the day on which it is notified under subsection (2.2), the institution or part shall notify the organization whether or not the institution or part objects to the organization complying with the request. The institution or part may object only if the institution or part is of the opinion that compliance with the request could reasonably be expected to be injurious to

(a) national security, the defence of Canada or the conduct of international affairs;

(a.1) the detection, prevention or deterrence of money laundering; or

(b) the enforcement of any law of Canada, a province or a foreign jurisdiction, an investigation relating to the enforcement of any such law or the gathering of intelligence for the purpose of enforcing any such law.

Prohibition

(2.4) Despite clause 4.9 of Schedule 1, if an organization is notified under subsection (2.3) that the institution or part objects to the organization complying with the request, the organization

(a) shall refuse the request to the extent that it relates to paragraph (2.1)(a) or to information referred to in subparagraph (2.1)(a)(ii);

(b) shall notify the Commissioner, in writing and without delay, of the refusal; and

(c) shall not disclose to the individual

(i) any information that the organization has relating to a disclosure to a government institution or a part of a government institution under paragraph 7(3)(c), sub-paragraph 7(3)(c.1)(i) or (ii) or paragraph 7(3)(c.2) or (d) or to a request made by a government institution under either of those subparagraphs,

(ii) that the organization notified an institution or part under paragraph (2.2)(a) or the Commissioner under paragraph (b), or

(iii) that the institution or part objects.

When access may be refused

(3) Despite the note that accompanies clause 4.9 of Schedule 1, an organization is not required to give access to personal information only if

(a) the information is protected by solicitor-client privilege;

(b) to do so would reveal confidential commercial information;

(c) to do so could reasonably be expected to threaten the life or security of another individual;

(c.1) the information was collected under paragraph 7(1)(b); or

(d) the information was generated in the course of a formal dispute resolution process.

However, in the circumstances described in paragraph (b) or (c), if giving access to the information would reveal confidential commercial information or could reasonably be expected to threaten the life or security of another individual, as the case may be, and that information is severable from the record containing any other information for which access is requested, the organization shall give the individual access after severing.

Limit

(4) Subsection (3) does not apply if the individual needs the information because an individual's life, health or security is threatened.

Notice

(5) If an organization decides not to give access to personal information in the circumstances set out in paragraph (3)(c.1), the organization shall, in writing, so notify the Commissioner, and shall include in the notification any information that the Commissioner may specify.

Sensory disability

10. An organization shall give access to personal information in an alternative format to an individual with a sensory disability who has a right of access to personal information under this Part and who requests that it be transmitted in the alternative format if

(a) a version of the information already exists in that format; or

(b) its conversion into that format is reasonable and necessary in order for the individual to be able to exercise rights under this Part.

DIVISION 2

REMEDIES

Filing of Complaints

Contravention

11. (1) An individual may file with the Commissioner a written complaint against an organization for contravening a provision of Division 1 or for not following a recommendation set out in Schedule 1.

Commissioner may initiate complaint

(2) If the Commissioner is satisfied that there are reasonable grounds to investigate a matter under this Part, the Commissioner may initiate a complaint in respect of the matter.

Time limit

(3) A complaint that results from the refusal to grant a request under section 8 must be filed within six months, or any longer period that the Commissioner allows, after the refusal or after the expiry of the time limit for responding to the request, as the case may be.

Notice

(4) The Commissioner shall give notice of a complaint to the organization against which the complaint was made.

Investigations of Complaints

Powers of Commissioner

12. (1) The Commissioner shall conduct an investigation in respect of a complaint and, for that purpose, may

(a) summon and enforce the appearance of persons before the Commissioner and compel them to give oral or written evidence on oath and to produce any records and things that the Commissioner considers necessary to investigate the complaint, in the same manner and to the same extent as a superior court of record;

(b) administer oaths;

(c) receive and accept any evidence and other information, whether on oath, by affidavit or otherwise, that the Commissioner sees fit, whether or not it is or would be admissible in a court of law;

(d) at any reasonable time, enter any premises, other than a dwelling-house, occupied by an organization on satisfying any security requirements of the organization relating to the premises;

(e) converse in private with any person in any premises entered under paragraph (d) and otherwise carry out in those premises any inquiries that the Commissioner sees fit; and

(f) examine or obtain copies of or extracts from records found in any premises entered under paragraph (d) that contain any matter relevant to the investigation.

Dispute resolution mechanisms

(2) The Commissioner may attempt to resolve complaints by means of dispute resolution mechanisms such as mediation and conciliation.

Delegation

(3) The Commissioner may delegate any of the powers set out in subsection (1) or (2).

Return of records

(4) The Commissioner or the delegate shall return to a person or an organization any record or thing that they produced under this section within ten days after they make a request to the Commissioner or the delegate, but nothing precludes the Commissioner or the delegate from again requiring that the record or thing be produced.

Certificate of delegation

(5) Any person to whom powers set out in subsection (1) are delegated shall be given a certificate of the delegation and the delegate shall produce the certificate, on request, to the person in charge of any premises to be entered under paragraph (1)(d).

Commissioner's Report

Contents

13. (1) The Commissioner shall, within one year after the day on which a complaint is filed or is initiated by the Commissioner, prepare a report that contains

(a) the Commissioner's findings and recommendations;

(b) any settlement that was reached by the parties;

(c) if appropriate, a request that the organization give the Commissioner, within a specified time, notice of any action taken or proposed to be taken to implement the recommendations contained in the report or reasons why no such action has been or is proposed to be taken; and

(d) the recourse, if any, that is available under section 14.

Where no report

(2) The Commissioner is not required to prepare a report if the Commissioner is satisfied that

> (a) the complainant ought first to exhaust grievance or review procedures otherwise reasonably available;

> (b) the complaint could more appropriately be dealt with, initially or completely, by means of a procedure provided for under the laws of Canada, other than this Part, or the laws of a province;

> (c) the length of time that has elapsed between the date when the subject-matter of the complaint arose and the date when the complaint was filed is such that a report would not serve a useful purpose; or

> (d) the complaint is trivial, frivolous or vexatious or is made in bad faith.

If a report is not to be prepared, the Commissioner shall inform the complainant and the organization and give reasons.

Report to parties

(3) The report shall be sent to the complainant and the organization without delay.

Hearing by Court

Application

14. (1) A complainant may, after receiving the Commissioner's report, apply to the Court for a hearing in respect of any matter in respect of which the complaint was made, or that is referred to in the Commissioner's report, and that is referred to in clause 4.1.3, 4.2, 4.3.3, 4.4, 4.6, 4.7 or 4.8 of Schedule 1, in clause 4.3, 4.5 or 4.9 of that Schedule as modified or clarified by Division 1, in subsection 5(3) or 8(6) or (7) or in section 10.

Time of application

(2) The application must be made within forty-five days after the report is sent or within any further time that the Court may, either before or after the expiry of those forty-five days, allow.

For greater certainty

(3) For greater certainty, subsections (1) and (2) apply in the same manner to complaints referred to in subsection 11(2) as to complaints referred to in subsection 11(1).

Commissioner may apply or appear

15. The Commissioner may, in respect of a complaint that the Commissioner did not initiate,

(a) apply to the Court, within the time limited by section 14, for a hearing in respect of any matter described in that section, if the Commissioner has the consent of the complainant;

(b) appear before the Court on behalf of any complainant who has applied for a hearing under section 14; or

(c) with leave of the Court, appear as a party to any hearing applied for under section 14.

Remedies

16. The Court may, in addition to any other remedies it may give,

(a) order an organization to correct its practices in order to comply with sections 5 to 10;

(b) order an organization to publish a notice of any action taken or proposed to paragraph (a); and

(c) award damages to the complainant, including damages for any humiliation that the complainant has suffered.

Summary hearings

17. (1) An application made under section 14 or 15 shall be heard and determined without delay and in a summary way unless the Court considers it inappropriate to do so.

Precautions

(2) In any proceedings arising from an application made under section 14 or 15, the Court shall take every reasonable precaution, including, when appropriate, receiving representations ex parte and conducting hearings in camera, to avoid the disclosure by the Court or any person of any information or other material that the organization would be authorized to refuse to disclose if it were requested under clause 4.9 of Schedule 1.

DIVISION 3

AUDITS

To ensure compliance

18. (1) The Commissioner may, on reasonable notice and at any reasonable time, audit the personal information management practices of an organization if the Commissioner has reasonable grounds to believe that the organization is contravening a provision of Division 1 or is not following a recommendation set out in Schedule 1, and for that purpose may

(a) summon and enforce the appearance of persons before the Commissioner and compel them to give oral or written evidence on oath and to produce any records and things that the Commissioner considers necessary for the audit, in the same manner and to the same extent as a superior court of record;

(b) administer oaths;

(c) receive and accept any evidence and other information, whether on oath, by affidavit or otherwise, that the Commissioner sees fit, whether or not it is or would be admissible in a court of law;

(d) at any reasonable time, enter any premises, other than a dwelling-house, occupied by the organization on satisfying any security requirements of the organization relating to the premises;

(e) converse in private with any person in any premises entered under paragraph (d) and otherwise carry out in those premises any inquiries that the Commissioner sees fit; and

(f) examine or obtain copies of or extracts from records found in any premises entered under paragraph (d) that contain any matter relevant to the audit.

Delegation

(2) The Commissioner may delegate any of the powers set out in subsection (1).

Return of records

(3) The Commissioner or the delegate shall return to a person or an organization any record or thing they produced under this section within ten days after they make a request to the Commissioner or the delegate, but nothing precludes the Commissioner or the delegate from again requiring that the record or thing be produced.

Certificate of delegation

(4) Any person to whom powers set out in subsection (1) are delegated shall be given a certificate of the delegation and the delegate shall produce the certificate, on request, to the person in charge of any premises to be entered under paragraph (1)(d).

Report of findings and recommendations

19. (1) After an audit, the Commissioner shall provide the audited organization with a report that contains the findings of the audit and any recommendations that the Commissioner considers appropriate.

Reports may be included in annual reports

(2) The report may be included in a report made under section 25.

DIVISON 4

GENERAL

Confidentiality

20. (1) Subject to subsections (2) to (5), 13(3) and 19(1), the Commissioner or any person acting on behalf or under the direction of the Commissioner shall not disclose any information that comes to their knowledge as a result of the performance or exercise of any of the Commissioner's duties or powers under this Part.

Public interest

(2) The Commissioner may make public any information relating to the personal information management practices of an organization if the Commissioner considers that it is in the public interest to do so.

Disclosure of necessary information

(3) The Commissioner may disclose, or may authorize any person acting on behalf or under the direction of the Commissioner to disclose, information that in the Commissioner's opinion is necessary to

(a) conduct an investigation or audit under this Part; or

(b) establish the grounds for findings and recommendations contained in any report under this Part.

Disclosure in the course of proceedings

(4) The Commissioner may disclose, or may authorize any person acting on behalf or under the direction of the Commissioner to disclose, information in the course of

(a) a prosecution for an offence under section 28;

(b) a prosecution for an offence under section 132 of the *Criminal Code* (perjury) in respect of a statement made under this Part;

(c) a hearing before the Court under this Part; or

(d) an appeal from a decision of the Court.

Disclosure of offence authorized

(5) The Commissioner may disclose to the Attorney General of Canada or of a province, as the case may be, information relating to the commission of an offence against any law of Canada or a province on the part of an officer or employee of an organization if, in the Commissioner's opinion, there is evidence of an offence.

Not competent witness

21. The Commissioner or person acting on behalf or under the direction of the Commissioner is not a competent witness in respect of any matter that comes to their knowledge as a result of the performance or exercise of any of the Commissioner's duties or powers under this Part in any proceeding other than

(a) a prosecution for an offence under section 28;

(b) a prosecution for an offence under section 132 of the *Criminal Code* (perjury) in respect of a statement made under this Part;

(c) a hearing before the Court under this Part; or

(d) an appeal from a decision of the Court.

Protection of Commissioner

22. (1) No criminal or civil proceedings lie against the Commissioner, or against any person acting on behalf or under the direction of the Commissioner, for anything done, reported or said in good faith as a result of the performance or exercise or purported performance or exercise of any duty or power of the Commissioner under this Part.

Libel or slander

(2) For the purposes of any law relating to libel or slander,

(a) anything said, any information supplied or any record or thing produced in good faith in the course of an investigation or audit carried out by or on behalf of the Commissioner under this Part is privileged; and

(b) any report made in good faith by the Commissioner under this Part and any fair and accurate account of the report made in good faith for the purpose of news reporting is privileged.

Consultations with provinces

23. (1) If the Commissioner considers it appropriate to do so, or on the request of an interested person, the Commissioner may, in order to ensure that personal information is protected in as consistent a manner as possible, consult with any person who, under provincial legislation that is substantially similar to this Part, has powers and duties similar to those of the Commissioner.

Agreements

(2) The Commissioner may enter into agreements with any person with whom the Commissioner may consult under subsection (1)

(a) to coordinate the activities of their offices and the office of the Commissioner, including to provide for mechanisms for the handling of any complaint in which they are mutually interested;

(b) to undertake and publish research related to the protection of personal information; and

(c) to develop model contracts for the protection of personal information that is collected, used or disclosed interprovincially or internationally.

Promoting the purposes of the Part

24. The Commissioner shall

(a) develop and conduct information programs to foster public understanding, and recognition of the purposes, of this Part;

(b) undertake and publish research that is related to the protection of personal information, including any such research that is requested by the Minister of Industry;

(c) encourage organizations to develop detailed policies and practices, including organizational codes of practice, to comply with sections 5 to 10; and

(d) promote, by any means that the Commissioner considers appropriate, the purposes of this Part.

Annual report

25. (1) The Commissioner shall, as soon as practicable after the end of each calendar year, submit to Parliament a report concerning the application of this Part, the extent to which the provinces have enacted legislation that is substantially similar to this Part and the application of any such legislation.

Consultation

(2) Before preparing the report, the Commissioner shall consult with those persons in the provinces who, in the Commissioner's opinion, are in a position to assist the Commissioner in reporting respecting personal information that is collected, used or disclosed interprovincially or internationally.

Regulations

26. (1) The Governor in Council may make regulations

(a) specifying, by name or by class, what is a government institution or part of a government institution for the purposes of any provision of this Part;

(a.01) specifying, by name or by class, what is an investigative body for the purposes of paragraph 7(3)(d) or (h.2);

(a.1) specifying information or classes of information for the purpose of paragraph 7(1)(d), (2)(c.1) or (3)(h.1); and

(b) for carrying out the purposes and provisions of this Part.

Orders

(2) The Governor in Council may, by order,

(a) provide that this Part is binding on any agent of Her Majesty in right of Canada to which the *Privacy Act* does not apply; and

(b) if satisfied that legislation of a province that is substantially similar to this Part applies to an organization, a class of organizations, an activity or a class of activities, exempt the organization, activity or class from the application of this Part in respect of the collection, use or disclosure of personal information that occurs within that province.

Whistleblowing

27. (1) Any person who has reasonable grounds to believe that a person has contravened or intends to contravene a provision of Division 1, may notify the Commissioner of the particulars of the matter and may request that their identity be kept confidential with respect to the notification.

Confidentiality

(2) The Commissioner shall keep confidential the identity of a person who has notified the Commissioner under subsection (1) and to whom an assurance of confidentiality has been provided by the Commissioner.

Prohibition

27.1 (1) No employer shall dismiss, suspend, demote, discipline, harass or otherwise disadvantage an employee, or deny an employee a benefit of employment, by reason that

(a) the employee, acting in good faith and on the basis of reasonable belief, has disclosed to the Commissioner that the employer or any other person has contravened or intends to contravene a provision of Division 1;

(b) the employee, acting in good faith and on the basis of reasonable belief, has refused or stated an intention of refusing to do anything that is a contravention of a provision of Division 1;

(c) the employee, acting in good faith and on the basis of reasonable belief, has done or stated an intention of doing anything that is required to be done in order that a provision of Division 1 not be contravened; or

(d) the employer believes that the employee will do anything referred to in paragraph (a), (b) or (c).

Saving

(2) Nothing in this section impairs any right of an employee either at law or under an employment contract or collective agreement.

Definitions

(3) In this section, "employee" includes an independent contractor and "employer" has a corresponding meaning.

Offence and punishment

28. Every person who knowingly contravenes subsection 8(8) or 27.1(1) or who obstructs the Commissioner or the Commissioner's delegate in the investigation of a complaint or in conducting an audit is guilty of

(a) an offence punishable on summary conviction and liable to a fine not exceeding $10,000; or

(b) an indictable offence and liable to a fine not exceeding $100,000.

Review of Part by parliamentary committee

29. (1) The administration of this Part shall, every five years after this Part comes into force, be reviewed by the committee of the House of Commons, or of both Houses of Parliament, that may be designated or established by Parliament for that purpose.

Review and report

(2) The committee shall undertake a review of the provisions and operation of this Part and shall, within a year after the review is undertaken or within any further period that the House of Commons may authorize, submit a report to Parliament that includes a statement of any changes to this Part or its administration that the committee recommends.

DIVISION 5

TRANSITIONAL PROVISIONS

Application

30. (1) This Part does not apply to any organization in respect of personal information that it collects, uses or discloses within a province whose legislature has the power to regulate the collection, use or disclosure of the information, unless the organization does it in connection with the operation of a federal work, undertaking or business or the organization discloses the information outside the province for consideration.

Application

(1.1) This Part does not apply to any organization in respect of personal health information that it collects, uses or discloses.

Expiry date

(2) Subsection (1) ceases to have effect three years after the day on which this section comes into force.

Expiry date

(2.1) Subsection (1.1) ceases to have effect one year after the day on which this section comes into force.

PART 2

ELECTRONIC DOCUMENTS

Interpretation

Definitions

31. (1) The definitions in this subsection apply in this Part.

"data"

"data" means representations of information or concepts, in any form.

"electronic document"

"electronic document" means data that is recorded or stored on any medium in or by a computer system or other similar device and that can be read or perceived by a person or a computer system or other similar device. It includes a display, printout or other output of that data.

"electronic signature"

"electronic signature" means a signature that consists of one or more letters, characters, numbers or other symbols in digital form incorporated in, attached to or associated with an electronic document.

"federal law"

"federal law" means an Act of Parliament or an instrument, regardless of its name, issued, made or established under an Act of Parliament or a prerogative of the Crown, other than an instrument issued, made or established under the Yukon Act, the Northwest Territories Act or the Nunavut Act.

"responsible authority"

"responsible authority", in respect of a provision of a federal law, means

(a) if the federal law is an Act of Parliament, the Minister responsible for that provision;

(b) if the federal law is an instrument issued, made or established under an Act of Parliament or a prerogative of the Crown, the person or body who issued, made or established the instrument; or

(c) despite paragraph (a) or (b), the person or body designated by the Governor in Council under subsection (2).

"secure electronic signature"

"secure electronic signature" means an electronic signature that results from the application of a technology or process prescribed by regulations made under subsection 48(1).

Designation

(2) The Governor in Council may, by order, for the purposes of this Part, designate any person, including any member of the Queen's Privy Council for Canada, or body to be the responsible authority in respect of a provision of a federal law if the Governor in Council is of the opinion that it is appropriate to do so in the circumstances.

Purpose

Purpose

32. The purpose of this Part is to provide for the use of electronic alternatives in the manner provided for in this Part where federal laws contemplate the use of paper to record or communicate information or transactions.

Electronic Alternatives

Collection, storage, etc.

33. A Minister of the Crown and any department, branch, office, board, agency, commission, corporation or body for the administration of affairs of which a Minister of the Crown is accountable to the Parliament of Canada may use electronic means to create, collect, receive, store, transfer, distribute, publish or otherwise deal with documents or information whenever a federal law does not specify the manner of doing so.

Electronic payment

34. A payment that is required to be made to the Government of Canada may be made in electronic form in any manner specified by the Receiver General.

Electronic version of statutory form

35. (1) If a provision of an Act of Parliament establishes a form, the responsible authority in respect of that provision may make regulations respecting an electronic form that is substantially the same as the form established in the provision, and the electronic form may be used for the same purposes as the form established in the provision.

Statutory manner of filing documents

(2) If a non-electronic manner of filing a document is set out in a provision of an Act of Parliament, the responsible authority in respect of that provision may make regulations respecting the filing of an electronic version of the document, and an electronic version of the document filed in accordance with those regulations is to be considered as a document filed in accordance with the provision.

Statutory manner of submitting information

(3) If a non-electronic manner of submitting information is set out in a provision of an Act of Parliament, the responsible authority in respect of that provision may make regulations respecting the manner of submitting the information using electronic means, and information submitted in accordance with those regulations is to be considered as information submitted in accordance with the provision.

Authority to prescribe form, etc.

(4) The authority under a federal law to issue, prescribe or in any other manner establish a form, or to establish the manner of filing a document or submitting information, includes the authority to issue, prescribe or establish an electronic form, or to establish an electronic manner of filing the document or submitting information, as the case may be.

Meaning of "filing"

(5) In this section, "filing" includes all manner of submitting, regardless of how it is designated.

Documents as evidence or proof

36. A provision of a federal law that provides that a certificate or other document signed by a Minister or public officer is proof of any matter or thing, or is admissible in evidence, is, subject to the federal law, satisfied by an electronic version of the certificate or other document if the electronic version is signed by the Minister or public officer with that person's secure electronic signature.

Retention of documents

37. A requirement under a provision of a federal law to retain a document for a specified period is satisfied, with respect to an electronic document, by the retention of the electronic document if

(a) the electronic document is retained for the specified period in the format in which it was made, sent or received, or in a format that does not change the information contained in the electronic document that was originally made, sent or received;

(b) the information in the electronic document will be readable or perceivable by any person who is entitled to have access to the electronic document or who is authorized to require the production of the electronic document; and

(c) if the electronic document was sent or received, any information that identifies the origin and destination of the electronic document and the date and time when it was sent or received is also retained.

Notarial act

38. A reference in a provision of a federal law to a document recognized as a notarial act in the province of Quebec is deemed to include an electronic version of the document if

(a) the electronic version of the document is recognized as a notarial act under the laws of the province of Quebec; and

(b) the federal law or the provision is listed in Schedule 2 or 3.

Seals

39. A requirement under a provision of a federal law for a person's seal is satisfied by a secure electronic signature that identifies the secure electronic signature as the person's seal if the federal law or the provision is listed in Schedule 2 or 3.

Requirements to provide documents or information

40. A provision of a federal law requiring a person to provide another person with a document or information, other than a provision referred to in any of sections 41 to 47, is satisfied by the provision of the document or information in electronic form if

(a) the federal law or the provision is listed in Schedule 2 or 3;

(b) both persons have agreed to the document or information being provided in electronic form; and

(c) the document or information in electronic form will be under the control of the person to whom it is provided and will be readable or perceivable so as to be usable for subsequent reference.

Writing requirements

41. A requirement under a provision of a federal law for a document to be in writing is satisfied by an electronic document if

(a) the federal law or the provision is listed in Schedule 2 or 3; and

(b) the regulations respecting the application of this section to the provision have been complied with.

Original documents

42. A requirement under a provision of a federal law for a document to be in its original form is satisfied by an electronic document if

(a) the federal law or the provision is listed in Schedule 2 or 3;

(b) the electronic document contains a secure electronic signature that was added when the electronic document was first generated in its final form and that can be used to verify that the electronic document has not been changed since that time; and

(c) the regulations respecting the application of this section to the provision have been complied with.

Signatures

43. Subject to sections 44 to 46, a requirement under a provision of a federal law for a signature is satisfied by an electronic signature if

(a) the federal law or the provision is listed in Schedule 2 or 3; and

(b) the regulations respecting the application of this section to the provision have been complied with.

Statements made under oath

44. A statement required to be made under oath or solemn affirmation under a provision of a federal law may be made in electronic form if

(a) the person who makes the statement signs it with that person's secure electronic signature;

(b) the person before whom the statement was made, and who is authorized to take statements under oath or solemn affirmation, signs it with that person's secure electronic signature;

(c) the federal law or the provision is listed in Schedule 2 or 3; and

(d) the regulations respecting the application of this section to the provision have been complied with.

Statements declaring truth, etc.

45. A statement required to be made under a provision of a federal law declaring or certifying that any information given by a person making the statement is true, accurate or complete may be made in electronic form if

(a) the person signs it with that person's secure electronic signature;

(b) the federal law or the provision is listed in Schedule 2 or 3; and

(c) the regulations respecting the application of this section to the provision have been complied with.

Witnessed signatures

46. A requirement under a provision of a federal law for a signature to be witnessed is satisfied with respect to an electronic document if

(a) each signatory and each witness signs the electronic document with their secure electronic signature;

(b) the federal law or the provision is listed in Schedule 2 or 3; and

(c) the regulations respecting the application of this section to the provision have been complied with.

Copies

47. A requirement under a provision of a federal law for one or more copies of a document to be submitted is satisfied by the submission of an electronic document if

(a) the federal law or the provision is listed in Schedule 2 or 3; and

(b) the regulations respecting the application of this section to the provision have been complied with.

Regulations and Orders

Regulations

48. (1) Subject to subsection (2), the Governor in Council may, on the recommendation of the Treasury Board, make regulations prescribing technologies or processes for the purpose of the definition "secure electronic signature" in subsection 31(1).

Characteristics

(2) The Governor in Council may prescribe a technology or process only if the Governor in Council is satisfied that it can be proved that

(a) the electronic signature resulting from the use by a person of the technology or process is unique to the person;

(b) the use of the technology or process by a person to incorporate, attach or associate the person's electronic signature to an electronic document is under the sole control of the person;

(c) the technology or process can be used to identify the person using the technology or process; and

(d) the electronic signature can be linked with an electronic document in such a way that it can be used to determine whether the electronic document has been changed since the electronic signature was incorporated in, attached to or associated with the electronic document.

Effect of amendment or repeal

(3) An amendment to or repeal of any provision of a regulation made under subsection (1) that has the effect of removing a prescribed technology or process from the regulation does not, by itself, affect the validity of any electronic signature resulting from the use of that technology or process while it was prescribed.

Amendment of schedules

49. For the purposes of sections 38 to 47, the responsible authority in respect of a provision of a federal law may, by order, amend Schedule 2 or 3 by adding or striking out a reference to that federal law or provision.

Regulations

50. (1) For the purposes of sections 41 to 47, the responsible authority in respect of a provision of a federal law may make regulations respecting the application of those sections to the provision.

Contents

(2) Without restricting the generality of subsection (1), the regulations that may be made may include rules respecting any of the following:

(a) the technology or process that must be used to make or send an electronic document;

(b) the format of an electronic document;

(c) the place where an electronic document is to be made or sent;

(d) the time and circumstances when an electronic document is to be considered to be sent or received and the place where it is considered to have been sent or received;

(e) the technology or process to be used to make or verify an electronic signature and the manner in which it is to be used; and

(f) any matter necessary for the purposes of the application of sections 41 to 47.

Minimum rules

(3) Without restricting the generality of subsection (1), if a provision referred to in any of sections 41 to 47 requires a person to provide another person with a document or information, the rules set out in the regulations respecting the application of that section to the provision may be that

(a) both persons have agreed to the document or information being provided in electronic form; and

(b) the document or information in electronic form will be under the control of the person to whom it is provided and will be readable or perceivable so as to be usable for subsequent reference.

Incorporation by reference

(4) Regulations may incorporate by reference the standards or specifications of any government, person or organization, either as they read at a fixed time or as they are amended from time to time.

Effect of striking out listed provision

51. The striking out of a reference to a federal law or provision in Schedule 2 or 3 does not affect the validity of anything done in compliance with any regulation made under section 50 that relates to that federal law or provision while it was listed in that Schedule.

PART 3

AMENDMENTS TO THE CANADA EVIDENCE ACT

52. Section 19 of the *Canada Evidence Act* is replaced by the following: Copies by Queen's Printer

19. Every copy of any Act of Parliament, public or private, published by the Queen's Printer, is evidence of that Act and of its contents, and every copy purporting to be published by the Queen's Printer shall be deemed to be so published, unless the contrary is shown.

53. Paragraph 20(c) of the Act is replaced by the following:

(c) by the production of a copy of them purporting to be published by the Queen's Printer.

54. Paragraphs 21(b) and (c) of the Act are replaced by the following:

(b) by the production of a copy of the proclamation, order, regulation or appointment, purporting to be published by the Queen's Printer;

(c) by the production of a copy of the treaty purporting to be published by the Queen's Printer;

55. Paragraph 22(1)(b) of the Act is replaced by the following:

(b) by the production of a copy of the proclamation, order, regulation or appointment purporting to be published by the government or Queen's Printer for the province; and

56. The Act is amended by adding the following after section 31:

Authentication of electronic documents

31.1 Any person seeking to admit an electronic document as evidence has the burden of proving its authenticity by evidence capable of supporting a finding that the electronic document is that which it is purported to be.

Application of best evidence rule—electronic documents

31.2 (1) The best evidence rule in respect of an electronic document is satisfied

(a) on proof of the integrity of the electronic documents system by or in which the electronic document was recorded or stored; or

(b) if an evidentiary presumption established under section 31.4 applies.

Printouts

(2) Despite subsection (1), in the absence of evidence to the contrary, an electronic document in the form of a printout satisfies the best evidence rule if the printout has been manifestly or consistently acted on, relied on or used as a record of the information recorded or stored in the printout.

Presumption of integrity

31.3 For the purposes of subsection 31.2(1), in the absence of evidence to the contrary, the integrity of an electronic documents system by or in which an electronic document is recorded or stored is proven

(a) by evidence capable of supporting a finding that at all material times the computer system or other similar device used by the electronic documents system was operating properly or, if it was not, the fact of its not operating properly did not affect the integrity of the electronic document and there are no other reasonable grounds to doubt the integrity of the electronic documents system;

(b) if it is established that the electronic document was recorded or stored by a party who is adverse in interest to the party seeking to introduce it; or

(c) if it is established that the electronic document was recorded or stored in the usual and ordinary course of business by a person who is not a party and who did not record or store it under the control of the party seeking to introduce it.

Presumptions regarding secure electronic signatures

31.4 The Governor in Council may make regulations establishing evidentiary presumptions in relation to electronic documents signed with secure electronic signatures, including regulations respecting

(a) the association of secure electronic signatures with persons; and

(b) the integrity of information contained in electronic documents signed with secure electronic signatures.

Standards may be considered

31.5 For the purpose of determining under any rule of law whether an electronic document is admissible, evidence may be presented in respect of any standard, procedure, usage or practice concerning the manner in which electronic documents are to be recorded or stored, having regard to the type of business, enterprise or endeavour that used, recorded or stored the electronic document and the nature and purpose of the electronic document.

Proof by affidavit

31.6 (1) The matters referred to in subsection 31.2(2) and sections 31.3 and 31.5 and in regulations made under section 31.4 may be established by affidavit.

Cross-examination

(2) A party may cross-examine a deponent of an affidavit referred to in subsection (1) that has been introduced in evidence

(a) as of right, if the deponent is an adverse party or is under the control of an adverse party; and

(b) with leave of the court, in the case of any other deponent.

Application

31.7 Sections 31.1 to 31.4 do not affect any rule of law relating to the admissibility of evidence, except the rules relating to authentication and best evidence.

Definitions

31.8 The definitions in this section apply in sections 31.1 to 31.6.

"computer system"

"computer system" means a device that, or a group of interconnected or related devices one or more of which,

(a) contains computer programs or other data; and

(b) pursuant to computer programs, performs logic and control, and may perform any other function.

"data"

"data" means representations of information or of concepts, in any form.

"electronic document"

"electronic document" means data that is recorded or stored on any medium in or by a computer system or other similar device and that can be read or perceived by a person or a computer system or other similar device. It includes a display, printout or other output of that data.

"electronic documents system"

"electronic documents system" includes a computer system or other similar device by or in which data is recorded or stored and any procedures related to the recording or storage of electronic documents.

"secure electronic signature"

"secure electronic signature" means a secure electronic signature as defined in subsection 31(1) of the *Personal Information Protection and Electronic Documents Act.*

57. Subsection 32(2) of the Act is replaced by the following:

Copies published in Canada Gazette

(2) All copies of official and other notices, advertisements and documents published in the Canada Gazette are admissible in evidence as proof, in the absence of evidence to the contrary, of the originals and of their contents.

PART 4

AMENDMENTS TO THE STATUTORY INSTRUMENTS ACT

58. Section 10 of the *Statutory Instruments Act* is renumbered as subsection 10(1) and is amended by adding the following:

Publication

(2) The Governor in Council may determine the form and manner in which the *Canada Gazette*, or any part of it, is published, including publication by electronic means.

59. Subsection 16(3) of the Act is replaced by the following:

Deemed publication in Canada Gazette

(3) For the purposes of this section,

> (a) if a regulation is included in a copy of the Consolidated Regulations of Canada, 1978 purporting to be printed by the Queen's Printer, that regulation is deemed to have been published in the *Canada Gazette*; and

> (b) if a regulation is included in a copy of a revision of regulations purporting to be printed by the Queen's Printer, that regulation is deemed to have been published in the *Canada Gazette*.

PART 5

AMENDMENTS TO THE STATUTE REVISION ACT

60. Section 1 of the *Statute Revision Act* is replaced by the following:

Short title

1. This Act may be cited as the *Legislation Revision and Consolidation Act*.

61. (1) The definition "revision" in section 2 of the Act is replaced by the following:

"revision"

"revision" means

(a) for the purposes of Part I, the arrangement, revision and consolidation of the public general statutes of Canada authorized under that Part; and

(b) for the purposes of Part II, the arrangement, revision and consolidation of the regulations authorized under that Part.

(2) Section 2 of the Act is amended by adding the following in alphabetical order:

"regulation"

"regulations" means

(a) statutory orders and regulations published in the Consolidated Regulations of Canada, 1978,

(b) regulations, statutory instruments and other documents published in the *Canada Gazette*, Part II, after the publication of the Consolidated Regulations of Canada, 1978, and

(c) any other regulations, statutory instruments or documents that, in the opinion of the Minister, are of continuing effect or apply to more than one person or body and that are not exempted from publication pursuant to regulations made under paragraph 20(c) of the *Statutory Instruments Act*;

62. Section 5 of the Act is replaced by the following:

Revision of statutes

5. The Commission shall, from time to time, revise the public general statutes of Canada.

63. The heading before section 8 and sections 8 to 10 of the Act are repealed.

64. The heading before section 11 and sections 11 and 12 of the Act are replaced by the following:

Revision

Revision of Regulations

10. The Commission shall, from time to time, revise the regulations.

Powers of Commission

11. In preparing and maintaining the Revised Regulations and in keeping the Revised Regulations up to date, the Commission may exercise, in respect of the regulations, the powers that it has under section 6 in respect of a revision under Part I.

Deposit of revision

12. (1) On receipt of a written report from the Commission in respect of the completion of all or any part of the Revised Regulations, the Governor in Council may cause a printed Roll of the regulations, attested under the signature of the Minister and the President of the Privy Council, to be deposited in the office of the Clerk of the Privy Council, and the Roll shall be held to be the original of the regulations included in it.

Schedule

(2) There shall be appended to each Roll a schedule similar in form to the Schedule to Appendix I appended to the Revised Statutes of Canada, 1985, and the Commission may include in the schedule a list of all regulations and parts of regulations that, although not expressly repealed, are superseded by the regulations included in the Roll, or are inconsistent with them, and a list of all regulations and parts of regulations that were for a temporary purpose the force of which is spent.

65. (1) Subsection 13(2) of the Act is replaced by the following:

Effect

(2) On the day referred to in subsection (1) in respect of any Roll, the regulations included in that Roll shall accordingly come into force and have effect as law as part of the Revised Regulations to all intents as if each regulation had been made by the appropriate regulation-making authority and all the requirements with respect to the making of that regulation had been complied with.

(2) Subsection 13(3) of the English version of the Act is replaced by the following:

Repeal

(3) On the day referred to in subsection (1), all regulations and parts of regulations listed in the schedule to the Roll are repealed to the extent mentioned in that schedule.

66. Sections 15 to 17 of the Act are replaced by the following:

Bound volumes

17. If the Commission has, as of a day selected by it, revised all the regulations that it is required to revise under section 10 to that day, it shall cause the Revised Regulations to be published in the form of bound volumes, and the regulations to be included in them shall be those that have been revised as of that day, and that day shall be indicated in each of the volumes.

67. (1) Subsection 18(1) of the English version of the Act is replaced by the following:

Old regulations not revived

18. (1) The repeal of the regulations and parts of regulations listed in the schedule appended to a Roll does not

(a) revive any regulation or part of any regulation so repealed;

(b) affect any saving clause in the regulations or parts of regulations so repealed; or

(c) prevent the application of any of those regulations or parts of regulations, or of any regulation or any part of a regulation formerly in force, to any transaction, matter or thing before the repeal to which they would otherwise apply.

(2) Subsections 18(2) to (4) of the Act are replaced by the following:

Not new law

(2) A regulation included in the Revised Regulations shall not be held to operate as a new regulation, but shall be construed and have effect as a consolidation and as declaratory of the law as contained in the regulation and parts of regulations as revised, and for which the regulation included in the Revised Regulations is substituted.

Where revision differs

(3) Where, on any point, the provisions of a regulation included in the Revised Regulations are not in effect the same as those of the repealed provisions for which they are substituted, in respect of all transactions, matters and things subsequent to the time when the regulation included in the Revised Regulations takes effect, the provisions contained in that regulation prevail, but in respect of all transactions, matters and things before that time, the repealed provisions prevail.

Construction of references

(4) A reference in any regulation remaining in force and not revised, or in any instrument or document, to any regulation or part of a regulation repealed under subsection 13(3) by inclusion in the Revised Regulations

shall, after the regulation in the Revised Regulations takes effect, be deemed, in respect of any subsequent transaction, matter or thing, to be a reference to the regulation or part of a regulation in the Revised Regulations having the same effect as the repealed regulation or part of a regulation.

68. Sections 19 to 21 of the Act are replaced by the following:

Effect of inclusion in schedule

19. (1) The inclusion of any regulation or part of a regulation in the schedule appended to a Roll shall not be considered to be a declaration that the regulation or part was or was not in force immediately before the coming into force of the portion of the Revised Regulations that includes that regulation or part.

Paragraph 16(3)(b) *Statutory Instruments Act*

(2) The whole or any part of the Revised Regulations shall be construed to be a revision of regulations referred to in paragraph 16(3)(b) of the *Statutory Instruments Act.*

Scrutiny Committees of Parliament

(3) A regulation that is included in the Consolidated Regulations of Canada, 1978 or in the Revised Regulations stands permanently referred to any Committee or Committees of Parliament established under section 19 of the *Statutory Instruments Act.*

Citation of Revised Regulations

20. (1) Any regulation included in the Revised Regulations may be cited and referred to in any Act, regulation, proceeding, instrument or document whatever either by its short or long title or by using the expression "Revised Regulations of Canada, chapter ...", or "Revised Regulations, chapter ...", or "Chapter ... of the Revised Regulations", or the abbreviation "R.R.C., c. ...", adding in each case the number of the particular chapter.

Amendments included

(2) The citation of any chapter of the Revised Regulations in accordance with subsection (1) is deemed to include any amendments made after the publication of that regulation in the Revised Regulations.

Electronic publishing

21. (1) The Queen's Printer may publish an edition of the Revised Regulations in electronic form and every copy of a revised regulation published in electronic form by the Queen's Printer is evidence of that regulation and of its contents, and every copy purporting to be published by the Queen's Printer is deemed to be so published, unless the contrary is shown.

Inconsistencies in regulations

(2) In the event of an inconsistency between a revised regulation published by the Queen's Printer in electronic form and the original of the regulation as printed in the Roll deposited in the office of the Clerk of the Privy Council under section 12, the original of the regulation prevails to the extent of the inconsistency.

69. Subsection 22(1) of the Act is replaced by the following:

Request to remake regulations

22. (1) If the Clerk of the Privy Council, after consultation with the Deputy Minister of Justice, is of the opinion that any particular regulations should be remade by the regulation-making authority instead of being revised under this Act, the Clerk of the Privy Council may request that authority or any person acting on behalf of that authority to make new regulations.

70. Section 23 of the Act is replaced by the following:

Indices

23. The Commission may cause indices to the Revised Regulations to be prepared and published for the convenience of the public.

Citation of Consolidated Regulations, 1978

24. (1) Any regulation included in the Consolidated Regulations of Canada, 1978 may be cited and referred to in any Act, regulation, proceeding, instrument or document whatever either by its short or long title or by using the expression "Consolidated Regulations of Canada, chapter ...", or "Consolidated Regulations, chapter ...", or "Chapter ... of the Consolidated Regulations", or the abbreviation "C.R.C., c. ...", adding in each case the number of the particular chapter.

Amendments included

(2) The citation of any chapter of the Consolidated Regulations of Canada, 1978 in accordance with subsection (1) is deemed to include any amendments made after the publication of that regulation in the Consolidated Regulations of Canada, 1978.

71. Part III of the Act is replaced by the following:

PART III

CONSOLIDATED STATUTES AND REGULATIONS OF CANADA

Interpretation

Definitions

25. The definitions in this section apply in this Part.

"consolidated regulations"

"consolidated regulations" means the consolidated regulations of Canada maintained by the Minister under this Part.

"consolidated statutes"

"consolidated statutes" means the consolidated statutes of Canada maintained by the Minister under this Part.

Consolidation of the Statutes and Regulations

Authority to maintain

26. The Minister may maintain a consolidation of the public statutes of Canada and a consolidation of the regulations of Canada.

Powers of Minister

27. In maintaining a consolidation of the statutes or regulations, the Minister may

(a) omit any Act or regulation, or any part of an Act or a regulation, that has expired, has been repealed or has had its effect;

(b) include historical references or other information that enhances the value of the consolidation;

(c) correct grammatical and typographical errors without changing the substance of any enactment; and

(d) set out as a separate Act or regulation any Act or regulation enacted by another Act or regulation.

Publication and Distribution

Authority to publish

28. (1) The Minister may cause the consolidated statutes or consolidated regulations to be published in printed or electronic form, and in any manner and frequency that the Minister considers appropriate.

Differences in form

(2) A publication in an electronic form may differ from a publication in another form to accommodate the needs of the electronic form if the differences do not change the substance of any enactment.

Free distribution

29. Copies of the consolidated statutes and consolidated regulations must be distributed without charge to the persons or classes of persons, and in the form and manner, that the Governor in Council, on the recommendation of the Minister, directs.

Effect of Consolidation

Consolidation not new law

30. The consolidated statutes and consolidated regulations do not operate as new law.

Published consolidation is evidence

31. (1) Every copy of a consolidated statute or consolidated regulation published by the Minister under this Act in either print or electronic form is evidence of that statute or regulation and of its contents and every copy purporting to be published by the Minister is deemed to be so published, unless the contrary is shown.

Inconsistencies in Acts

(2) In the event of an inconsistency between a consolidated statute published by the Minister under this Act and the original statute or a subsequent amendment as certified by the Clerk of the Parliaments under the *Publication of Statutes Act*, the original statute or amendment prevails to the extent of the inconsistency.

Inconsistencies in regulations

(3) In the event of an inconsistency between a consolidated regulation published by the Minister under this Act and the original regulation or a subsequent amendment as registered by the Clerk of the Privy Council under the *Statutory Instruments Act*, the original regulation or amendment prevails to the extent of the inconsistency.

Co-publishing Agreements

Agreements

32. The Minister may enter into agreements for the production of the consolidated statutes or consolidated regulations and for their publication, sale or distribution.

PART 6

COMING INTO FORCE

Coming into force

72. Parts 1 to 5 or any provision of those Parts come into force on a day or days to be fixed by order of the Governor in Council made on the recommendation of

(a) in the case of Parts 1 and 2 or any provision of those Parts, the Minister of Industry; and

(b) in the case of Parts 3 to 5 or any provision of those Parts, the Minister of Justice.

SCHEDULE 1

(Section 5)

PRINCIPLES SET OUT IN THE NATIONAL STANDARD OF CANADA ENTITLED *MODEL CODE FOR THE PROTECTION OF PERSONAL INFORMATION,* CAN/CSA-Q830-96

4.1 Principle 1 — Accountability

An organization is responsible for personal information under its control and shall designate an individual or individuals who are accountable for the organization's compliance with the following principles.

4.1.1

Accountability for the organization's compliance with the principles rests with the designated individual(s), even though other individuals within the organization may be responsible for the day-to-day collection and processing of personal information. In addition, other individuals within the organization may be delegated to act on behalf of the designated individual(s).

4.1.2

The identity of the individual(s) designated by the organization to oversee the organization's compliance with the principles shall be made known upon request.

4.1.3

An organization is responsible for personal information in its possession or custody, including information that has been transferred to a third party for processing. The organization shall use contractual or other means to provide a comparable level of protection while the information is being processed by a third party.

4.1.4

Organizations shall implement policies and practices to give effect to the principles, including

(a) implementing procedures to protect personal information;

(b) establishing procedures to receive and respond to complaints and inquiries;

(c) training staff and communicating to staff information about the organization's policies and practices; and

(d) developing information to explain the organization's policies and procedures.

4.2 Principle 2 — Identifying Purposes

The purposes for which personal information is collected shall be identified by the organization at or before the time the information is collected.

4.2.1

The organization shall document the purposes for which personal information is collected in order to comply with the Openness principle (Clause 4.8) and the Individual Access principle (Clause 4.9).

4.2.2

Identifying the purposes for which personal information is collected at or before the time of collection allows organizations to determine the information they need to collect to fulfil these purposes. The Limiting Collection principle (Clause 4.4) requires an organization to collect only that information necessary for the purposes that have been identified.

4.2.3

The identified purposes should be specified at or before the time of collection to the individual from whom the personal information is collected. Depending upon the way in which the information is collected, this can be done orally or in writing. An application form, for example, may give notice of the purposes.

4.2.4

When personal information that has been collected is to be used for a purpose not previously identified, the new purpose shall be identified prior to use. Unless the new purpose is required by law, the consent of the individual is required before information can be used for that purpose. For an elaboration on consent, please refer to the Consent principle (Clause 4.3).

4.2.5

Persons collecting personal information should be able to explain to individuals the purposes for which the information is being collected.

4.2.6

This principle is linked closely to the Limiting Collection principle (Clause 4.4) and the Limiting Use, Disclosure, and Retention principle (Clause 4.5).

4.3 Principle 3 — Consent

The knowledge and consent of the individual are required for the collection, use, or disclosure of personal information, except where inappropriate.

Note: In certain circumstances personal information can be collected, used, or disclosed without the knowledge and consent of the individual. For example, legal, medical, or security reasons may make it impossible or impractical to seek consent. When information is being collected for the detection and prevention of fraud or for law enforcement, seeking the consent of the individual might defeat the purpose of collecting the information. Seeking consent may be impossible or inappropriate when the individual is a minor, seriously ill, or mentally incapacitated. In addition, organizations that do not have a direct relationship with the individual may not always be able to seek consent. For example, seeking consent may be impractical for a charity or a direct-marketing firm that wishes to acquire a mailing list from another organization. In such cases, the organization providing the list would be expected to obtain consent before disclosing personal information.

4.3.1

Consent is required for the collection of personal information and the subsequent use or disclosure of this information. Typically, an organization will seek consent for the use or disclosure of the information at the time of collection. In certain circumstances, consent with respect to use or disclosure may be sought after the information has been collected but before use (for example, when an organization wants to use information for a purpose not previously identified).

4.3.2

The principle requires "knowledge and consent". Organizations shall make a reasonable effort to ensure that the individual is advised of the purposes for which the information will be used. To make the consent meaningful, the purposes must be stated in such a manner that the individual can reasonably understand how the information will be used or disclosed.

4.3.3

An organization shall not, as a condition of the supply of a product or service, require an individual to consent to the collection, use, or disclosure of information beyond that required to fulfil the explicitly specified, and legitimate purposes.

4.3.4

The form of the consent sought by the organization may vary, depending upon the circumstances and the type of information. In determining the form of consent to use, organizations shall take into account the sensitivity of the information. Although some information (for example, medical records and income records) is almost always considered to be sensitive, any information can be sensitive, depending on the context. For example, the names and addresses of subscribers to a newsmagazine would generally not be considered sensitive information. However, the names and addresses of subscribers to some special-interest magazines might be considered sensitive.

4.3.5

In obtaining consent, the reasonable expectations of the individual are also relevant. For example, an individual buying a subscription to a magazine should reasonably expect that the organization, in addition to using the individual's name and address for mailing and billing purposes, would also contact the person to solicit the renewal of the subscription. In this case, the organization can assume that the individual's request constitutes consent for specific purposes. On the other hand, an individual would not reasonably expect that personal information given to a health-care professional would be given to a company selling health-care products, unless consent were obtained. Consent shall not be obtained through deception.

4.3.6

The way in which an organization seeks consent may vary, depending on the circumstances and the type of information collected. An organization should generally seek express consent when the information is likely to be considered sensitive. Implied consent would generally be appropriate when the information is less sensitive. Consent can also be given by an authorized representative (such as a legal guardian or a person having power of attorney).

4.3.7

Individuals can give consent in many ways. For example:

(a) an application form may be used to seek consent, collect information, and inform the individual of the use that will be made of the information. By completing and signing the form, the individual is giving consent to the collection and the specified uses;

(b) a checkoff box may be used to allow individuals to request that their names and addresses not be given to other organizations. Individuals who do not check the box are assumed to consent to the transfer of this information to third parties;

(c) consent may be given orally when information is collected over the telephone; or

(d) consent may be given at the time that individuals use a product or service.

4.3.8

An individual may withdraw consent at any time, subject to legal or contractual restrictions and reasonable notice. The organization shall inform the individual of the implications of such withdrawal.

4.4 Principle 4 — Limiting Collection

The collection of personal information shall be limited to that which is necessary for the purposes identified by the organization. Information shall be collected by fair and lawful means.

4.4.1

Organizations shall not collect personal information indiscriminately. Both the amount and the type of information collected shall be limited to that which is necessary to fulfil the purposes identified. Organizations shall specify the type of information collected as part of their information-handling policies and practices, in accordance with the Openness principle (Clause 4.8).

4.4.2

The requirement that personal information be collected by fair and lawful means is intended to prevent organizations from collecting information by misleading or deceiving individuals about the purpose for which information is being collected. This requirement implies that consent with respect to collection must not be obtained through deception.

4.4.3

This principle is linked closely to the Identifying Purposes principle (Clause 4.2) and the Consent principle (Clause 4.3).

4.5 Principle 5 — Limiting Use, Disclosure, and Retention

Personal information shall not be used or disclosed for purposes other than those for which it was collected, except with the consent of the individual or as required by law. Personal information shall be retained only as long as necessary for the fulfilment of those purposes.

4.5.1

Organizations using personal information for a new purpose shall document this purpose (see Clause 4.2.1).

4.5.2

Organizations should develop guidelines and implement procedures with respect to the retention of personal information. These guidelines should include minimum and maximum retention periods. Personal information that has been used to make a decision about an individual shall be retained long enough to allow the individual access to the information after the decision has been made. An organization may be subject to legislative requirements with respect to retention periods.

4.5.3

Personal information that is no longer required to fulfil the identified purposes should be destroyed, erased, or made anonymous. Organizations shall develop guidelines and implement procedures to govern the destruction of personal information.

4.5.4

This principle is closely linked to the Consent principle (Clause 4.3), the Identifying Purposes principle (Clause 4.2), and the Individual Access principle (Clause 4.9).

4.6 Principle 6 — Accuracy

Personal information shall be as accurate, complete, and up-to-date as is necessary for the purposes for which it is to be used.

4.6.1

The extent to which personal information shall be accurate, complete, and up-to-date will depend upon the use of the information, taking into account the interests of the individual. Information shall be sufficiently accurate, complete, and up-to-date to minimize the possibility that inappropriate information may be used to make a decision about the individual.

4.6.2

An organization shall not routinely update personal information, unless such a process is necessary to fulfil the purposes for which the information was collected.

4.6.3

Personal information that is used on an ongoing basis, including information that is disclosed to third parties, should generally be accurate and up-to-date, unless limits to the requirement for accuracy are clearly set out.

4.7 Principle 7 — Safeguards

Personal information shall be protected by security safeguards appropriate to the sensitivity of the information.

4.7.1

The security safeguards shall protect personal information against loss or theft, as well as unauthorized access, disclosure, copying, use, or modification. Organizations shall protect personal information regardless of the format in which it is held.

4.7.2

The nature of the safeguards will vary depending on the sensitivity of the information that has been collected, the amount, distribution, and format of the information, and the method of storage. More sensitive information should be safeguarded by a higher level of protection. The concept of sensitivity is discussed in Clause 4.3.4.

4.7.3

The methods of protection should include

(a) physical measures, for example, locked filing cabinets and restricted access to offices;

(b) organizational measures, for example, security clearances and limiting access on a "need-to-know" basis; and

(c) technological measures, for example, the use of passwords and encryption.

4.7.4

Organizations shall make their employees aware of the importance of maintaining the confidentiality of personal information.

4.7.5

Care shall be used in the disposal or destruction of personal information, to prevent unauthorized parties from gaining access to the information (see Clause 4.5.3).

4.8 Principle 8 — Openness

An organization shall make readily available to individuals specific information about its policies and practices relating to the management of personal information.

4.8.1

Organizations shall be open about their policies and practices with respect to the management of personal information. Individuals shall be able to acquire information about an organization's policies and practices without unreasonable effort. This information shall be made available in a form that is generally understandable.

4.8.2

The information made available shall include

(a) the name or title, and the address, of the person who is accountable for the organization's policies and practices and to whom complaints or inquiries can be forwarded;

(b) the means of gaining access to personal information held by the organization;

(c) a description of the type of personal information held by the organization, including a general account of its use;

(d) a copy of any brochures or other information that explain the organization's policies, standards, or codes; and

(e) what personal information is made available to related organizations (e.g., subsidiaries).

4.8.3

An organization may make information on its policies and practices available in a variety of ways. The method chosen depends on the nature of its business and other considerations. For example, an organization may choose to make brochures available in its place of business, mail information to its customers, provide online access, or establish a toll-free telephone number.

4.9 Principle 9 — Individual Access

Upon request, an individual shall be informed of the existence, use, and disclosure of his or her personal information and shall be given access to that information. An individual shall be able to challenge the accuracy and completeness of the information and have it amended as appropriate.

Note: In certain situations, an organization may not be able to provide access to all the personal information it holds about an individual. Exceptions to the access requirement should be limited and specific. The reasons for denying access should be provided to the individual upon request. Exceptions may include information that is prohibitively costly to provide, information that contains references to other individuals, information that cannot be disclosed for legal, security, or commercial proprietary reasons, and information that is subject to solicitor-client or litigation privilege.

4.9.1

Upon request, an organization shall inform an individual whether or not the organization holds personal information about the individual. Organizations are encouraged to indicate the source of this information. The organization shall allow the individual access to this information. However, the organization may choose to make sensitive medical information available through a medical practitioner. In addition, the organization shall provide an account of the use that has been made or is being made of this information and an account of the third parties to which it has been disclosed.

4.9.2

An individual may be required to provide sufficient information to permit an organization to provide an account of the existence, use, and disclosure of personal information. The information provided shall only be used for this purpose.

4.9.3

In providing an account of third parties to which it has disclosed personal information about an individual, an organization should attempt to be as specific as possible. When it is not possible to provide a list of the organizations to which it has actually disclosed information about an individual, the organization shall provide a list of organizations to which it may have disclosed information about the individual.

4.9.4

An organization shall respond to an individual's request within a reasonable time and at minimal or no cost to the individual. The requested information shall be provided or made available in a form that is generally understandable. For example, if the organization uses abbreviations or codes to record information, an explanation shall be provided.

4.9.5

When an individual successfully demonstrates the inaccuracy or incompleteness of personal information, the organization shall amend the information as required. Depending upon the nature of the information challenged, amendment involves the correction, deletion, or addition of information. Where appropriate, the amended information shall be transmitted to third parties having access to the information in question.

4.9.6

When a challenge is not resolved to the satisfaction of the individual, the substance of the unresolved challenge shall be recorded by the organization. When appropriate, the existence of the unresolved challenge shall be transmitted to third parties having access to the information in question.

4.10 Principle 10 — Challenging Compliance

An individual shall be able to address a challenge concerning compliance with the above principles to the designated individual or individuals accountable for the organization's compliance.

4.10.1

The individual accountable for an organization's compliance is discussed in Clause 4.1.1.

4.10.2

Organizations shall put procedures in place to receive and respond to complaints or inquiries about their policies and practices relating to the handling of personal information. The complaint procedures should be easily accessible and simple to use.

4.10.3

Organizations shall inform individuals who make inquiries or lodge complaints of the existence of relevant complaint procedures. A range of these procedures may exist. For example, some regulatory bodies accept complaints about the personal-information handling practices of the companies they regulate.

4.10.4

An organization shall investigate all complaints. If a complaint is found to be justified, the organization shall take appropriate measures, including, if necessary, amending its policies and practices.

SCHEDULE 2

(Sections 38 to 47, 49 and 51)

ACTS OF PARLIAMENT

SCHEDULE 3

(Sections 38 To 47, 49 And 51)

REGULATIONS AND OTHER INSTRUMENTS

GUIDELINES GOVERNING THE PROTECTION OF PRIVACY AND TRANSBORDER FLOWS OF PERSONAL DATA

Printed with permission from OECD. Copyright OECD, 1980, document available on the OECD Web site at <http://www.oecd.org/dsti/sti/it/secur/index.htm>.

PART ONE. GENERAL DEFINITIONS

1. For the purposes of these Guidelines:

    a) "data controller" means a party who, according to domestic law, is competent to decide about the contents and use of personal data regardless of whether or not such data are collected, stored, processed or disseminated by that party or by an agent on its behalf;

    b) "personal data" means any information relating to an identified or identifiable individual (data subject);

    c) "transborder flows of personal data" means movements of personal data across national borders.

Scope of Guidelines

2. These Guidelines apply to personal data, whether in the public or private sectors, which, because of the manner in which they are processed, or because of their nature or the context in which they are used, pose a danger to privacy and individual liberties.

3. These Guidelines should not be interpreted as preventing:

   a) the application, to different categories of personal data, of different protective measures depending upon their nature and the context in which they are collected, stored, processed or disseminated;

   b) the exclusion from the application of the Guidelines of personal data which obviously do not contain any risk to privacy and individual liberties; or

   c) the application of the Guidelines only to automatic processing of personal data.

4. Exceptions to the Principles contained in Parts Two and Three of these Guidelines, including those relating to national sovereignty, national security and public policy ("order public"), should be:

   a) as few as possible, and

   b) made known to the public.

5. In the particular case of Federal countries the observance of these Guidelines may be affected by the division of powers in the Federation.

6. These Guidelines should be regarded as minimum standards which are capable of being supplemented by additional measures for the protection of privacy and individual liberties.

PART TWO. BASIC PRINCIPLES OF NATIONAL APPLICATION

Collection Limitation Principle

7. There should be limits to the collection of personal data and any such data should be obtained by lawful and fair means and, where appropriate, with the knowledge or consent of the data subject.

Data Quality Principle

8. Personal data should be relevant to the purposes for which they are to be used, and, to the extent necessary for those purposes, should be accurate, complete and kept up-to-date.

Purpose Specification Principle

9. The purposes for which personal data are collected should be specified not later than at the time of data collection and the subsequent use limited to the fulfilment of those purposes or such others as are not incompatible with those purposes and as are specified on each occasion of change of purpose.

Use Limitation Principle

10. Personal data should not be disclosed, made available or otherwise used for purposes other than those specified in accordance with Paragraph 9 except:

    (a) with the consent of the data subject; or

    (b) by the authority of law.

Security Safeguards Principle

11. Personal data should be protected by reasonable security safeguards against such risks as loss or unauthorised access, destruction, use, modification or disclosure of data.

Openness Principle

12. There should be a general policy of openness about developments, practices and policies with respect to personal data. Means should be readily available of establishing the existence and nature of personal data, and the main purposes of their use, as well as the identity and usual residence of the data controller.

Individual Participation Principle

13. An individual should have the right:

    (a) to obtain from a data controller, or otherwise, confirmation of whether or not the data controller has data relating to him;

    (b) to have communicated to him, data relating to him

        (i) within a reasonable time;

        (ii) at a charge, if any, that is not excessive;

        (iii) in a reasonable manner; and

        (iv) in a form that is readily intelligible to him;

    (c) to be given reasons if a request made under subparagraphs (a) and (b) is denied, and to be able to challenge such denial; and

    (d) to challenge data relating to him and, if the challenge is successful, to have the data erased, rectified, completed or amended.

Accountability Principle

14. A data controller should be accountable for complying with measures which give effect to the principles stated above.

PART THREE. BASIC PRINCIPLES OF INTERNATIONAL APPLICATION: FREE FLOW AND LEGITIMATE RESTRICTIONS

15. Member countries should take into consideration the implications for other Member countries of domestic processing and re-export of personal data.

16. Member countries should take all reasonable and appropriate steps to ensure that transborder flows of personal data, including transit through a Member country, are uninterrupted and secure.

17. A Member country should refrain from restricting transborder flows of personal data between itself and another Member country except where the latter does not yet substantially observe these Guidelines or where the re-export of such data would circumvent its domestic privacy legislation. A Member country may also impose restrictions in respect of certain categories of personal data for which its domestic privacy legislation includes specific regulations in view of the nature of those data and for which the other Member country provides no equivalent protection.

18. Member countries should avoid developing laws, policies and practices in the name of the protection of privacy and individual liberties, which would create obstacles to transborder flows of personal data that would exceed requirements for such protection.

PART FOUR. NATIONAL IMPLEMENTATION

19. In implementing domestically the principles set forth in Parts Two and Three, Member countries should establish legal, administrative or other procedures or institutions for the protection of privacy and individual liberties in respect of personal data. Member countries should in particular endeavour to:

(a) adopt appropriate domestic legislation;

(b) encourage and support self-regulation, whether in the form of codes of conduct or otherwise;

(c) provide for reasonable means for individuals to exercise their rights;

(d) provide for adequate sanctions and remedies in case of failures to comply with measures which implement the principles set forth in Parts Two and Three; and

(e) ensure that there is no unfair discrimination against data subjects.

PART FIVE. INTERNATIONAL CO-OPERATION

20. Member countries should, where requested, make known to other Member countries details of the observance of the principles set forth in these Guidelines. Member countries should also ensure that procedures for transborder flows of personal data and for the protection of privacy and individual liberties are simple and compatible with those of other Member countries which comply with these Guidelines.

21. Member countries should establish procedures to facilitate:

    (i) information exchange related to these Guidelines, and

    (ii) mutual assistance in the procedural and investigative matters involved.

22. Member countries should work towards the development of principles, domestic and international, to govern the applicable law in the case of transborder flows of personal data.

Directive 95/46/EC of the European Parliament and of the Council of 24 October 1995 on the protection of individuals with regard to the processing of personal data and on the free movement of such data

Official Journal L281 (1995) 0031–0050

Text:

Directive 95/46/Ec Of The European Parliament And Of The Council Of 24 October 1995 on the protection of individuals with regard to the processing of personal data and on the free movement of such data

THE EUROPEAN PARLIAMENT AND THE COUNCIL OF THE EUROPEAN UNION,

Having regard to the Treaty establishing the European Community, and in particular Article 100a thereof, Having regard to the proposal from the Commission,[1]

Having regard to the opinion of the Economic and Social Committee,[2]

Acting in accordance with the procedure referred to in Article 189b of the Treaty,[3]

---

[1] OJ No C 277, 5.11.1990, p. 3 and OJ No C 311, 27.11.1992, p. 30.

[2] OJ No C 159, 17.6.1991, p. 38.

[3] Opinion of the European Parliament of 11 March 1992 (OJ No C 94, 13.4.1992, p. 198), confirmed on 2 December 1993 (OJ No C 342, 20.12.1993, p. 30); Council common position of 20 February 1995 (OJ No C 93, 13.4.1995, p. 1) and Decision of the European Parliament of 15 June 1995 (OJ No C 166, 3.7.1995).

(1) Whereas the objectives of the Community, as laid down in the Treaty, as amended by the Treaty on European Union, include creating an ever closer union among the peoples of Europe, fostering closer relations between the States belonging to the Community, ensuring economic and social progress by common action to eliminate the barriers which divide Europe, encouraging the constant improvement of the living conditions of its peoples, preserving and strengthening peace and liberty and promoting democracy on the basis of the fundamental rights recognized in the constitution and laws of the Member States and in the European Convention for the Protection of Human Rights and Fundamental Freedoms;

(2) Whereas data-processing systems are designed to serve man; whereas they must, whatever the nationality or residence of natural persons, respect their fundamental rights and freedoms, notably the right to privacy, and contribute to economic and social progress, trade expansion and the well-being of individuals;

(3) Whereas the establishment and functioning of an internal market in which, in accordance with Article 7a of the Treaty, the free movement of goods, persons, services and capital is ensured require not only that personal data should be able to flow freely from one Member State to another, but also that the fundamental rights of individuals should be safeguarded;

(4) Whereas increasingly frequent recourse is being had in the Community to the processing of personal data in the various spheres of economic and social activity; whereas the progress made in information technology is making the processing and exchange of such data considerably easier;

(5) Whereas the economic and social integration resulting from the establishment and functioning of the internal market within the meaning of Article 7a of the Treaty will necessarily lead to a substantial increase in cross-border flows of personal data between all those involved in a private or public capacity in economic and social activity in the Member States; whereas the exchange of personal data between undertakings in different Member States is set to increase; whereas the national authorities in the various Member States are being called upon by virtue of Community law to collaborate and exchange personal data so as to be able to perform their duties or carry out tasks on behalf of an authority in another Member State within the context of the area without internal frontiers as constituted by the internal market;

(6) Whereas, furthermore, the increase in scientific and technical cooperation and the coordinated introduction of new telecommunications networks in the Community necessitate and facilitate cross-border flows of personal data;

(7) Whereas the difference in levels of protection of the rights and freedoms of individuals, notably the right to privacy, with regard to the processing of personal data afforded in the Member States may prevent the transmission of such data from the territory of one Member State to that of another Member State; whereas this difference may therefore constitute an obstacle to the pursuit of a number of economic activities at Community level, distort competition and impede authorities in the discharge of their responsibilities under Community law; whereas this difference in levels of protection is due to the existence of a wide variety of national laws, regulations and administrative provisions;

(8) Whereas, in order to remove the obstacles to flows of personal data, the level of protection of the rights and freedoms of individuals with regard to the processing of such data must be equivalent in all Member States; whereas this objective is vital to the internal market but cannot be achieved by the Member States alone, especially in view of the scale of the divergences which currently exist between the relevant laws in the Member States and the need to coordinate the laws of the Member States so as to ensure that the cross-border flow of personal data is regulated in a consistent manner that is in keeping with the objective of the internal market as provided for in Article 7a of the Treaty; whereas Community action to approximate those laws is therefore needed;

(9) Whereas, given the equivalent protection resulting from the approximation of national laws, the Member States will no longer be able to inhibit the free movement between them of personal data on grounds relating to protection of the rights and freedoms of individuals, and in particular the right to privacy; whereas Member States will be left a margin for manoeuvre, which may, in the context of implementation of the Directive, also be exercised by the business and social partners; whereas Member States will therefore be able to specify in their national law the general conditions governing the lawfulness of data processing; whereas in doing so the Member States shall strive to improve the protection currently provided by their legislation; whereas, within the limits of this margin for manoeuvre and in accordance with Community law, disparities could arise in the implementation of the Directive, and this could have an effect on the movement of data within a Member State as well as within the Community;

(10) Whereas the object of the national laws on the processing of personal data is to protect fundamental rights and freedoms, notably the right to privacy, which is recognized both in Article 8 of the European Convention for the Protection of Human Rights and Fundamental Freedoms and in the general principles of Community law; whereas, for that reason, the approximation of those laws must not result in any lessening of the protec-

tion they afford but must, on the contrary, seek to ensure a high level of protection in the Community;

(11) Whereas the principles of the protection of the rights and freedoms of individuals, notably the right to privacy, which are contained in this Directive, give substance to and amplify those contained in the Council of Europe Convention of 28 January 1981 for the Protection of Individuals with regard to Automatic Processing of Personal Data;

(12) Whereas the protection principles must apply to all processing of personal data by any person whose activities are governed by Community law; whereas there should be excluded the processing of data carried out by a natural person in the exercise of activities which are exclusively personal or domestic, such as correspondence and the holding of records of addresses;

(13) Whereas the activities referred to in Titles V and VI of the Treaty on European Union regarding public safety, defence, State security or the activities of the State in the area of criminal laws fall outside the scope of Community law, without prejudice to the obligations incumbent upon Member States under Article 56 (2), Article 57 or Article 100a of the Treaty establishing the European Community; whereas the processing of personal data that is necessary to safeguard the economic well-being of the State does not fall within the scope of this Directive where such processing relates to State security matters;

(14) Whereas, given the importance of the developments under way, in the framework of the information society, of the techniques used to capture, transmit, manipulate, record, store or communicate sound and image data relating to natural persons, this Directive should be applicable to processing involving such data;

(15) Whereas the processing of such data is covered by this Directive only if it is automated or if the data processed are contained or are intended to be contained in a filing system structured according to specific criteria relating to individuals, so as to permit easy access to the personal data in question;

(16) Whereas the processing of sound and image data, such as in cases of video surveillance, does not come within the scope of this Directive if it is carried out for the purposes of public security, defence, national security or in the course of State activities relating to the area of criminal law or of other activities which do not come within the scope of Community law;

(17) Whereas, as far as the processing of sound and image data carried out for purposes of journalism or the purposes of literary or artistic expression is concerned, in particular in the audiovisual field, the principles of the Directive are to apply in a restricted manner according to the provisions laid down in Article 9;

(18) Whereas, in order to ensure that individuals are not deprived of the protection to which they are entitled under this Directive, any processing of personal data in the Community must be carried out in accordance with the law of one of the Member States; whereas, in this connection, processing carried out under the responsibility of a controller who is established in a Member State should be governed by the law of that State;

(19) Whereas establishment on the territory of a Member State implies the effective and real exercise of activity through stable arrangements; whereas the legal form of such an establishment, whether simply branch or a subsidiary with a legal personality, is not the determining factor in this respect; whereas, when a single controller is established on the territory of several Member States, particularly by means of subsidiaries, he must ensure, in order to avoid any circumvention of national rules, that each of the establishments fulfils the obligations imposed by the national law applicable to its activities;

(20) Whereas the fact that the processing of data is carried out by a person established in a third country must not stand in the way of the protection of individuals provided for in this Directive; whereas in these cases, the processing should be governed by the law of the Member State in which the means used are located, and there should be guarantees to ensure that the rights and obligations provided for in this Directive are respected in practice;

(21) Whereas this Directive is without prejudice to the rules of territoriality applicable in criminal matters;

(22) Whereas Member States shall more precisely define in the laws they enact or when bringing into force the measures taken under this Directive the general circumstances in which processing is lawful; whereas in particular Article 5, in conjunction with Articles 7 and 8, allows Member States, independently of general rules, to provide for special processing conditions for specific sectors and for the various categories of data covered by Article 8;

(23) Whereas Member States are empowered to ensure the implementation of the protection of individuals both by means of a general law on the protection of individuals as regards the processing of personal data and by sectorial laws such as those relating, for example, to statistical institutes;

(24) Whereas the legislation concerning the protection of legal persons with regard to the processing data which concerns them is not affected by this Directive;

(25) Whereas the principles of protection must be reflected, on the one hand, in the obligations imposed on persons, public authorities, enterprises, agencies or other bodies responsible for processing, in particular regarding data quality, technical security, notification to the supervisory

authority, and the circumstances under which processing can be carried out, and, on the other hand, in the right conferred on individuals, the data on whom are the subject of processing, to be informed that processing is taking place, to consult the data, to request corrections and even to object to processing in certain circumstances;

(26) Whereas the principles of protection must apply to any information concerning an identified or identifiable person; whereas, to determine whether a person is identifiable, account should be taken of all the means likely reasonably to be used either by the controller or by any other person to identify the said person; whereas the principles of protection shall not apply to data rendered anonymous in such a way that the data subject is no longer identifiable; whereas codes of conduct within the meaning of Article 27 may be a useful instrument for providing guidance as to the ways in which data may be rendered anonymous and retained in a form in which identification of the data subject is no longer possible;

(27) Whereas the protection of individuals must apply as much to automatic processing of data as to manual processing; whereas the scope of this protection must not in effect depend on the techniques used, otherwise this would create a serious risk of circumvention; whereas, nonetheless, as regards manual processing, this Directive covers only filing systems, not unstructured files; whereas, in particular, the content of a filing system must be structured according to specific criteria relating to individuals allowing easy access to the personal data; whereas, in line with the definition in Article 2 (c), the different criteria for determining the constituents of a structured set of personal data, and the different criteria governing access to such a set, may be laid down by each Member State; whereas files or sets of files as well as their cover pages, which are not structured according to specific criteria, shall under no circumstances fall within the scope of this Directive;

(28) Whereas any processing of personal data must be lawful and fair to the individuals concerned; whereas, in particular, the data must be adequate, relevant and not excessive in relation to the purposes for which they are processed; whereas such purposes must be explicit and legitimate and must be determined at the time of collection of the data; whereas the purposes of processing further to collection shall not be incompatible with the purposes as they were originally specified;

(29) Whereas the further processing of personal data for historical, statistical or scientific purposes is not generally to be considered incompatible with the purposes for which the data have previously been collected provided that Member States furnish suitable safeguards; whereas these safeguards must in particular rule out the use of the data in support of measures or decisions regarding any particular individual;

(30) Whereas, in order to be lawful, the processing of personal data must in addition be carried out with the consent of the data subject or be necessary for the conclusion or performance of a contract binding on the data subject, or as a legal requirement, or for the performance of a task carried out in the public interest or in the exercise of official authority, or in the legitimate interests of a natural or legal person, provided that the interests or the rights and freedoms of the data subject are not overriding; whereas, in particular, in order to maintain a balance between the interests involved while guaranteeing effective competition, Member States may determine the circumstances in which personal data may be used or disclosed to a third party in the context of the legitimate ordinary business activities of companies and other bodies; whereas Member States may similarly specify the conditions under which personal data may be disclosed to a third party for the purposes of marketing whether carried out commercially or by a charitable organization or by any other association or foundation, of a political nature for example, subject to the provisions allowing a data subject to object to the processing of data regarding him, at no cost and without having to state his reasons;

(31) Whereas the processing of personal data must equally be regarded as lawful where it is carried out in order to protect an interest which is essential for the data subject's life;

(32) Whereas it is for national legislation to determine whether the controller performing a task carried out in the public interest or in the exercise of official authority should be a public administration or another natural or legal person governed by public law, or by private law such as a professional association;

(33) Whereas data which are capable by their nature of infringing fundamental freedoms or privacy should not be processed unless the data subject gives his explicit consent; whereas, however, derogations from this prohibition must be explicitly provided for in respect of specific needs, in particular where the processing of these data is carried out for certain health-related purposes by persons subject to a legal obligation of professional secrecy or in the course of legitimate activities by certain associations or foundations the purpose of which is to permit the exercise of fundamental freedoms;

(34) Whereas Member States must also be authorized, when justified by grounds of important public interest, to derogate from the prohibition on processing sensitive categories of data where important reasons of public interest so justify in areas such as public health and social protection — especially in order to ensure the quality and cost-effectiveness of the procedures used for settling claims for benefits and services in the health insurance system — scientific research and government statistics; whereas it is

incumbent on them, however, to provide specific and suitable safeguards so as to protect the fundamental rights and the privacy of individuals;

(35) Whereas, moreover, the processing of personal data by official authorities for achieving aims, laid down in constitutional law or international public law, of officially recognized religious associations is carried out on important grounds of public interest;

(36) Whereas where, in the course of electoral activities, the operation of the democratic system requires in certain Member States that political parties compile data on people's political opinion, the processing of such data may be permitted for reasons of important public interest, provided that appropriate safeguards are established;

(37) Whereas the processing of personal data for purposes of journalism or for purposes of literary or artistic expression, in particular in the audiovisual field, should qualify for exemption from the requirements of certain provisions of this Directive in so far as this is necessary to reconcile the fundamental rights of individuals with freedom of information and notably the right to receive and impart information, as guaranteed in particular in Article 10 of the European Convention for the Protection of Human Rights and Fundamental Freedoms; whereas Member States should therefore lay down exemptions and derogations necessary for the purpose of balance between fundamental rights as regards general measures on the legitimacy of data processing, measures on the transfer of data to third countries and the power of the supervisory authority; whereas this should not, however, lead Member States to lay down exemptions from the measures to ensure security of processing; whereas at least the supervisory authority responsible for this sector should also be provided with certain ex-post powers, e.g. to publish a regular report or to refer matters to the judicial authorities;

(38) Whereas, if the processing of data is to be fair, the data subject must be in a position to learn of the existence of a processing operation and, where data are collected from him, must be given accurate and full information, bearing in mind the circumstances of the collection;

(39) Whereas certain processing operations involve data which the controller has not collected directly from the data subject; whereas, furthermore, data can be legitimately disclosed to a third party, even if the disclosure was not anticipated at the time the data were collected from the data subject; whereas, in all these cases, the data subject should be informed when the data are recorded or at the latest when the data are first disclosed to a third party;

(40) Whereas, however, it is not necessary to impose this obligation if the data subject already has the information; whereas, moreover, there will be no such obligation if the recording or disclosure are expressly provided for by law or if the provision of information to the data subject proves impossible or would involve disproportionate efforts, which could be the case where processing is for historical, statistical or scientific purposes; whereas, in this regard, the number of data subjects, the age of the data, and any compensatory measures adopted may be taken into consideration;

(41) Whereas any person must be able to exercise the right of access to data relating to him which are being processed, in order to verify in particular the accuracy of the data and the lawfulness of the processing; whereas, for the same reasons, every data subject must also have the right to know the logic involved in the automatic processing of data concerning him, at least in the case of the automated decisions referred to in Article 15 (1); whereas this right must not adversely affect trade secrets or intellectual property and in particular the copyright protecting the software; whereas these considerations must not, however, result in the data subject being refused all information;

(42) Whereas Member States may, in the interest of the data subject or so as to protect the rights and freedoms of others, restrict rights of access and information; whereas they may, for example, specify that access to medical data may be obtained only through a health professional;

(43) Whereas restrictions on the rights of access and information and on certain obligations of the controller may similarly be imposed by Member States in so far as they are necessary to safeguard, for example, national security, defence, public safety, or important economic or financial interests of a Member State or the Union, as well as criminal investigations and prosecutions and action in respect of breaches of ethics in the regulated professions; whereas the list of exceptions and limitations should include the tasks of monitoring, inspection or regulation necessary in the three last-mentioned areas concerning public security, economic or financial interests and crime prevention; whereas the listing of tasks in these three areas does not affect the legitimacy of exceptions or restrictions for reasons of State security or defence;

(44) Whereas Member States may also be led, by virtue of the provisions of Community law, to derogate from the provisions of this Directive concerning the right of access, the obligation to inform individuals, and the quality of data, in order to secure certain of the purposes referred to above;

(45) Whereas, in cases where data might lawfully be processed on grounds of public interest, official authority or the legitimate interests of a natural or legal person, any data subject should nevertheless be entitled, on legiti-

mate and compelling grounds relating to his particular situation, to object to the processing of any data relating to himself; whereas Member States may nevertheless lay down national provisions to the contrary;

(46) Whereas the protection of the rights and freedoms of data subjects with regard to the processing of personal data requires that appropriate technical and organizational measures be taken, both at the time of the design of the processing system and at the time of the processing itself, particularly in order to maintain security and thereby to prevent any unauthorized processing; whereas it is incumbent on the Member States to ensure that controllers comply with these measures; whereas these measures must ensure an appropriate level of security, taking into account the state of the art and the costs of their implementation in relation to the risks inherent in the processing and the nature of the data to be protected;

(47) Whereas where a message containing personal data is transmitted by means of a telecommunications or electronic mail service, the sole purpose of which is the transmission of such messages, the controller in respect of the personal data contained in the message will normally be considered to be the person from whom the message originates, rather than the person offering the transmission services; whereas, nevertheless, those offering such services will normally be considered controllers in respect of the processing of the additional personal data necessary for the operation of the service;

(48) Whereas the procedures for notifying the supervisory authority are designed to ensure disclosure of the purposes and main features of any processing operation for the purpose of verification that the operation is in accordance with the national measures taken under this Directive;

(49) Whereas, in order to avoid unsuitable administrative formalities, exemptions from the obligation to notify and simplification of the notification required may be provided for by Member States in cases where processing is unlikely adversely to affect the rights and freedoms of data subjects, provided that it is in accordance with a measure taken by a Member State specifying its limits; whereas exemption or simplification may similarly be provided for by Member States where a person appointed by the controller ensures that the processing carried out is not likely adversely to affect the rights and freedoms of data subjects; whereas such a data protection official, whether or not an employee of the controller, must be in a position to exercise his functions in complete independence;

(50) Whereas exemption or simplification could be provided for in cases of processing operations whose sole purpose is the keeping of a register intended, according to national law, to provide information to the public and open to consultation by the public or by any person demonstrating a legitimate interest;

(51) Whereas, nevertheless, simplification or exemption from the obligation to notify shall not release the controller from any of the other obligations resulting from this Directive;

(52) Whereas, in this context, ex post facto verification by the competent authorities must in general be considered a sufficient measure;

(53) Whereas, however, certain processing operations are likely to pose specific risks to the rights and freedoms of data subjects by virtue of their nature, their scope or their purposes, such as that of excluding individuals from a right, benefit or a contract, or by virtue of the specific use of new technologies; whereas it is for Member States, if they so wish, to specify such risks in their legislation;

(54) Whereas with regard to all the processing undertaken in society, the amount posing such specific risks should be very limited; whereas Member States must provide that the supervisory authority, or the data protection official in cooperation with the authority, check such processing prior to it being carried out; whereas following this prior check, the supervisory authority may, according to its national law, give an opinion or an authorization regarding the processing; whereas such checking may equally take place in the course of the preparation either of a measure of the national parliament or of a measure based on such a legislative measure, which defines the nature of the processing and lays down appropriate safeguards;

(55) Whereas, if the controller fails to respect the rights of data subjects, national legislation must provide for a judicial remedy; whereas any damage which a person may suffer as a result of unlawful processing must be compensated for by the controller, who may be exempted from liability if he proves that he is not responsible for the damage, in particular in cases where he establishes fault on the part of the data subject or in case of force majeure; whereas sanctions must be imposed on any person, whether governed by private or public law, who fails to comply with the national measures taken under this Directive;

(56) Whereas cross-border flows of personal data are necessary to the expansion of international trade; whereas the protection of individuals guaranteed in the Community by this Directive does not stand in the way of transfers of personal data to third countries which ensure an adequate level of protection; whereas the adequacy of the level of protection afforded by a third country must be assessed in the light of all the circumstances surrounding the transfer operation or set of transfer operations;

(57) Whereas, on the other hand, the transfer of personal data to a third country which does not ensure an adequate level of protection must be prohibited;

(58) Whereas provisions should be made for exemptions from this prohibition in certain circumstances where the data subject has given his consent, where the transfer is necessary in relation to a contract or a legal claim, where protection of an important public interest so requires, for example in cases of international transfers of data between tax or customs administrations or between services competent for social security matters, or where the transfer is made from a register established by law and intended for consultation by the public or persons having a legitimate interest; whereas in this case such a transfer should not involve the entirety of the data or entire categories of the data contained in the register and, when the register is intended for consultation by persons having a legitimate interest, the transfer should be made only at the request of those persons or if they are to be the recipients;

(59) Whereas particular measures may be taken to compensate for the lack of protection in a third country in cases where the controller offers appropriate safeguards; whereas, moreover, provision must be made for procedures for negotiations between the Community and such third countries;

(60) Whereas, in any event, transfers to third countries may be effected only in full compliance with the provisions adopted by the Member States pursuant to this Directive, and in particular Article 8 thereof;

(61) Whereas Member States and the Commission, in their respective spheres of competence, must encourage the trade associations and other representative organizations concerned to draw up codes of conduct so as to facilitate the application of this Directive, taking account of the specific characteristics of the processing carried out in certain sectors, and respecting the national provisions adopted for its implementation;

(62) Whereas the establishment in Member States of supervisory authorities, exercising their functions with complete independence, is an essential component of the protection of individuals with regard to the processing of personal data;

(63) Whereas such authorities must have the necessary means to perform their duties, including powers of investigation and intervention, particularly in cases of complaints from individuals, and powers to engage in legal proceedings; whereas such authorities must help to ensure transparency of processing in the Member States within whose jurisdiction they fall;

(64) Whereas the authorities in the different Member States will need to assist one another in performing their duties so as to ensure that the rules of protection are properly respected throughout the [4] European Union;

---

[4]   OJ No L 197, 18.7.1987, p. 33.

(65) Whereas, at Community level, a Working Party on the Protection of Individuals with regard to the Processing of Personal Data must be set up and be completely independent in the performance of its functions; whereas, having regard to its specific nature, it must advise the Commission and, in particular, contribute to the uniform application of the national rules adopted pursuant to this Directive;

(66) Whereas, with regard to the transfer of data to third countries, the application of this Directive calls for the conferment of powers of implementation on the Commission and the establishment of a procedure as laid down in Council Decision 87/373/EEC;

(67) Whereas an agreement on a modus vivendi between the European Parliament, the Council and the Commission concerning the implementing measures for acts adopted in accordance with the procedure laid down in Article 189b of the EC Treaty was reached on 20 December 1994;

(68) Whereas the principles set out in this Directive regarding the protection of the rights and freedoms of individuals, notably their right to privacy, with regard to the processing of personal data may be supplemented or clarified, in particular as far as certain sectors are concerned, by specific rules based on those principles;

(69) Whereas Member States should be allowed a period of not more than three years from the entry into force of the national measures transposing this Directive in which to apply such new national rules progressively to all processing operations already under way; whereas, in order to facilitate their cost-effective implementation, a further period expiring 12 years after the date on which this Directive is adopted will be allowed to Member States to ensure the conformity of existing manual filing systems with certain of the Directive's provisions; whereas, where data contained in such filing systems are manually processed during this extended transition period, those systems must be brought into conformity with these provisions at the time of such processing;

(70) Whereas it is not necessary for the data subject to give his consent again so as to allow the controller to continue to process, after the national provisions taken pursuant to this Directive enter into force, any sensitive data necessary for the performance of a contract concluded on the basis of free and informed consent before the entry into force of these provisions;

(71) Whereas this Directive does not stand in the way of a Member State's regulating marketing activities aimed at consumers residing in territory in so far as such regulation does not concern the protection of individuals with regard to the processing of personal data;

(72) Whereas this Directive allows the principle of public access to official documents to be taken into account when implementing the principles set out in this Directive,

HAVE ADOPTED THIS DIRECTIVE:

CHAPTER I: GENERAL PROVISIONS

Article 1

Object of the Directive

1. In accordance with this Directive, Member States shall protect the fundamental rights and freedoms of natural persons, and in particular their right to privacy with respect to the processing of personal data.

2. Member States shall neither restrict nor prohibit the free flow of personal data between Member States for reasons connected with the protection afforded under paragraph 1.

Article 2

Definitions

For the purposes of this Directive:

(a) 'personal data' shall mean any information relating to an identified or identifiable natural person ('data subject'); an identifiable person is one who can be identified, directly or indirectly, in particular by reference to an identification number or to one or more factors specific to his physical, physiological, mental, economic, cultural or social identity;

(b) 'processing of personal data' ('processing') shall mean any operation or set of operations which is performed upon personal data, whether or not by automatic means, such as collection, recording, organization, storage, adaptation or alteration, retrieval, consultation, use, disclosure by transmission, dissemination or otherwise making available, alignment or combination, blocking, erasure or destruction;

(c) 'personal data filing system' ('filing system') shall mean any structured set of personal data which are accessible according to specific criteria, whether centralized, decentralized or dispersed on a functional or geographical basis;

(d) 'controller' shall mean the natural or legal person, public authority, agency or any other body which alone or jointly with others determines the purposes and means of the processing of personal data; where the purposes and means of processing are determined by national or Community laws or regulations, the controller or the specific criteria for his nomination may be designated by national or Community law;

(e) 'processor' shall mean a natural or legal person, public authority, agency or any other body which processes personal data on behalf of the controller;

(f) 'third party' shall mean any natural or legal person, public authority, agency or any other body other than the data subject, the controller, the processor and the persons who, under the direct authority of the controller or the processor, are authorized to process the data;

(g) 'recipient' shall mean a natural or legal person, public authority, agency or any other body to whom data are disclosed, whether a third party or not; however, authorities which may receive data in the framework of a particular inquiry shall not be regarded as recipients;

(h) 'the data subject's consent' shall mean any freely given specific and informed indication of his wishes by which the data subject signifies his agreement to personal data relating to him being processed.

Article 3
Scope

1. This Directive shall apply to the processing of personal data wholly or partly by automatic means, and to the processing otherwise than by automatic means of personal data which form part of a filing system or are intended to form part of a filing system.

2. This Directive shall not apply to the processing of personal data:

– in the course of an activity which falls outside the scope of Community law, such as those provided for by Titles V and VI of the Treaty on European Union and in any case to processing operations concerning public security, defence, State security (including the economic well-being of the State when the processing operation relates to State security matters) and the activities of the State in areas of criminal law,

– by a natural person in the course of a purely personal or household activity.

Article 4
National law applicable

1. Each Member State shall apply the national provisions it adopts pursuant to this Directive to the processing of personal data where:

(a) the processing is carried out in the context of the activities of an establishment of the controller on the territory of the Member State; when the same controller is established on the territory of several Member States, he must take the necessary measures to ensure that each of these establishments complies with the obligations laid down by the national law applicable;

(b) the controller is not established on the Member State's territory, but in a place where its national law applies by virtue of international public law;

(c) the controller is not established on Community territory and, for purposes of processing personal data makes use of equipment, automated or otherwise, situated on the territory of the said Member State, unless such equipment is used only for purposes of transit through the territory of the Community.

2. In the circumstances referred to in paragraph 1 (c), the controller must designate a representative established in the territory of that Member State, without prejudice to legal actions which could be initiated against the controller himself.

CHAPTER II: GENERAL RULES ON THE LAWFULNESS OF THE PROCESSING OF PERSONAL DATA

Article 5

Member States shall, within the limits of the provisions of this Chapter, determine more precisely the conditions under which the processing of personal data is lawful.

SECTION I
PRINCIPLES RELATING TO DATA QUALITY

Article 6

1. Member States shall provide that personal data must be:

(a) processed fairly and lawfully;

(b) collected for specified, explicit and legitimate purposes and not further processed in a way incompatible with those purposes. Further processing of data for historical, statistical or scientific purposes shall not be considered as incompatible provided that Member States provide appropriate safeguards;

(c) adequate, relevant and not excessive in relation to the purposes for which they are collected and/or further processed;

(d) accurate and, where necessary, kept up to date; every reasonable step must be taken to ensure that data which are inaccurate or incomplete, having regard to the purposes for which they were collected or for which they are further processed, are erased or rectified;

(e) kept in a form which permits identification of data subjects for no longer than is necessary for the purposes for which the data were collected or for which they are further processed. Member States shall lay down appropriate safeguards for personal data stored for longer periods for historical, statistical or scientific use.

2. It shall be for the controller to ensure that paragraph 1 is complied with.

SECTION II
CRITERIA FOR MAKING DATA PROCESSING LEGITIMATE

Article 7

Member States shall provide that personal data may be processed only if:

(a) the data subject has unambiguously given his consent; or

(b) processing is necessary for the performance of a contract to which the data subject is party or in order to take steps at the request of the data subject prior to entering into a contract; or

(c) processing is necessary for compliance with a legal obligation to which the controller is subject; or

(d) processing is necessary in order to protect the vital interests of the data subject; or

(e) processing is necessary for the performance of a task carried out in the public interest or in the exercise of official authority vested in the controller or in a third party to whom the data are disclosed; or

(f) processing is necessary for the purposes of the legitimate interests pursued by the controller or by the third party or parties to whom the data are disclosed, except where such interests are overridden by the interests for fundamental rights and freedoms of the data subject which require protection under Article 1 (1).

SECTION III
SPECIAL CATEGORIES OF PROCESSING

Article 8

The processing of special categories of data

1. Member States shall prohibit the processing of personal data revealing racial or ethnic origin, political opinions, religious or philosophical beliefs, trade-union membership, and the processing of data concerning health or sex life.

2. Paragraph 1 shall not apply where:

(a) the data subject has given his explicit consent to the processing of those data, except where the laws of the Member State provide that the prohibition referred to in paragraph 1 may not be lifted by the data subject's giving his consent; or

(b) processing is necessary for the purposes of carrying out the obligations and specific rights of the controller in the field of employment law in so far as it is authorized by national law providing for adequate safeguards; or

(c) processing is necessary to protect the vital interests of the data subject or of another person where the data subject is physically or legally incapable of giving his consent; or

(d) processing is carried out in the course of its legitimate activities with appropriate guarantees by a foundation, association or any other non-profit-seeking body with a political, philosophical, religious or trade-union aim and on condition that the processing relates solely to the members of the body or to persons who have regular contact with it in connection with its purposes and that the data are not disclosed to a third party without the consent of the data subjects; or

(e) the processing relates to data which are manifestly made public by the data subject or is necessary for the establishment, exercise or defence of legal claims.

3. Paragraph 1 shall not apply where processing of the data is required for the purposes of preventive medicine, medical diagnosis, the provision of care or treatment or the management of health-care services, and where those data are processed by a health professional subject under national law or rules established by national competent bodies to the obligation of professional secrecy or by another person also subject to an equivalent obligation of secrecy.

4. Subject to the provision of suitable safeguards, Member States may, for reasons of substantial public interest, lay down exemptions in addition to those laid down in paragraph 2 either by national law or by decision of the supervisory authority.

5. Processing of data relating to offences, criminal convictions or security measures may be carried out only under the control of official authority, or if suitable specific safeguards are provided under national law, subject to derogations which may be granted by the Member State under national provisions providing suitable specific safeguards. However, a complete register of criminal convictions may be kept only under the control of official authority.

Member States may provide that data relating to administrative sanctions or judgements in civil cases shall also be processed under the control of official authority.

6. Derogations from paragraph 1 provided for in paragraphs 4 and 5 shall be notified to the Commission.

7. Member States shall determine the conditions under which a national identification number or any other identifier of general application may be processed.

Article 9

Processing of personal data and freedom of expression

Member States shall provide for exemptions or derogations from the provisions of this Chapter, Chapter IV and Chapter VI for the processing of personal data carried out solely for journalistic purposes or the purpose of artistic or literary expression only if they are necessary to reconcile the right to privacy with the rules governing freedom of expression.

SECTION IV
INFORMATION TO BE GIVEN TO THE DATA SUBJECT

Article 10

Information in cases of collection of data from the data subject

Member States shall provide that the controller or his representative must provide a data subject from whom data relating to himself are collected with at least the following information, except where he already has it:

(a) the identity of the controller and of his representative, if any;

(b) the purposes of the processing for which the data are intended;

(c) any further information such as

– the recipients or categories of recipients of the data,

– whether replies to the questions are obligatory or voluntary, as well as the possible consequences of failure to reply,

– the existence of the right of access to and the right to rectify the data concerning him in so far as such further information is necessary, having regard to the specific circumstances in which the data are collected, to guarantee fair processing in respect of the data subject.

Article 11

Information where the data have not been obtained from the data subject

1. Where the data have not been obtained from the data subject, Member States shall provide that the controller or his representative must at the time of undertaking the recording of personal data or if a disclosure to a third party is envisaged, no later than the time when the data are first disclosed provide the data subject with at least the following information, except where he already has it:

(a) the identity of the controller and of his representative, if any;

(b) the purposes of the processing;

(c) any further information such as

– the categories of data concerned,

– the recipients or categories of recipients,

– the existence of the right of access to and the right to rectify the data concerning him in so far as such further information is necessary, having regard to the specific circumstances in which the data are processed, to guarantee fair processing in respect of the data subject.

2. Paragraph 1 shall not apply where, in particular for processing for statistical purposes or for the purposes of historical or scientific research, the provision of such information proves impossible or would involve a disproportionate effort or if recording or disclosure is expressly laid down by law. In these cases Member States shall provide appropriate safeguards.

SECTION V
THE DATA SUBJECT'S RIGHT OF ACCESS TO DATA

Article 12

Right of access

Member States shall guarantee every data subject the right to obtain from the controller:

(a) without constraint at reasonable intervals and without excessive delay or expense:

– confirmation as to whether or not data relating to him are being processed and information at least as to the purposes of the processing, the categories of data concerned, and the recipients or categories of recipients to whom the data are disclosed,

– communication to him in an intelligible form of the data undergoing processing and of any available information as to their source,

– knowledge of the logic involved in any automatic processing of data concerning him at least in the case of the automated decisions referred to in Article 15 (1);

(b) as appropriate the rectification, erasure or blocking of data the processing of which does not comply with the provisions of this Directive, in particular because of the incomplete or inaccurate nature of the data;

(c) notification to third parties to whom the data have been disclosed of any rectification, erasure or blocking carried out in compliance with (b), unless this proves impossible or involves a disproportionate effort.

SECTION VI
EXEMPTIONS AND RESTRICTIONS

Article 13
Exemptions and restrictions

1. Member States may adopt legislative measures to restrict the scope of the obligations and rights provided for in Articles 6 (1), 10, 11 (1), 12 and 21 when such a restriction constitutes a necessary measure to safeguard:

(a) national security;

(b) defence;

(c) public security;

(d) the prevention, investigation, detection and prosecution of criminal offences, or of breaches of ethics for regulated professions;

(e) an important economic or financial interest of a Member State or of the European Union, including monetary, budgetary and taxation matters;

(f) a monitoring, inspection or regulatory function connected, even occasionally, with the exercise of official authority in cases referred to in (c), (d) and (e);

(g) the protection of the data subject or of the rights and freedoms of others.

2. Subject to adequate legal safeguards, in particular that the data are not used for taking measures or decisions regarding any particular individual, Member States may, where there is clearly no risk of breaching the privacy of the data subject, restrict by a legislative measure the rights provided for in Article 12 when data are processed solely for purposes of scientific research or are kept in personal form for a period which does not exceed the period necessary for the sole purpose of creating statistics.

SECTION VII
THE DATA SUBJECT'S RIGHT TO OBJECT

Article 14
The data subject's right to object

Member States shall grant the data subject the right:

(a) at least in the cases referred to in Article 7 (e) and (f), to object at any time on compelling legitimate grounds relating to his particular situation to the processing of data relating to him, save where otherwise provided by national legislation. Where there is a justified objection, the processing instigated by the controller may no longer involve those data;

(b) to object, on request and free of charge, to the processing of personal data relating to him which the controller anticipates being processed for the purposes of direct marketing, or to be informed before personal data are disclosed for the first time to third parties or used on their behalf for the purposes of direct marketing, and to be expressly offered the right to object free of charge to such disclosures or uses.

Member States shall take the necessary measures to ensure that data subjects are aware of the existence of the right referred to in the first subparagraph of (b).

Article 15
Automated individual decisions

1. Member States shall grant the right to every person not to be subject to a decision which produces legal effects concerning him or significantly affects him and which is based solely on automated processing of data intended to evaluate certain personal aspects relating to him, such as his performance at work, creditworthiness, reliability, conduct, etc.

2. Subject to the other Articles of this Directive, Member States shall provide that a person may be subjected to a decision of the kind referred to in paragraph 1 if that decision:

(a) is taken in the course of the entering into or performance of a contract, provided the request for the entering into or the performance of the contract, lodged by the data subject, has been satisfied or that there are suitable measures to safeguard his legitimate interests, such as arrangements allowing him to put his point of view; or

(b) is authorized by a law which also lays down measures to safeguard the data subject's legitimate interests.

SECTION VIII
CONFIDENTIALITY AND SECURITY OF PROCESSING

Article 16
Confidentiality of processing

Any person acting under the authority of the controller or of the processor, including the processor himself, who has access to personal data must not process them except on instructions from the controller, unless he is required to do so by law.

Article 17

Security of processing

1. Member States shall provide that the controller must implement appropriate technical and organizational measures to protect personal data against accidental or unlawful destruction or accidental loss, alteration, unauthorized disclosure or access, in particular where the processing involves the transmission of data over a network, and against all other unlawful forms of processing.

Having regard to the state of the art and the cost of their implementation, such measures shall ensure a level of security appropriate to the risks represented by the processing and the nature of the data to be protected.

2. The Member States shall provide that the controller must, where processing is carried out on his behalf, choose a processor providing sufficient guarantees in respect of the technical security measures and organizational measures governing the processing to be carried out, and must ensure compliance with those measures.

3. The carrying out of processing by way of a processor must be governed by a contract or legal act binding the processor to the controller and stipulating in particular that:

– the processor shall act only on instructions from the controller,

– the obligations set out in paragraph 1, as defined by the law of the Member State in which the processor is established, shall also be incumbent on the processor.

4. For the purposes of keeping proof, the parts of the contract or the legal act relating to data protection and the requirements relating to the measures referred to in paragraph 1 shall be in writing or in another equivalent form.

SECTION IX
NOTIFICATION

Article 18

Obligation to notify the supervisory authority

1. Member States shall provide that the controller or his representative, if any, must notify the supervisory authority referred to in Article 28 before carrying out any wholly or partly automatic processing operation or set of such operations intended to serve a single purpose or several related purposes.

2. Member States may provide for the simplification of or exemption from notification only in the following cases and under the following conditions:

– where, for categories of processing operations which are unlikely, taking account of the data to be processed, to affect adversely the rights and freedoms of data subjects, they specify the purposes of the processing, the data or categories of data undergoing processing, the category or categories of data subject, the recipients or categories of recipient to whom the data are to be disclosed and the length of time the data are to be stored, and/or

– where the controller, in compliance with the national law which governs him, appoints a personal data protection official, responsible in particular:

– for ensuring in an independent manner the internal application of the national provisions taken pursuant to this Directive,

– for keeping the register of processing operations carried out by the controller, containing the items of information referred to in Article 21 (2), thereby ensuring that the rights and freedoms of the data subjects are unlikely to be adversely affected by the processing operations.

3. Member States may provide that paragraph 1 does not apply to processing whose sole purpose is the keeping of a register which according to laws or regulations is intended to provide information to the public and which is open to consultation either by the public in general or by any person demonstrating a legitimate interest.

4. Member States may provide for an exemption from the obligation to notify or a simplification of the notification in the case of processing operations referred to in Article 8 (2) (d).

5. Member States may stipulate that certain or all non-automatic processing operations involving personal data shall be notified, or provide for these processing operations to be subject to simplified notification.

Article 19
Contents of notification

1. Member States shall specify the information to be given in the notification. It shall include at least:

(a) the name and address of the controller and of his representative, if any;

(b) the purpose or purposes of the processing;

(c) a description of the category or categories of data subject and of the data or categories of data relating to them;

(d) the recipients or categories of recipient to whom the data might be disclosed;

(e) proposed transfers of data to third countries;

(f) a general description allowing a preliminary assessment to be made of the appropriateness of the measures taken pursuant to Article 17 to ensure security of processing.

2. Member States shall specify the procedures under which any change affecting the information referred to in paragraph 1 must be notified to the supervisory authority.

Article 20
Prior checking

1. Member States shall determine the processing operations likely to present specific risks to the rights and freedoms of data subjects and shall check that these processing operations are examined prior to the start thereof.

2. Such prior checks shall be carried out by the supervisory authority following receipt of a notification from the controller or by the data protection official, who, in cases of doubt, must consult the supervisory authority.

3. Member States may also carry out such checks in the context of preparation either of a measure of the national parliament or of a measure based on such a legislative measure, which define the nature of the processing and lay down appropriate safeguards.

Article 21
Publicizing of processing operations

1. Member States shall take measures to ensure that processing operations are publicized.

2. Member States shall provide that a register of processing operations notified in accordance with Article 18 shall be kept by the supervisory authority.

The register shall contain at least the information listed in Article 19 (1) (a) to (e).

The register may be inspected by any person.

3. Member States shall provide, in relation to processing operations not subject to notification, that controllers or another body appointed by the Member States make available at least the information referred to in Article 19 (1) (a) to (e) in an appropriate form to any person on request.

Member States may provide that this provision does not apply to processing whose sole purpose is the keeping of a register which according to laws or regulations is intended to provide information to the public and which is open to consultation either by the public in general or by any person who can provide proof of a legitimate interest.

CHAPTER III: JUDICIAL REMEDIES, LIABILITY AND SANCTIONS

Article 22

Remedies

Without prejudice to any administrative remedy for which provision may be made, inter alia before the supervisory authority referred to in Article 28, prior to referral to the judicial authority, Member States shall provide for the right of every person to a judicial remedy for any breach of the rights guaranteed him by the national law applicable to the processing in question.

Article 23

Liability

1. Member States shall provide that any person who has suffered damage as a result of an unlawful processing operation or of any act incompatible with the national provisions adopted pursuant to this Directive is entitled to receive compensation from the controller for the damage suffered.

2. The controller may be exempted from this liability, in whole or in part, if he proves that he is not responsible for the event giving rise to the damage.

Article 24

Sanctions

The Member States shall adopt suitable measures to ensure the full implementation of the provisions of this Directive and shall in particular lay down the sanctions to be imposed in case of infringement of the provisions adopted pursuant to this Directive.

CHAPTER IV: TRANSFER OF PERSONAL DATA TO THIRD COUNTRIES

Article 25

Principles

1. The Member States shall provide that the transfer to a third country of personal data which are undergoing processing or are intended for processing after transfer may take place only if, without prejudice to compliance with the national provisions adopted pursuant to the other provisions of this Directive, the third country in question ensures an adequate level of protection.

2. The adequacy of the level of protection afforded by a third country shall be assessed in the light of all the circumstances surrounding a data transfer operation or set of data transfer operations; particular consideration shall be given to the nature of the data, the purpose and duration of the pro-

posed processing operation or operations, the country of origin and country of final destination, the rules of law, both general and sectoral, in force in the third country in question and the professional rules and security measures which are complied with in that country.

3. The Member States and the Commission shall inform each other of cases where they consider that a third country does not ensure an adequate level of protection within the meaning of paragraph 2.

4. Where the Commission finds, under the procedure provided for in Article 31 (2), that a third country does not ensure an adequate level of protection within the meaning of paragraph 2 of this Article, Member States shall take the measures necessary to prevent any transfer of data of the same type to the third country in question.

5. At the appropriate time, the Commission shall enter into negotiations with a view to remedying the situation resulting from the finding made pursuant to paragraph 4.

6. The Commission may find, in accordance with the procedure referred to in Article 31 (2), that a third country ensures an adequate level of protection within the meaning of paragraph 2 of this Article, by reason of its domestic law or of the international commitments it has entered into, particularly upon conclusion of the negotiations referred to in paragraph 5, for the protection of the private lives and basic freedoms and rights of individuals.

Member States shall take the measures necessary to comply with the Commission's decision.

Article 26

Derogations

1. By way of derogation from Article 25 and save where otherwise provided by domestic law governing particular cases, Member States shall provide that a transfer or a set of transfers of personal data to a third country which does not ensure an adequate level of protection within the meaning of Article 25 (2) may take place on condition that:

(a) the data subject has given his consent unambiguously to the proposed transfer; or

(b) the transfer is necessary for the performance of a contract between the data subject and the controller or the implementation of precontractual measures taken in response to the data subject's request; or

(c) the transfer is necessary for the conclusion or performance of a contract concluded in the interest of the data subject between the controller and a third party; or

(d) the transfer is necessary or legally required on important public interest grounds, or for the establishment, exercise or defence of legal claims; or

(e) the transfer is necessary in order to protect the vital interests of the data subject; or

(f) the transfer is made from a register which according to laws or regulations is intended to provide information to the public and which is open to consultation either by the public in general or by any person who can demonstrate legitimate interest, to the extent that the conditions laid down in law for consultation are fulfilled in the particular case.

2. Without prejudice to paragraph 1, a Member State may authorize a transfer or a set of transfers of personal data to a third country which does not ensure an adequate level of protection within the meaning of Article 25 (2), where the controller adduces adequate safeguards with respect to the protection of the privacy and fundamental rights and freedoms of individuals and as regards the exercise of the corresponding rights; such safeguards may in particular result from appropriate contractual clauses.

3. The Member State shall inform the Commission and the other Member States of the authorizations it grants pursuant to paragraph 2.

If a Member State or the Commission objects on justified grounds involving the protection of the privacy and fundamental rights and freedoms of individuals, the Commission shall take appropriate measures in accordance with the procedure laid down in Article 31 (2).

Member States shall take the necessary measures to comply with the Commission's decision.

4. Where the Commission decides, in accordance with the procedure referred to in Article 31 (2), that certain standard contractual clauses offer sufficient safeguards as required by paragraph 2, Member States shall take the necessary measures to comply with the Commission's decision.

CHAPTER V: CODES OF CONDUCT

Article 27

1. The Member States and the Commission shall encourage the drawing up of codes of conduct intended to contribute to the proper implementation of the national provisions adopted by the Member States pursuant to this Directive, taking account of the specific features of the various sectors.

2. Member States shall make provision for trade associations and other bodies representing other categories of controllers which have drawn up draft national codes or which have the intention of amending or extending

existing national codes to be able to submit them to the opinion of the national authority.

Member States shall make provision for this authority to ascertain, among other things, whether the drafts submitted to it are in accordance with the national provisions adopted pursuant to this Directive. If it sees fit, the authority shall seek the views of data subjects or their representatives.

3. Draft Community codes, and amendments or extensions to existing Community codes, may be submitted to the Working Party referred to in Article 29. This Working Party shall determine, among other things, whether the drafts submitted to it are in accordance with the national provisions adopted pursuant to this Directive. If it sees fit, the authority shall seek the views of data subjects or their representatives. The Commission may ensure appropriate publicity for the codes which have been approved by the Working Party.

CHAPTER VI: SUPERVISORY AUTHORITY AND WORKING PARTY ON THE PROTECTION OF INDIVIDUALS WITH REGARD TO THE PROCESSING OF PERSONAL DATA

Article 28
Supervisory authority

1. Each Member State shall provide that one or more public authorities are responsible for monitoring the application within its territory of the provisions adopted by the Member States pursuant to this Directive.

These authorities shall act with complete independence in exercising the functions entrusted to them.

2. Each Member State shall provide that the supervisory authorities are consulted when drawing up administrative measures or regulations relating to the protection of individuals' rights and freedoms with regard to the processing of personal data.

3. Each authority shall in particular be endowed with:

– investigative powers, such as powers of access to data forming the subject-matter of processing operations and powers to collect all the information necessary for the performance of its supervisory duties,

– effective powers of intervention, such as, for example, that of delivering opinions before processing operations are carried out, in accordance with Article 20, and ensuring appropriate publication of such opinions, of ordering the blocking, erasure or destruction of data, of imposing a temporary or definitive ban on processing, of warning or admonishing the controller, or that of referring the matter to national parliaments or other political institutions,

– the power to engage in legal proceedings where the national provisions adopted pursuant to this Directive have been violated or to bring these violations to the attention of the judicial authorities.

Decisions by the supervisory authority which give rise to complaints may be appealed against through the courts.

4. Each supervisory authority shall hear claims lodged by any person, or by an association representing that person, concerning the protection of his rights and freedoms in regard to the processing of personal data. The person concerned shall be informed of the outcome of the claim.

Each supervisory authority shall, in particular, hear claims for checks on the lawfulness of data processing lodged by any person when the national provisions adopted pursuant to Article 13 of this Directive apply. The person shall at any rate be informed that a check has taken place.

5. Each supervisory authority shall draw up a report on its activities at regular intervals. The report shall be made public.

6. Each supervisory authority is competent, whatever the national law applicable to the processing in question, to exercise, on the territory of its own Member State, the powers conferred on it in accordance with paragraph 3. Each authority may be requested to exercise its powers by an authority of another Member State.

The supervisory authorities shall cooperate with one another to the extent necessary for the performance of their duties, in particular by exchanging all useful information.

7. Member States shall provide that the members and staff of the supervisory authority, even after their employment has ended, are to be subject to a duty of professional secrecy with regard to confidential information to which they have access.

Article 29
Working Party on the Protection of Individuals with regard to the Processing of Personal Data

1. A Working Party on the Protection of Individuals with regard to the Processing of Personal Data, hereinafter referred to as 'the Working Party', is hereby set up.

It shall have advisory status and act independently.

2. The Working Party shall be composed of a representative of the supervisory authority or authorities designated by each Member State and of a representative of the authority or authorities established for the Community institutions and bodies, and of a representative of the Commission.

Each member of the Working Party shall be designated by the institution, authority or authorities which he represents. Where a Member State has designated more than one supervisory authority, they shall nominate a joint representative. The same shall apply to the authorities established for Community institutions and bodies.

3. The Working Party shall take decisions by a simple majority of the representatives of the supervisory authorities.

4. The Working Party shall elect its chairman. The chairman's term of office shall be two years. His appointment shall be renewable.

5. The Working Party's secretariat shall be provided by the Commission.

6. The Working Party shall adopt its own rules of procedure.

7. The Working Party shall consider items placed on its agenda by its chairman, either on his own initiative or at the request of a representative of the supervisory authorities or at the Commission's request.

Article 30

1. The Working Party shall:

(a) examine any question covering the application of the national measures adopted under this Directive in order to contribute to the uniform application of such measures;

(b) give the Commission an opinion on the level of protection in the Community and in third countries;

(c) advise the Commission on any proposed amendment of this Directive, on any additional or specific measures to safeguard the rights and freedoms of natural persons with regard to the processing of personal data and on any other proposed Community measures affecting such rights and freedoms;

(d) give an opinion on codes of conduct drawn up at Community level.

2. If the Working Party finds that divergences likely to affect the equivalence of protection for persons with regard to the processing of personal data in the Community are arising between the laws or practices of Member States, it shall inform the Commission accordingly.

3. The Working Party may, on its own initiative, make recommendations on all matters relating to the protection of persons with regard to the processing of personal data in the Community.

4. The Working Party's opinions and recommendations shall be forwarded to the Commission and to the committee referred to in Article 31.

5. The Commission shall inform the Working Party of the action it has taken in response to its opinions and recommendations. It shall do so in a report which shall also be forwarded to the European Parliament and the Council. The report shall be made public.

6. The Working Party shall draw up an annual report on the situation regarding the protection of natural persons with regard to the processing of personal data in the Community and in third countries, which it shall transmit to the Commission, the European Parliament and the Council. The report shall be made public.

CHAPTER VII: COMMUNITY IMPLEMENTING MEASURES

Article 31

The Committee

1. The Commission shall be assisted by a committee composed of the representatives of the Member States and chaired by the representative of the Commission.

2. The representative of the Commission shall submit to the committee a draft of the measures to be taken. The committee shall deliver its opinion on the draft within a time limit which the chairman may lay down according to the urgency of the matter.

The opinion shall be delivered by the majority laid down in Article 148 (2) of the Treaty. The votes of the representatives of the Member States within the committee shall be weighted in the manner set out in that Article. The chairman shall not vote.

The Commission shall adopt measures which shall apply immediately. However, if these measures are not in accordance with the opinion of the committee, they shall be communicated by the Commission to the Council forthwith. In that event:

– the Commission shall defer application of the measures which it has decided for a period of three months from the date of communication,

– the Council, acting by a qualified majority, may take a different decision within the time limit referred to in the first indent.

FINAL PROVISIONS

Article 32

1. Member States shall bring into force the laws, regulations and administrative provisions necessary to comply with this Directive at the latest at the end of a period of three years from the date of its adoption.

When Member States adopt these measures, they shall contain a reference to this Directive or be accompanied by such reference on the occasion of their official publication. The methods of making such reference shall be laid down by the Member States.

2. Member States shall ensure that processing already under way on the date the national provisions adopted pursuant to this Directive enter into force, is brought into conformity with these provisions within three years of this date.

By way of derogation from the preceding subparagraph, Member States may provide that the processing of data already held in manual filing systems on the date of entry into force of the national provisions adopted in implementation of this Directive shall be brought into conformity with Articles 6, 7 and 8 of this Directive within 12 years of the date on which it is adopted. Member States shall, however, grant the data subject the right to obtain, at his request and in particular at the time of exercising his right of access, the rectification, erasure or blocking of data which are incomplete, inaccurate or stored in a way incompatible with the legitimate purposes pursued by the controller.

3. By way of derogation from paragraph 2, Member States may provide, subject to suitable safeguards, that data kept for the sole purpose of historical research need not be brought into conformity with Articles 6, 7 and 8 of this Directive.

4. Member States shall communicate to the Commission the text of the provisions of domestic law which they adopt in the field covered by this Directive.

Article 33

The Commission shall report to the Council and the European Parliament at regular intervals, starting not later than three years after the date referred to in Article 32 (1), on the implementation of this Directive, attaching to its report, if necessary, suitable proposals for amendments. The report shall be made public.

The Commission shall examine, in particular, the application of this Directive to the data processing of sound and image data relating to natural persons and shall submit any appropriate proposals which prove to be necessary, taking account of developments in information technology and in the light of the state of progress in the information society.

Article 34

This Directive is addressed to the Member States.

Done at Luxembourg, 24 October 1995.
For the European Parliament
The President
K. Haensch
For the Council
The President
L. Atienza Serna

FEDERAL COURT OF CANADA REGISTRY OFFICES

Note: Telecommunications Device for the Hearing Impaired: (TDD)

PRINCIPAL REGISTRY OFFICE

90 Elgin Street
Ottawa, Ontario
K1A 0H9

Appeal Division: (613) 996-6795
Facsimile: (613) 952-7226
(TDD): (613) 947-0407

Trial Division
(Non-Immigration): (613) 992-4238
Facsimile: (613) 952-3653
(TDD): (613) 947-0406

Trial Division (Immigration):
(613) 995-9177
Facsimile: (613) 947-2141
(TDD): (613) 947-4098

ALBERTA

Calgary

635 Eight Avenue, S.W.
3rd and 4th Floors
Calgary, Alberta T2P 3M3

Telephone: (403) 292-5920
Facsimile: (403) 292-5329
(TDD): (403) 292-5879

Edmonton

Scotia Place
10060 Jasper Avenue
Tower 1, Suite 530
P.O. Box 51
Edmonton, Alberta T5J 3R8

Telephone: (780) 495-4651
Facsimile: 495-4681
(TDD): 495-2428

BRITISH COLUMBIA

Vancouver

Pacific Centre
P.O. Box 10065
700 West Georgia Street, 16th Floor
Toronto Dominion Tower
Vancouver, British Columbia V7Y 1B6

Telephone: (604) 666-3232
Facsimile: (604) 666-8181
(TDD): (604) 666-9228

MANITOBA

Winnipeg

363 Broadway
4th Floor
Winnipeg, Manitoba R3C 3N9

Telephone: (204) 983-2509
Facsimile: (204) 983-7636
(TDD): (204) 984-4440

NEW BRUNSWICK

Fredericton

82 Westmorland Street
Suite 100
Fredericton, New Brunswick E3B 3L3

Telephone: (506)452-3016
Facsimile: 452-3584
(TDD): 452-3036

Saint John

The Provincial Building
110 Charlotte Street
4th Floor, Room 413
Saint John, New Brunswick E2L 2J4

Telephone: (506) 636-4990
Facsimile: (506) 658-3070

NEWFOUNDLAND

St. John's

The Court House
Duckworth Street
P.O. Box 937
St. John's, Newfoundland A1C 5M3

Telephone: (709) 772-2884
Facsimile: (709) 772-6351

NORTHWEST TERRITORIES

Yellowknife

The Court House
4905 - 49th Street
P.O. Box 1320
Yellowknife, Northwest Territories X1A 2L9

Telephone: (867) 873-2044
Facsimile: (867) 873-0291

NOVA SCOTIA

Halifax

1801 Hollis Street, 17th Floor
Suite 1720
Halifax, Nova Scotia
B3J 3N4

Courtroom:
Courtroom # 5
The Law Courts Building
1815 Upper Water Street
Halifax, Nova Scotia
B3J 1S7

Telephone: (902)426-3282
Facsimile: 426-5514
(TDD): 426-9776

ONTARIO

Toronto

Canada Life Building
330 University Avenue, 7th Floor
Toronto, Ontario
M5G 1R7

Courtrooms:
330 University Avenue, 5th, 8th and 9th
Floors
361 University Avenue, Courtroom 4-10

Telephone: (416) 973-3356
Facsimile: 973-2154
(TDD): 954-4245

PRINCE EDWARD ISLAND

Charlottetown

Sir Louis Henry Davies Law Courts
42 Water Street
Box 2000
Charlottetown, Prince Edward Island
C1A 7N8

Telephone: (902) 368-0179
Facsimile: (902) 368-0266

QUEBEC

Montreal

30 McGill Street
Montreal, Quebec H2Y 3Z7

Telephone: (514) 283-4820
Fax: (514) 283-6004
(TDD): (514) 283-3017

Quebec

Palais de Justice

300 Jean Lesage Blvd
Room 500A
Quebec, Quebec G1K 8K6

Telephone: (418) 648-4920
Fax: (418) 648-4051
(TDD): (418) 648-4644

SASKATCHEWAN

Regina

The Court House
2425 Victoria Avenue
Regina, Saskatchewan S4P 3V7

Telephone: (306) 780-5268
Facsimile: (306) 787-7217

Saskatoon

The Court House
520 Spadina Crescent East
Saskatoon, Saskatchewan S7K 2H6

Telephone: (306) 975-4509
Facsimile: (306) 975-4818

YUKON TERRITORY

Whitehorse

Andrew A. Phillipsen Law Centre
2134 Second Avenue
Whitehorse, Yukon Territory Y1A 5H6

Mailing Address:
P.O. Box 2703
Whitehorse, Yukon Territory Y1A 2C6

Telephone: (867) 667-5441
Facsimile: (867) 393-6212

PRIVACY IMPACT ASSESSMENTS: AN ESSENTIAL TOOL FOR DATA PROTECTION[1]

1. Introduction

At the dawn of the twenty-first century, privacy and data protection commissioners, and indeed privacy advocates themselves, are facing a continuing stream of technological innovations that have to be evaluated systematically to measure compliance with the fair information practices or data protection principles that are at the heart of all data protection legislation.[2] Data protectors are facing such arduous responsibilities in the face of an increasing work burden, more and more complex and bureaucratic legislation — such as the European Directive on Data Protection and the national legislation that implements it — and a very fast pace of technological innovation.

Privacy impact assessments form an additional tool in the arsenal of the data protector. The idea is to require the preparation of privacy impact assessments for new products, practices, databases, and delivery systems involving personal information. In the last five years, privacy specialists have developed an assessment model for the application of a new technology or the introduction of a new service, which has good potential for raising privacy alarms at an early stage in an organization's planning process in

---

[1] This section on privacy impact assessments has been adapted from David H. Flaherty's presentation to a plenary session on "New Technologies, Security and Freedom" at the 22nd Annual Meeting of Privacy and Data Protection Officials (Venice, 27–30 September 2000). See David Flaherty, "Privacy Impact Assessments: An Essential Tool for Data Protection" (2000) 7:5 Privacy Law & Policy Reporter 85.

[2] See Colin J. Bennett, *Regulating Privacy: Data Protection and Public Policy in Europe and the United States* (Ithaca and London: Cornell University Press, 1992).

either the public or private sectors. Various models exist for privacy impact assessments that can be customized to the needs of any organization. The essential goal is to describe personal dataflows as fully as possible to understand what impact the innovation or modification may have on the personal privacy of employees or customers and how fair information practices may be complied with. Ultimately, a privacy impact assessment is a risk-assessment tool for decision makers to address not only the legal, but the moral and ethical, issues posed by whatever is being proposed. This idea of using privacy impact assessments to address certain types of data protection problems was pioneered during the last half decade by New Zealand and by certain Canadian provinces, including Ontario, British Columbia, and Alberta.[3]

The preparation of a privacy impact assessment, in cooperation with a data protection office, can be extremely useful in helping to avoid an overly legalistic focus in the detailed work of privacy protection. The core of an effective privacy impact assessment is a careful description of how a system, (or any application of technology to personal information), actually works. In this process, specific privacy issues can be segregated and addressed in a comprehensive manner. Conducting a privacy impact assessment is also an effective method of engaging a team of persons at any organization, including technology, policy, legal, and privacy specialists, to work together to identify and resolve data protection problems.

2. Description of a Privacy Impact Assessment

Simply put, a privacy impact assessment seeks to set forth, in as much detail as required to promote necessary understanding, the essential components of any personal information system or any system that contains significant amounts of personal information. The following generic categories of information should be considered for inclusion in an informative and informed privacy impact assessment.[4]

---

[3]   One of the earliest references to privacy impact assessments comes from a Privacy Issues Forum held in Christchurch, New Zealand (13 June 1996). The presenters were Blair Stewart of the New Zealand Privacy Commissioner's office and Elizabeth Longworth, a leading New Zealand privacy practitioner. Stewart published a series of articles on privacy impact assessments in (1996) 3 Privacy Law & Policy Reporter, 61–64, 134–38; and (1999) 5:8, *ibid.*, 147–49. These reflected, from a critical perspective, his experience with the process in New Zealand.

[4]   These specific headings can be reduced to seven broad headings: Introduction and Overview; Description; Data Collection; Disclosure and Use of Data; Privacy Standards and Security Measures; Conclusions; and Sources.

Table of Contents for a Model Privacy Impact Assessment

1. Introduction and Overview
2. Description
3. General Goals
4. The Need for a System
5. Current and Intended Scope
6. Key Objectives
7. Conceptual Technical Architecture
8. Risk Management
9. Statutory Authorities for the Collection, Use, and Disclosure of Personal Information
10. Privacy Standards and Concerns
11. Original Purposes of Data Collection
12. Information Collected
13. Sources of Data
14. Limits on Data Collected
15. Location of Data
16. Data Retention/Destruction
17. Consent Issues
18. Access Rights for Individuals to their Personal Data
19. Users of Personal Information
20. Disclosure of Personal Information
21. Record Linkages as a Privacy Issue
22. Security Safeguards
23. Disclosure Avoidance Practices
24. The Implications of Future Developments
25. Conclusions about the Privacy Impact
26. Sources of Information for a Privacy Impact Assessment

Issues of definition and description of the central components of a privacy impact assessment also involve initial questions of whether an organization really needs to prepare one in specific circumstances. In 1999, the Information and Privacy Commissioner for British Columbia had to deal with an issue involving detailed patient waiting lists by specialist for many hospitals in the Lower Mainland and Vancouver Island. The advice of staff was that a privacy impact assessment was not necessary, but the Commissioner was concerned about the accuracy of the information about the medical practices of individual physicians and whether physicians themselves had agreed to, or were at least aware of, the personal data to be disseminated in the context of their patient waiting lists. The British Columbia Ministry of Health was initially reluctant to do the work involved but ultimately prepared a privacy impact assessment, which the Privacy Commissioner approved. It was then posted on the Ministry of Health's Web site with the announcement of the waiting list registry.[5]

In the early stages of the development of a system, it is difficult to decide if a privacy impact assessment is required.[6] A better approach is simply to indicate to organizations that privacy impact assessments are highly desirable for significant changes to existing personal information systems or the creation of new ones. Ideally, those responsible for central government oversight of compliance with an Act will ensure that organizations prepare such privacy impact assessments on their own initiative, which can ultimately be reviewed by central government and the Privacy Commissioner's office at an appropriate later step in the process. A similar model can work in the corporate world. A data protection office has to download as much work as possible to avoid being swamped.[7]

Organizations must prepare privacy-impact assessments in such a manner as to identify key problems, not gloss over, or skip by, them, because the specialists in the offices of privacy commissioners will focus on them in the long term. "Solutions" to such issues as consent, for example, will likely also be transferable from one privacy impact assessment to another, if the thought processes of the team involved are insightful and creative.

3. Guides to Preparing a Privacy Impact Assessment

A variety of informed groups in Canada and the United States have detailed guides on how to prepare privacy impact assessments. These include the U.S. Internal Revenue Service; Treasury Board Canada, which oversees the federal government's central administration of compliance with the Canadian federal *Privacy Act*; and the Ontario Management Board of Cabinet, which plays a comparable role with respect to Ontario's *Freedom of Informa-*

---

[5]   This particular privacy impact assessment is a simple model of what can be done; it can be found at <http://www.hlth.gov.bc.ca/waitlist/privacy.html>.

[6]   In an ideal world, any personal information system should have its own privacy impact assessment available for continuing updating and revision. But the amount of work required to complete a competent privacy impact assessment makes this goal unrealistic in some cases. The issue is much more clear-cut for any privacy-intensive organization that collects and uses significant amounts of personal data.

[7]   See David H. Flaherty, *Protecting Privacy In Surveillance Societies: The Federal Republic of Germany, Sweden, France, Canada, and the United States* (Chapel Hill, NC: University of North Carolina Press, 1989) at 57, 385–91.

tion and Protection of Privacy Act.[8] One major criticism of these guides is that they appear too complicated and burdensome for users at organizations that will be asked to do the actual work in what is, after all, a largely voluntary activity on the part of those being regulated. In British Columbia, the Information, Science, and Technology Agency (ISTA) and the Office of the Information and Privacy Commissioner have published user-friendly model forms for the completion of privacy impact assessments.[9]

4. Challenges in the Preparation of Privacy Impact Assessments

- Having outside consultants to research and prepare a privacy impact assessment can be expensive to execute and difficult to accomplish in practical terms, because the consultant comes from outside the project team and is not one of the developers or proponents. In theory, it would be preferable for someone inside the project to draft a privacy impact assessment and keep it up to date, but the lack of readily available models and privacy expertise to date has made that approach difficult for any organization. However, to put costs in perspective, in one particular situation, the cost of the preparation of the privacy impact assessment was less than one percent of the development costs for the complex delivery system.
- From the beginnings of system design, proponents often have every intention of complying with privacy, confidentiality, and security requirements and legislation. But the burdens of building the innovative system often mean that this commitment smacks of lip service in terms of the actual contents of the substantial project reports that the consultant is able to review and that serve as the basis for the privacy impact assessment.

---

[8]   See Treasury Board Canada, "Model Cross-Jurisdiction Privacy Impact Assessment Guide," (Draft, October 1999); Ontario, "Privacy Impact Assessment Guidelines," (March 2000, 83 pp.) at <http://www.gov.on.ca/MBS/english/fip/pia/>; U.S. Internal Revenue Service, "Model Information Technology Privacy Impact Assessment," (Version 1.3, 17 December 1996, 17 pp.) at <http://www.cio.gov/docs/IRS.htm>. This U.S. model contains a help list of "privacy questions" to guide those preparing an initial privacy impact assessment for review with the IRS's Privacy Advocate. The Ontario Management Board of Cabinet now requires a privacy impact assessment of any submission to it from a government department "seeking approval to begin the detailed design phase or to request funding approval for product acquisition or system development work." (*ibid.* at 6) It also has lists of helpful questions associated with each component of the privacy impact assessment.

[9]   ISTA's guidelines include some sample language under each box on the privacy impact assessment form to assist in preparation. See <www.ista.gov.bc.ca>. The Office of the Information and Privacy Commissioner model provides a detailed worksheet, including critical questions. See <http://oipcbc.org/publications/pia>.

- A project development team may itself lack the trained resources to prepare a proper privacy impact assessment and to resolve critical data protection issues in a systematic manner. After all, their priority is to build a sophisticated and innovative data collection and data display system.

- There is no use building a system that is so privacy compliant, in terms of disclosure avoidance practices in particular, that it would be of absolutely no use to the professionals who are the sole intended users. Some pragmatic rules and solutions need to be found to serve all sides of the public good in the case of the public sector, or corporate goals in the private sector. A cost-benefit analysis and a privacy impact assessment are useful vehicles for balancing competing interests.

- The people involved in promoting and executing a project need to document their activities as much as possible so that those following in their footsteps, such as in the preparation of a privacy impact assessment, can understand as much as they need to know of how the system operates and the levels of personal microdata involved at each stage of creation, use, and disclosure of the data.

- A basic function of a draft privacy impact assessment is to ask probing, detailed questions of the proponents, builders, and designers to promote comprehension. The role is in effect that of a devil's advocate.

- The person preparing the assessment should obtain a demonstration or simulation of the system at an early stage. The ideal privacy impact assessment of any project is prepared by someone from inside the project and with an up-front demonstration of just how it works or is supposed to work. However, some of these internally generated assessments lack sophistication and skip over large and small data protection issues, which can be admittedly problematic to deal with in a bureaucratic world where everyone seems to have too much work to do. Internal advocates of innovative systems are naturally reluctant to be too critical of their scheme. The best protection for such a project is for the difficult data protection questions to be posed and then answered by means of appropriate solutions as required.

- The reality is that it is difficult to find someone building any automated system who knows enough about data protection principles and fair information practices to be able to apply them in a sophisticated manner to the project in question. The evidence is that few persons understand intuitively what fair information practices are all about.

- Executing a successful privacy impact assessment for any application also presupposes a capacity to understand and explain security practices in a manner that the lay reader of any privacy impact assessment will be able to understand. Cutting through jargon is an essential task of the activity.

- A related technical issue is the all-important one of disclosure avoidance practices. It is one thing for a critic to raise specific privacy issues around such questions as the risk of re-identification, for example, in the conduct of research and statistical uses of information, but it is much more difficult to measure the real risks and then to decide how to manage them in a reasonable manner. These are methodological issues that require technical assistance from specialists.

5. The Uses of Privacy Impact Assessments

- The primary purpose of a privacy impact assessment is to allow the organization building or operating a personal information system to decide whether it is in compliance with relevant data protection legislation at any particular stage in time.[10] An important secondary goal is to meet the privacy expectations of the public with respect to moral and ethical considerations. The Office of a Privacy or Data Protection Commissioner could have a role to play in both activities. An organization that has a fully-functioning and experienced Chief Privacy Officer may not need to involve the oversight body.

- A secondary purpose of a privacy impact assessment is to serve as an educational and negotiating tool for the system operators to use for purposes of compliance reviews by senior management and by the external data protection agent or agency. The privacy impact assessment should make it relatively easy for executives and the privacy commissioner and his or her staff to understand how the system works and what the privacy issues and risks are, if indeed there are any. The contents of a privacy impact assessment should deliver all the necessary details and not skirt over real issues. The completion of an effective and meaningful privacy impact assessment requires a dialogue (not a diatribe) between the regulator and the regulated.

- In some cases, political reality and real costs to taxpayers or consumers should influence whether a privacy impact assessment could be used to obtain a waiver of, or relaxation from, any requirement of a data protection act. Fair information practices need to be customized to work in practice, and minimal benefits would need to be balanced against excessive costs. For example, a cost of half a million dollars for the Workers' Compensation Board in British Columbia to replace the use of Social Insurance Numbers to keep track of workers in the province whose hearing was tested regularly over a period of years was judged excessive by the Privacy Commissioner's office in terms of the benefits of linking the testing records by an efficient method.

---

10   The Ontario Management Board Guidelines, above note 9 at 25, state: "The end result of a privacy impact assessment process is documented assurance that all privacy issues have been appropriately identified and either adequately addressed or, in the case of outstanding privacy issues, brought forward to senior management for further direction."

- A privacy impact assessment is a protean document in the sense that it is likely to continue to evolve over time with the continued development of a particular system. This is one of its most important characteristics, since the privacy impact assessment can be used to monitor important changes in any system, especially those with potentially negative implications for the privacy of individuals.[11] It is an early warning system for management and responsible Ministers or executives.

- Public bodies and other organizations in the private sector should post any privacy impact assessment on their Web site, so that it is available to everyone, including privacy advocates who may wish to second-guess the choices that have been made. An effective privacy impact assessment can also be a guide to others seeking to emulate a particular application, especially within the complex federal, provincial, and territorial political system in Canada.

- One of the perhaps semantic issues with a privacy impact assessment is whether or not a Privacy Commissioner really has to approve the finished product.[12] The model process for a privacy impact assessment is for the staff of the Privacy Commissioner and the staff of the public body to meet and discuss planned innovations in information systems. If the matter is significant enough, the initial meeting may be with the Commissioner, who will naturally express a strong interest in wanting to fully understand how the personal information system will work in practice in the form of a developed privacy impact assessment. It takes a lot of staff time and persistent effort to figure out what the flows of personal information are in any information system. Any ministry or organization has the right to be told that it is acting in compliance with the data protection act, if the staff executed their plans according to the privacy impact assessment developed in coordination with the Commissioner's staff. It is customary in such instances to suggest that the Commissioner's views are subject to later revision on the basis of new information or a privacy complaint, but this rarely happens. If privacy concerns are to be taken seriously by public bodies and other organizations that are privacy intensive in terms of their use of personal informa-

---

[11] The Ontario Management Board Guidelines, above note 9 at 11, state: "While the completion of a full and detailed privacy impact assessment may only be possible at later stages in the system development and acquisition phase, the privacy impact assessment is best approached as an evolving document which will grow increasingly detailed over time."

[12] The Alberta Information and Privacy Commissioner issued two press releases in August 1999 announcing his "acceptance" of two privacy impact assessments submitted to his office by Alberta Health and Wellness and alberta we//net. They are located under "reports," and "privacy impact assessments" on the office's Web site at <www.oipc.ab.ca>.

tion, then they have the right, after the exercise of due diligence on both sides, to positive expressions about the privacy impact assessment from the Privacy Commissioner. Clearly this model of close cooperation is not viable for all organizations in the private sector. Nevertheless there may be a place for an industry organization to discuss methodologies on behalf of its members.

6. Conclusions

A successful privacy impact assessment can be a very effective instrument in the toolkit of the twenty-first century Data Protection Commissioner. It can also be very helpful to senior public servants and their elected Ministers who do not wish to be blindsided by privacy disasters, such as happened to the Canadian Minister of Human Resources Development in May 2000.[13] A proper privacy impact assessment that incorporated the informed observations of the Office of the Privacy Commissioner of Canada might have prevented a political and public relations disaster for that particular Minister and the federal government. Private sector organizations will find it useful to add these assessment instruments to their tool kits as well.

---

[13] In his final annual report as Privacy Commissioner of Canada, Bruce Phillips drew attention to some data protection problems with a massive research database maintained by HRDC. When his press release give pride of place to an issue that was otherwise buried in the bowels of the annual report, the media and Opposition political parties in Parliament picked up on the issue and made it front-page news for almost two weeks. An initially defensive Minister subsequently ordered the literal destruction of the linkage devices that had made the database possible. Many thousands of Canadians simultaneously demanded to know what information was held about them in the database in question.

EXAMPLES OF PRIVACY CODES

A. Sample Privacy Code for a Small Enterprise

B. Telus Privacy Code

C. Air Miles® Reward Program Privacy Commitment to the Protection of Customer Information

The authors wish to thank TELUS and the Loyalty Management Group Canada Inc. (Air Miles) for allowing their privacy codes to be reproduced in this book as examples of how two Canadian firms have responded to this legislation.

Example "A"
Privacy Code for A Small Enterprise

One of the key components of the rationale for having the CSA Code as the basis for the law was that the ten principles were an easy template for small business to follow in drafting their own codes and would make compliance relatively simple. Although larger organizations must take their information holdings apart and create several separate policies, a small business such as a services consultant, plumber, or corner store will typically have the following holdings:

- Personnel information for a few employees, including pay, insurance, tax, and in some cases, staff relations or hiring/firing information. This may include résumés for prospective employees, and information about dependents.
- Customer information, which may include credit cards, purchase habits, or personal information about their households. An architect or designer, for instance, may gather detailed information about how their customers live; a personal trainer will have detailed health information.

Organizations should decide, based on such things as the extent of the customer database, the kinds of personal information they maintain, and the number of staff and complexity of the records they hold concerning them, whether they wish to have one privacy code or two. Let's walk this through an example, a services organization called Perfect Plumbing.

Perfect Plumbing's Privacy Code   Commentary

CUSTOMER POLICY

Perfect Plumbing has established a customer privacy policy to ensure that your personal information is protected and that all our practices and procedures are compliant with relevant data protection law. We believe that we are fully compliant with Canada's *Personal Information Protection and Electronic Documents Act*, and the policy below is organized according to the principles of the Canadian Standards Association's Model Code, which forms the base of that law. We invite you to address any questions you may have about personal information and about our policies to Mary Smith.

Perfect Plumbing is a small business consisting of John Smith, a plumber; his wife, Mary, who does the accounting and customer service calls; two assistant plumbers, Harry and Harriet; and a revolving roster of apprentices who come and work for six months after graduating from the local technical college. John has an agreement with the technical college and the provincial and federal governments to participate in a job retraining program, so he has more extensive personnel records than a corner dry cleaner has. He elects to have two separate policies, one for customers and one for staff.

1. Accountability

Mary Smith is responsible for our privacy policies for both customer information and staff information. She trains all our staff in how to handle the personal information of customers. She also will be happy to provide any information about the policy and about your information, including copies of your personal information if we have that information. She can be reached at 613-908-1111, fax 613-907-1111, e-mail <address>. You may also write to Mary Smith, Perfect Plumbing, 111 Main Street, Smalltown, Ontario, Canada xxx yyy.

We regard any breach of the confidentiality of the personal information of our customers as a serious matter, and staff will be disciplined to the point of dismissal if they do not abide by this policy.

Mary, as the bookkeeper and records manager, is the logical person to take on this task. She also is the person answering the phone and dispatching the plumbers to the various jobs. Just as she trains everyone about what to do with the current paperwork, she has added the care of customer and staff information to her responsibilities.

2. Identifying Purposes

We gather customer information for the following purposes:

- to serve customers who need plumbing services, installation, and repair;
- to maintain customer records to ensure good follow-up, warranty, and future repair information;
- to bill and maintain payment records.

Mary has gone through their records and identified these collections and uses of information. It is important to remember that the purposes pertain to collection, use, and disclosure. If the company decides to participate in marketing campaigns, it may have to amend this list and include marketing. However, this is not likely to happen in the immediate future.

3. Consent

We do not gather information from anyone but our customers, and we tell you when we are asking for information what it will be used for. In the event that an individual moves from his current address without making arrangements to pay his bill, we reserve the right to seek the new address. In situations where bills are unpaid after six months and our efforts to make arrangements with the customer to address the issues have been fruitless, we turn these accounts over to Hawks R Us Collection Agency. We ask our customers to agree to this when they sign the work orders, which specify our terms of net 30 days.

Customers sign a work order when the serviceman arrives, or for new installation, when the original estimates are provided. Mary had designed a new form that included a new paragraph that asks for a separate signature agreeing that unpaid bills will be handed over to a collection agency. John and Mary feel strongly about this. As small business people, they have lost a significant amount of money to bad cheques and to landlords who order the work and ignore bills.

4. Limiting Collection

As indicated above, we limit the information we collect to that which is necessary to deliver service and to do standard billing and accounting practices. We keep on our customer files your name, address, phone numbers, fax, and e-mail if we have it, instructions on how to get to your residence or property, and any information you may have given us on what times are suitable to call.

5. Limiting Use, Disclosure, and Retention

We use our information only for the purposes outlined above, and we do not sell or lend out information to anyone else. Our staff do not have access to customer records, unless they are providing service to you. Law enforcement agencies have a right under various pieces of legislation to get information that may be necessary for investigations; we insist on warrants and lawful instruments before we provide any such information.

We have a record of all the plumbing work that we have done for you, and we keep these records in an active file for ten years. After that time, we store it in secure storage for twenty years. If you ask us, we will keep these records in perpetuity; otherwise, we will purge the files at that time. We keep the records this long because accurate records of what happened to your plumbing can help immeasurably when fixing problems many years later, and this can minimize the disruption that might be necessary to your house.

6. Accuracy

We ask our customers to sign work orders prior to work, and after the job is done. We encourage you to look closely at these documents to ensure that we have the correct personal information. These documents are held securely and are not altered unless you ask us, or we identify errors. If you have concerns about the accuracy of our records, please speak to Mary Smith and she will happy to assist you.

Sometimes customers who have difficulties with their plumbing will contest the scope or timing of earlier work. Experience has taught this company to keep good records of their work and of their discussions with the client, particularly if they warned them of the short-term nature of a repair that they suspect should have been a reinstallation and will result in pipes leaking behind a wall and causing damage.

7. Safeguards

We keep all our files in a locked fire-resistant cabinet. Staff do not have free access to the files, but must ask the Office Manager, Mary Smith. If a record needs to be taken to a site, a copy is made, and the original stays in the file. Our Internet presence is limited to information about our products and services, advertising, and our chat group "Ask a Plumber." Records from "Ask a Plumber" are kept without identifiers, and if you wish to participate anonymously on-line, you may do so by using your existing privacy protection software, or by following the links to a variety of privacy information sites where you may select and download one.

Mary has experimented with a Web site, and the company has set up a successful little chat group where John signs on and answers plumbing and repair questions. It has been very useful to build their brand, but they do not link the personal information and try to contact potential customers through this chat room. Landlords in particular were asking for anonymity, so the company did a bit of research and made links to a few privacy sites where individuals who wanted to keep their identities private could download software themselves.

8. Openness

This policy, and our staff policy, are freely available. Our accounting policies are also available to those who are interested.

A small company such as this one is not going to have a lot of written policy. This policy and information about how they handle credit card information are probably all that is necessary.

9. Individual Access

We will be happy to provide you with copies of all the records we have of your customer relationship with us. For competitive reasons, we will not provide information about our costs; they will be deleted in the event that records concerning the costing of materials we supplied to you happen to be in your records. If you feel that the information on your file is inaccurate, you are invited to bring it to the attention of our Office Manager and ask for it to be amended. In rare instances we may not agree to amend the information, but we will be happy to add your notations about the information to the file.

10. Challenging Compliance

We are anxious to ensure that our privacy policy meets your concerns and responds to your needs. Our Office Manager, Mary Smith, is available to receive your enquiries and complaints. We are members of the Better Business Bureau, who also are happy to discuss complaints related to customer satisfaction and billing practices. If you are unhappy with the results of these discussions, you may complain to the Office of the Federal Privacy Commissioner, 112 Kent Street, Ottawa, Ontario, **K1A 1H3**.

This may seem to be an obvious point, but in small businesses, often the costs of a job are included in the file and would have to be removed. It is good practice to make this clear before the individual has access to the file, or you will be explaining staples and paperclips that have no attachments once the original documents are removed. As it is rarely your happy customers who ask to see their files, it is prudent to be prepared for an adversarial experience. Properly handled, you can turn this into a positive opportunity to do customer relations. When dealing with requests for correction, it is best to develop a standard notation form to offer the customer.

It is not likely that the average business will need more than this. It is important that there is information about how to reach the responsible person, but it should be in one place — in this policy, right up front.

STAFF POLICY

Perfect Plumbing has established a staff privacy policy to ensure that your personal information is protected and that all our practices and procedures are compliant with relevant data protection law. We believe that we are fully compliant with Canada's *Personal Information Protection and Electronic Documents Act*, and the policy below is organized according to the principles of the Canadian Standards Association's Model Code, which forms the base of that law.

Personnel information is not actually covered by that law with respect to small enterprises like our own, but we feel that our staff are entitled to the same care and attention with respect to their personal information as our customers. We invite you to address any questions you may have about personal information and about our policies to Mary Smith.

1. Accountability

Mary Smith is responsible for our privacy policies for both customer information and staff information. She trains all our staff in how to handle the personal information of customers. She also will be happy to provide any information about the policy and about your information, including copies of your personal information. She can be reached at 613-908-1111, fax 613-907-1111, e-mail <address>. You may also write to Mary Smith, Perfect Plumbing, 111 Main Street, Smalltown, Ontario, Canada xxx yyy.

We regard any breach of the confidentiality of the personal information of our customers or our staff as a serious matter, and staff will be disciplined to the point of dismissal if they do not abide by this policy and the customer policy.

Once again, Mary, as the bookkeeper and records manager, is the logical person to take on this task. She also is the person who handles hiring and firing, medical insurance and leave issues, and pay. She trains staff in the areas of customer relations and ensures that they respect one another's privacy as well as their customers.

2. Identifying Purposes

We gather staff information for the following purposes:

- to review prospective candidates and select employees;
- to maintain staff records to ensure accurate pay and benefits, and all documentation required by law and by the various levels of government, in accordance with sound accounting practices;
- to maintain accurate and fair accounts of staff and customer relations disputes.

Mary has gone through their records and identified these collections and uses of information. It is important to remember that the purposes pertain to collection, use, and disclosure. Having had an issue where one of their staff got into an unpleasant situation involving an allegation of sexual harassment with a customer, they have taken the somewhat unusual step of setting up procedures for customer and staff relations, and have encouraged their staff to document any problems, in a report before they get out of control. Aware that these documents are potentially available to the customer, the reports have been standardized on a brief form that Mary has developed.

3. Consent

We do not gather information from any-one but our staff and our customers, and we tell you when we are asking for information what it will be used for. In the event that an individual leaves our employment and moves from his or her current address without making arrangements to keep in touch with us about such issues as tax and benefits, we reserve the right to seek out the new address of the individual.

Staff understand that they are involved with customers, that comments about them may be made on customer files, and that this is a part of working for Perfect Plumbing. We expect the most professional comportment from our staff, including complete compliance with our customer and staff privacy policies. Staff sign on to the privacy policies when they sign their contracts of employment, and recognize that failure to comply with the policies will result in disciplinary action and possibly firing.

4. Limiting Collection

As indicated above, we limit the information we collect to that which is necessary to administer pay and benefits, assign jobs, send staff on training courses, and manage customer and staff relations issues. It is our policy to keep the information collected to an absolute minimum. When dealing with staff and customer relations issues, the Office Manager has developed forms to record information that may be necessary to document a situation, in a form and level of detail that is professional and acceptable.

Mary has added a paragraph to the employment contract that requires staff to comply with the privacy policies.

Making sure that staff do not write inappropriate comments on their work reports or files is extremely important, given that customers now have access to those records. Training staff and reminding them of this is a daily task, and it is definitely worth a mention in the staff policy.

5. Limiting Use, Disclosure, and Retention

We use our information only for the purposes outlined above, and we do not sell or lend out information to anyone else. Only the Office Manager and the Owner of the company have access to the staff records. We disclose certain types of information to government organizations on a regular basis, and the retention period for this information is ten years. Law enforcement agencies have a right under various legislation to get information that may be necessary for investigations; we insist on warrants and lawful instruments before we provide any such information.

We have a record of all the plumbing work that we have done for customers, including the names, notes, and possibly other personal information about the staff who did the work. We keep these records in an active file for ten years. After that time, we store it in secure storage for twenty years. If customers ask us, we will keep these records in perpetuity; otherwise, we will purge the files at that time. We keep the records this long because accurate records of what happened to their plumbing can help immeasurably when fixing problems many years later, and this can minimize the disruption that might be necessary to their property.

Personnel information is not covered by the *Personal Information Protection and Electronic Documents Act*, but it is covered by provincial labour law in some respects; it is required to be shared with provincial and federal agencies by a number of other laws.

6. Accuracy

We ask our staff to fill out a number of documents when they start to work for us. We encourage you to look closely at these documents to ensure that we have the correct information, and to do this on a regular basis so that we can reflect change. These documents are held securely and are not altered unless you ask us, or we identify errors. If you have concerns about the accuracy of our records, please speak to Mary Smith and she will be happy to assist you. If we do not agree with a suggested amendment to your records, we will nevertheless be happy to attach the notation you request.

In the case of customer files, if any information about the staff is contained on that record or is generated in the context of a complaint, the individual staff member will be notified. unless the issue is significant enough to evoke solicitor-client privilege.

Staff should be encouraged to inspect their personnel records on a regular basis, to ensure accuracy and promote trust. It is in the company's interest, in the long term, for staff to make thorough and reliable notes of the jobs that they have done, in a manner that will pass muster when the customer accesses his file. The Office Manager has taken on the task of quality control, ensuring good notes that will be useful in the event that a customer comes back later and alleges that improper advice was given.

7. Safeguards

We keep all our files in a locked fire-resistant cabinet. Staff do not have free access to the files, but must ask the Office Manager, Mary Smith. If a customer record needs to be taken to a site, a copy is made and the original stays in the file. Our Internet presence is limited to information about our products and services, advertising, and our chat group "Ask a Plumber." Records from "Ask a Plumber" are kept without identifiers for customers, but if any staff member is asked to replace John Smith, they will be identified.

When John and Mary are on holidays, another plumber takes on the responsibility of the Web site.

8. Openness

This policy, and our customer policy, are freely available. Our accounting policies are also available to those who are interested.

A small company like this is not going to have a lot of written policy. This policy and information about how they handle accident and health information are probably all that is necessary. Staff may enquire about what information is sent to the various governments, and Mary is usually able to answer those questions.

9. Individual Access

We will be happy to provide staff with copies of all the records we have in their personnel files. As indicated above, we will be happy to amend records if we agree, and staff are always welcome to add their annotation to the record. A staff member may examine customer files that concern them and place an annotation on that file.

It is important to encourage staff to check their files. It leads to more accuracy, it generates trust, and it offers a teaching opportunity to engender a more careful approach to the handling of customer information.

10. Challenging Compliance

We are anxious to ensure that our privacy policy meets your concerns and responds to your needs. Our Office Manager, Mary Smith, is available to receive your enquiries and complaints. We are members of the Better Business Bureau, who also are happy to discuss complaints related to customer satisfaction and billing practices.

Until provinces act to legislate and act to protect employee information, there will be no oversight agency to look after employee complaints. Organizations would be well advised to get together and provide independent complaint mediation.

Example "B"
TELUS Privacy Code

Our Privacy Commitment to You

The TELUS Privacy Code incorporates the provisions of Part 1 of the *Personal Information Protection and Electronic Documents Act* (Statutes of Canada 2000, Chapter 5) and includes the ten principles of the Canadian Standards Association (CSA) Model Code for the Protection of Personal Information (CAN/CSA-Q830-96), which was published in March 1996 as a National Standard of Canada.

The TELUS Privacy Code was originally published in 1998 as part of our long-standing commitment to the protection of our customers' and employees' personal information. It was updated in September 2000 to reflect changes associated with the implementation of the new legislation referred to above.

TABLE OF CONTENTS

Introduction

Summary of Principles

Principle 1 — Accountability

Principle 2 — Identifying Purposes for Collection of Personal Information

Principle 3 — Obtaining Consent for Collection, Use or Disclosure of Personal Information

Principle 4 — Limiting Collection of Personal Information

Principle 5 — Limiting Use, Disclosure, and Retention of Personal Information

Principle 6 — Accuracy of Personal Information

Principle 7 — Security Safeguards

Principle 8 — Openness Concerning Policies and Practices

Principle 9 — Customer and Employee Access to Personal Information

Principle 10 — Challenging Compliance

Scope and Application

Definitions

The TELUS Privacy Code in Detail

Principle   1 — Accountability

Principle   2 — Identifying Purposes for Collection of Personal Information

Principle   3 — Obtaining Consent for Collection, Use or Disclosure of Personal Information

Principle   4 — Limiting Collection of Personal Information

Principle   5 — Limiting Use, Disclosure, and Retention of Personal Information

Principle   6 — Accuracy of Personal Information

Principle   7 — Security Safeguards

Principle   8 — Openness Concerning Policies and Practices

Principle   9 — Customer and Employee Access to Personal Information

Principle 10 — Challenging Compliance

Introduction

TELUS is Canada's second largest telecommunications company and provides a full range of advanced communication services and products connecting Canadians with the world. For TELUS, customer privacy is a high priority. We have a long-standing policy of protecting the privacy of customers in all of our business operations.

The TELUS Privacy Code is a formal statement of principles and guidelines concerning the minimum requirements for the protection of personal information provided by TELUS to its customers and employees. The objective of the TELUS Privacy Code is to promote responsible and transparent practices in the management of personal information, in accordance with the provisions of the *Personal Information Protection and Electronic Documents Act.*

TELUS will continue to review its Privacy Code to ensure it is relevant and remains current with changing technologies and laws. Most importantly, TELUS wants to ensure it continues to meet the evolving needs of our customers and employees.

Summary of Principles

Principle 1 — Accountability

TELUS is responsible for personal information under its control and shall designate one or more persons who are accountable for the company's compliance with the following principles.

Principle 2 — Identifying Purposes for Collection of Personal Information

TELUS shall identify the purposes for which personal information is collected at or before the time the information is collected.

Principle 3 — Obtaining Consent for Collection, Use or Disclosure of Personal Information

The knowledge and consent of a customer or employee are required for the collection, use, or disclosure of personal information, except where inappropriate.

Principle 4 — Limiting Collection of Personal Information

TELUS shall limit the collection of personal information to that which is necessary for the purposes identified by the company. TELUS shall collect personal information by fair and lawful means.

Principle 5 — Limiting Use, Disclosure, and Retention of Personal Information

TELUS shall not use or disclose personal information for purposes other than those for which it was collected, except with the consent of the individual or as required by law. TELUS shall retain personal information only as long as necessary for the fulfillment of those purposes.

Principle 6 — Accuracy of Personal Information

Personal information shall be as accurate, complete, and up-to-date as is necessary for the purposes for which it is to be used.

Principle 7 — Security Safeguards

TELUS shall protect personal information by security safeguards appropriate to the sensitivity of the information.

Principle 8 — Openness Concerning Policies and Practices

TELUS shall make readily available to customers and employees specific information about its policies and practices relating to the management of personal information.

Principle 9 — Customer and Employee Access to Personal Information

TELUS shall inform a customer or employee of the existence, use, and disclosure of his or her personal information upon request and shall give the individual access to that information. A customer or employee shall be able to challenge the accuracy and completeness of the information and have it amended as appropriate.

Principle 10 — Challenging Compliance

A customer or employee shall be able to address a challenge concerning compliance with the above principles to the designated person or persons accountable for TELUS' compliance with the TELUS Privacy Code.

Scope and Application

The ten principles, which form the basis of the TELUS Privacy Code, are interrelated and TELUS shall adhere to the ten principles as a whole. Each principle must be read in conjunction with the accompanying commentary. As permitted by the *Personal Information Protection and Electronic Documents Act*, the commentary in the TELUS Privacy Code has been tailored to reflect personal information issues specific to TELUS.

The scope and application of the TELUS Privacy Code are as follows:

- The Code applies to personal information about TELUS' customers and employees that is collected, used, or disclosed by TELUS.
- The Code applies to the management of personal information in any form whether oral, electronic or written.
- The Code does not impose any limits on the collection, use or disclosure of the following information by TELUS:

  a) a customer's name, address, telephone number and e-mail address, when listed in a directory or available through directory assistance;
  b) an employee's name, title, business address (including e-mail address) or business telephone or fax number; or
  c) other information about the customer or employee that is publicly available and is specified by regulation pursuant to the *Personal Information Protection and Electronic Documents Act*.

- The Code does not apply to information regarding TELUS' corporate customers; however, such information is protected by other TELUS policies and practices and through contractual arrangements.
- The application of the TELUS Privacy Code is subject to the requirements and provisions of Part 1 of the *Personal Information Protection and Electronic Documents Act*, the regulations enacted thereunder,

and any other applicable legislation or regulations, including any applicable regulations of the Canadian Radio-television and Telecommunications Commission.

Definitions

collection — the act of gathering, acquiring, recording, or obtaining personal information from any source, including third parties, by any means.

consent — voluntary agreement with the collection, use and disclosure of personal information for defined purposes. Consent can be either express or implied and can be provided directly by the individual or by an authorized representative. Express consent can be given orally, electronically or in writing, but is always unequivocal and does not require any inference on the part of TELUS. Implied consent is consent that can reasonably be inferred from an individual's action or inaction.

customer — an individual who uses, or applies to use, TELUS' products or services, where such individual is a residential customer or an individual carrying on business alone as a sole proprietorship or in partnership with other individuals.

disclosure — making personal information available to a third party.

employee — an employee of TELUS.

personal information — information about an identifiable customer or employee, but does not include aggregated information that cannot be associated with a specific individual.

> For a customer, such information includes a customer's credit information, billing records, service and equipment, and any recorded complaints. For an employee, such information includes information found in personal employment files, performance appraisals, and medical and benefits information, but does not include the employee's name, title, business address (including e-mail address) or business telephone or fax numbers.

TELUS — TELUS Corporation and its subsidiary companies, as they may exist from time to time. These include, without limitation, the subsidiaries which carry on business under the following names: TELUS, TELUS Communications, TELUS Mobility, TELUS Advanced Communications, TELUS Internet Services, TELUS Integrated Communications, TELUS Advertising Services, and ISM-BC. "TELUS" does not include independent dealers and distributors of TELUS products and services, The QuebecTel Group Inc. or its subsidiary companies.

third party — an individual or organization outside TELUS.

use — the treatment, handling, and management of personal information by and within TELUS.

The TELUS Privacy Code in Detail

Principle 1 — Accountability

TELUS is responsible for personal information under its control and shall designate one or more persons who are accountable for TELUS' compliance with the following principles.

1.1

Responsibility for ensuring compliance with the provisions of the TELUS Privacy Code rests with the senior management of TELUS, which shall designate one or more persons to be accountable for compliance with the Code. Other individuals within TELUS may be delegated to act on behalf of the designated person(s) or to take responsibility for the day-to-day collection and processing of personal information.

1.2

TELUS shall make known, upon request, the title of the person or persons designated to oversee TELUS' compliance with the TELUS Privacy Code.

1.3

TELUS is responsible for personal information in its possession or control. TELUS shall use appropriate means to provide a comparable level of protection while information is being processed by a third party (see Principle 7).

1.4

TELUS shall implement policies and procedures to give effect to the TELUS Privacy Code, including:

a) implementing procedures to protect personal information and to oversee TELUS' compliance with the TELUS Privacy Code;
b) establishing procedures to receive and respond to inquiries or complaints;
c) training and communicating to staff about TELUS' policies and practices; and
d) developing public information to explain TELUS' policies and practices.

Principle 2 — Identifying Purposes for Collection of Personal Information

TELUS shall identify the purposes for which personal information is collected at or before the time the information is collected.

2.1

TELUS collects personal information only for the following purposes:

a) to establish and maintain responsible commercial relations with customers and to provide ongoing service;
b) to understand customer needs and preferences;
c) to develop, enhance, market or provide products and services;
d) to manage and develop TELUS' business and operations, including personnel and employment matters; and
e) to meet legal and regulatory requirements.

Further references to "identified purposes" mean the purposes identified in this Principle.

2.2

TELUS shall specify orally, electronically or in writing the identified purposes to the customer or employee at or before the time personal information is collected. Upon request, persons collecting personal information shall explain these identified purposes or refer the individual to a designated person within TELUS who shall explain the purposes.

2.3

Unless required by law, TELUS shall not use or disclose for any new purpose personal information that has been collected without first identifying and documenting the new purpose and obtaining the consent of the customer or employee.

Principle 3 — Obtaining Consent for Collection, Use or Disclosure of Personal Information

The knowledge and consent of a customer or employee are required for the collection, use, or disclosure of personal information, except where inappropriate. In certain circumstances personal information can be collected, used, or disclosed without the knowledge and consent of the individual.

For example, TELUS may collect or use personal information without knowledge or consent if it is clearly in the interests of the individual and consent can not be obtained in a timely way, such as when the individual is seriously ill or mentally incapacitated.

TELUS may also collect, use or disclose personal information without knowledge or consent if seeking the consent of the individual might defeat the purpose of collecting the information, such as in the investigation of a breach of an agreement or a contravention of a federal or provincial law.

TELUS may also use or disclose personal information without knowledge or consent in the case of an emergency where the life, health or security of an individual is threatened.

TELUS may disclose personal information without knowledge or consent to a lawyer representing TELUS, to collect a debt, to comply with a subpoena, warrant or other court order, or as may be otherwise required or authorized by law.

3.1

In obtaining consent, TELUS shall use reasonable efforts to ensure that a customer or employee is advised of the identified purposes for which personal information will be used or disclosed. Purposes shall be stated in a manner that can be reasonably understood by the customer or employee.

3.2

Generally, TELUS shall seek consent to use and disclose personal information at the same time it collects the information. However, TELUS may seek consent to use and disclose personal information after it has been collected, but before it is used or disclosed for a new purpose.

3.3

TELUS will require customers to consent to the collection, use or disclosure of personal information as a condition of the supply of a product or service only if such collection, use or disclosure is required to fulfill the identified purposes.

3.4

In determining the appropriate form of consent, TELUS shall take into account the sensitivity of the personal information and the reasonable expectations of its customers and employees.

3.5

In general, the use of products and services by a customer, or the acceptance of employment or benefits by an employee, constitutes implied consent for TELUS to collect, use and disclose personal information for all identified purposes.

3.6

A customer may withdraw consent at any time, subject to legal or contractual restrictions and reasonable notice. Customers may contact TELUS for more information regarding the implications of withdrawing consent.

Principle 4 — Limiting Collection of Personal Information

TELUS shall limit the collection of personal information to that which is necessary for the purposes identified by TELUS. TELUS shall collect personal information by fair and lawful means.

4.1

TELUS collects personal information primarily from its customers or employees.

4.2

TELUS may also collect personal information from other sources including credit bureaus, employers or personal references, or other third parties who represent that they have the right to disclose the information.

Principle 5 — Limiting Use, Disclosure, and Retention of Personal Information

TELUS shall not use or disclose personal information for purposes other than those for which it was collected, except with the consent of the individual or as required by law. TELUS shall retain personal information only as long as necessary for the fulfillment of those purposes.

5.1

TELUS may disclose a customer's personal information to:

a) a person who in the reasonable judgment of TELUS is seeking the information as an agent of the customer;
b) another telecommunications company for the efficient and cost-effective provision of telecommunications services;
c) a company involved in supplying the customer with communications or communications directory related services;
d) a company or individual employed by TELUS to perform functions on its behalf, such as research or data processing;
e) another company or individual for the development, enhancement, marketing or provision of any of TELUS' products or services;
f) an agent used by TELUS to evaluate the customer's creditworthiness or to collect the customer's account;
g) a credit reporting agency;
h) a public authority or agent of a public authority, if in the reasonable judgment of TELUS, it appears that there is imminent danger to life or property which could be avoided or minimized by disclosure of the information; and
i) a third party or parties, where the customer consents to such disclosure or disclosure is required by law.

5.2

TELUS may disclose personal information about its employees:

a) for normal personnel and benefits administration;
b) in the context of providing references regarding current or former employees in response to requests from prospective employers; or
c) where disclosure is required by law.

5.3

Only TELUS' employees with a business need to know, or whose duties reasonably so require, are granted access to personal information about customers and employees.

5.4

TELUS shall keep personal information only as long as it remains necessary or relevant for the identified purposes or as required by law. Depending on the circumstances, where personal information has been used to make a decision about a customer or employee, TELUS shall retain, for a period of time that is reasonably sufficient to allow for access by the customer or employee, either the actual information or the rationale for making the decision.

5.5

TELUS shall maintain reasonable and systematic controls, schedules and practices for information and records retention and destruction which apply to personal information that is no longer necessary or relevant for the identified purposes or required by law to be retained. Such information shall be destroyed, erased or made anonymous.

Principle 6 — Accuracy of Personal Information

Personal information shall be as accurate, complete, and up-to-date as is necessary for the purposes for which it is to be used.

6.1

Personal information used by TELUS shall be sufficiently accurate, complete, and up-to-date to minimize the possibility that inappropriate information may be used to make a decision about a customer or employee.

6.2

TELUS shall update personal information about customers and employees as and when necessary to fulfill the identified purposes or upon notification by the individual.

Principle 7 — Security Safeguards

TELUS shall protect personal information by security safeguards appropriate to the sensitivity of the information.

7.1

TELUS shall protect personal information against such risks as loss or theft, unauthorized access, disclosure, copying, use, modification or destruction, through appropriate security measures. TELUS shall protect the information regardless of the format in which it is held.

7.2

TELUS shall protect personal information disclosed to third parties by contractual agreements stipulating the confidentiality of the information and the purposes for which it is to be used.

7.3

All of TELUS' employees with access to personal information shall be required to respect the confidentiality of that information.

Principle 8 — Openness Concerning Policies and Practices

TELUS shall make readily available to customers and employees specific information about its policies and practices relating to the management of personal information.

8.1

TELUS shall make information about its policies and practices easy to understand, including:

a) the title and address of the person or persons accountable for TELUS' compliance with the TELUS Privacy Code and to whom inquiries or complaints can be forwarded;
b) the means of gaining access to personal information held by TELUS; and
c) a description of the type of personal information held by TELUS, including a general account of its use.

8.2

TELUS shall make available information to help customers and employees exercise choices regarding the use of their personal information and the privacy-enhancing services available from TELUS.

Principle 9 — Customer and Employee Access to Personal Information

TELUS shall inform a customer or employee of the existence, use, and disclosure of his or her personal information upon request and shall give the individual access to that information. A customer or employee shall be able to challenge the accuracy and completeness of the information and have it amended as appropriate.

9.1

Upon request, TELUS shall afford customers and employees a reasonable opportunity to review the personal information in the individual's file. Personal information shall be provided in understandable form within a reasonable time, and at a minimal or no cost to the individual.

9.2

In certain situations, TELUS may not be able to provide access to all the personal information that it holds about a customer or employee. For example, TELUS may not provide access to information if doing so would likely reveal personal information about a third party or could reasonably be expected to threaten the life or security of another individual. Also, TELUS may not provide access to information if disclosure would reveal confidential commercial information, if the information is protected by solicitor — client privilege, if the information was generated in the course of a formal dispute resolution process, or if the information was collected in relation to the investigation of a breach of an agreement or a contravention of a federal or provincial law. If access to personal information cannot be provided, TELUS shall provide the reasons for denying access upon request.

9.3

Upon request, TELUS shall provide an account of the use and disclosure of personal information and, where reasonably possible, shall state the source of the information. In providing an account of disclosure, TELUS shall provide a list of organizations to which it may have disclosed personal information about the individual when it is not possible to provide an actual list.

9.4

In order to safeguard personal information, a customer or employee may be required to provide sufficient identification information to permit TELUS to account for the existence, use and disclosure of personal information and to authorize access to the individual's file. Any such information shall be used only for this purpose.

9.5

TELUS shall promptly correct or complete any personal information found to be inaccurate or incomplete. Any unresolved differences as to accuracy or completeness shall be noted in the individual's file. Where appropriate, TELUS shall transmit to third parties having access to the personal information in question any amended information or the existence of any unresolved differences.

9.6

Customers can obtain information or seek access to their individual files by contacting a designated representative at TELUS' business offices.

9.7

Employees can obtain information or seek access to their individual files by contacting their immediate supervisor within TELUS.

Principle 10 — Challenging Compliance

A customer or employee shall be able to address a challenge concerning compliance with the above principles to the designated person or persons accountable for TELUS' compliance with the TELUS Privacy Code.

10.1

TELUS shall maintain procedures for addressing and responding to all inquiries or complaints from its customers and employees about TELUS' handling of personal information.

10.2

TELUS shall inform its customers and employees about the existence of these procedures as well as the availability of complaint procedures.

10.3

The person or persons accountable for compliance with the TELUS Privacy Code may seek external advice where appropriate before providing a final response to individual complaints.

10.4

TELUS shall investigate all complaints concerning compliance with the TELUS Privacy Code. If a complaint is found to be justified, TELUS shall take appropriate measures to resolve the complaint including, if necessary, amending its policies and procedures. A customer or employee shall be informed of the outcome of the investigation regarding his or her complaint.

For more information on the TELUS privacy practices, contact: 1-800-567-0000.

For a copy of the *Personal Information Protection and Electronic Documents Act*, please access the Privacy Commissioner of Canada web site at

www.privcom.gc.ca.

For copies of the CSA Model Code for the Protection of Personal Information contact the Canadian Standards Association, 178 Rexdale Blvd., Etobicoke, Ontario M9W 1R3.

Example "C"
AIR MILES® Reward Program
Privacy Commitment to the Protection of Customer Information

Introduction

The Loyalty Group, as creator and manager of the AIR MILES® Reward Program in Canada, is demonstrating its commitment to protecting the privacy of Customers' Personal Information by developing and implementing this *Privacy Commitment to the Protection of Customer Information.*

The AIR MILES® *Privacy Commitment* complies with or exceeds the federal *Personal Information Protection and Electronic Documents Act,* the Canadian Marketing Association's *Code of Ethics and Standards of Practice,* and applicable provincial privacy laws. It was developed in conjunction with PricewaterhouseCoopers and is also based on the Canadian Standards Association's *Model Code for the Protection of Personal Information.*

This *Privacy Commitment* applies to the collection, storage, use, disclosure, protection, and accuracy of Personal Information collected and controlled by The Loyalty Group. It also applies to all Personal Information held in the AIR MILES databases and utilized by The Loyalty Group's business units.

Definitions

Collector — an individual, business or organization who or which has enrolled, or is applying for enrollment, in the AIR MILES® Reward Program, the AIR MILES For Business Program™ and/or AIR MILES INCENTIVES™, and for whom an AIR MILES account number has been established or is being established in the AIR MILES databases.

collect — to gather, acquire, or obtain Personal Information from any source, including third parties.

consent — voluntary agreement with what is being done or proposed. Consent can be either express or implied. Express consent is given explicitly, either orally or in writing. Express consent is unequivocal and does not require any inference on the part of The Loyalty Group. Implied consent arises where consent may reasonably be inferred from the action or inaction of the Collector, such as the presentation or usage of the AIR MILES Collector Card or number.

direct marketing — direct communications targeted to Collectors, including mail, telemarketing, fax or electronic mail, but not including Collector Summaries.

Personal Information — information about an identifiable Collector recorded in any form.

Sponsor — an organization, corporation or business that issues AIR MILES reward miles to build and maintain customer and employee loyalty.

Summary — a regular report to Collectors detailing their account balance and transactions, either by mail or electronic means, and which may include promotional material and AIR MILES® Reward Program updates.

Supplier — a company under contract to provide reward supply services, or data collection, processing and/or management services to The Loyalty Group.

The Loyalty Group — the creator and manager of the AIR MILES® Reward Program and the AIR MILES For Business Program™ in Canada. In addition, The Loyalty Group operates other businesses including EXTRA MILE TRAVEL™, EXTRA MILE *Flowers*™, EXTRA MILE Books.com™, AIR MILES INCENTIVES™ and Loyalty Consulting™.

™/® AIR MILES International Trading, B.V. Used under licence by Loyalty Management Group Canada Inc.

© 2000 Loyalty Management Group Canada Inc.

All rights reserved, including the right to reproduction, in whole or in part, in any form.

The Principles

Principle 1 — Accountability

The Loyalty Group is responsible for Personal Information under its control, including Personal Information disclosed by The Loyalty Group to a third party for data and list processing.

1.1   The Executive Committee of The Loyalty Group is accountable for The Loyalty Group's compliance with the AIR MILES® *Privacy Commitment.*

1.2   The Senior Vice President, AIR MILES® Business Programs and The Loyalty Group's Corporate Counsel oversee The Loyalty Group's compliance with the AIR MILES® *Privacy Commitment.*

1.3   The Loyalty Group uses legal agreements to provide a comparable level of protection for Personal Information while the information is being processed by an authorized third party.

1.4   The management of The Loyalty Group has established procedures to implement the AIR MILES *Privacy Commitment,* including

- procedures to protect Personal Information;
- procedures to receive and respond to complaints and inquiries;
- communications and training programs to provide information to The Loyalty Group's staff about privacy policies and practices;
- information for Sponsors, Collectors and The Loyalty Group's employees to explain the AIR MILES® *Privacy Commitment.*

Principle 2 — Identifying Purposes

The Loyalty Group collects Personal Information for three primary purposes: to ensure the proper functioning of the AIR MILES Reward Program; to meet the direct marketing, product development and research requirements of the AIR MILES Reward Program and its participating Sponsors; and to improve the promotional offers and services of the AIR MILES Reward Program and its participating Sponsors.

2.1   The Loyalty Group provides Collectors with information that explains: the purposes for which Personal Information is being collected; and

- how the Personal Information may be used or disclosed.

2.2   The Loyalty Group collects Personal Information for the following purposes:

- To administer the AIR MILES® Reward Program, the AIR MILES for Business Program™, and AIR MILES INCENTIVES™, including the management of Collector Accounts to accurately record and update reward mile balances;
- To process Collector redemptions, including the issuance of reward tickets and vouchers;
- To invoice Collector and Sponsor accounts as appropriate;
- To communicate information and offers to Collectors, Sponsors and Suppliers;
- To understand and analyze Collectors' responses, needs and preferences;
- To develop, enhance, market and/or provide products and services to meet those needs; and
- To enable Collectors to participate in promotions and contests.

2.3   AIR MILES Collectors can opt out of receiving marketing and promotional communications in electronic, printed or verbal format, other than AIR MILES Collector Summaries by writing AIR MILES Customer Service, P.O. Box 602, Station A, Scarborough, Ontario M1K 5K7 or by email to privacyoffice@airmiles.ca. The decision to opt out of additional communications does not affect the Collector's ability to collect or redeem reward miles in the AIR MILES Reward Program.

2.4 The Loyalty Group obtains a Collector's consent before using Personal Information for a purpose that has not been specified, unless the new purpose is required by law.

2.5 Employees of The Loyalty Group who collect Personal Information on behalf of the AIR MILES® Reward Program are able to provide information which explains the purposes for which it is being collected.

Principle 3 — Consent

The Loyalty Group makes a reasonable effort to ensure that Collectors understand how Personal Information will be used. The Loyalty Group obtains the consent of Collectors as required for the collection, use or disclosure of Personal Information, except where it is inappropriate to do so.

3.1 The Loyalty Group provides its Collectors with information about the way in which Personal Information will be used through printed materials, the AIR MILES Web site and other electronic means, its Interactive Voice Response system, and its Customer Service Centre.

3.2 The Loyalty Group obtains consent for the collection, use or disclosure of Personal Information. Typically, this consent is obtained on paper or electronic enrollment forms, survey forms, and/or during telephone conversations with Collectors.

3.3 The Loyalty Group does not, as a condition of participation in the AIR MILES® Reward Program, require a Collector to consent to the collection, use, or disclosure of Personal Information beyond that required to fulfill specified purposes.

3.4 Consent can be either express or implied. Express consent is given either verbally or in writing — e.g., on an AIR MILES® enrollment or survey form. Consent is implied when it can be reasonably understood by the action or inaction of the Collector. For example, if a Collector uses an AIR MILES® Card, The Loyalty Group assumes that the Collector has given consent to the collection of the transaction information required to fulfill specified purposes.

3.5 A Collector can withdraw consent at any time as per Section 2.3. If a Collector withdraws consent, The Loyalty Group makes the Collector aware of the consequences of this action.

Principle 4 — Limiting Collection

The collection of Personal Information is limited to that which is necessary for the purposes identified by The Loyalty Group. The Loyalty Group collects Personal Information by fair and lawful means.

4.1   The Loyalty Group does not collect Personal Information indiscriminately. Both the amount and the type of Personal Information collected are limited to that which is necessary to fulfill the purposes identified.

4.2   The Loyalty Group collects Personal Information from the Collector

- as a result of purchases by the Collector at Sponsor locations;
- through online and electronic activity with The Loyalty Group;
- through telephone, paper and online surveys and contests;
- through enrollment in the AIR MILES Reward Program; and
- through Collector redemption requests.

Principle 5 — Limiting Use, Disclosure and Retention

The Loyalty Group does not use or disclose Personal Information for purposes other than those for which it is collected, except with the consent of the Collector or as required by law. The Loyalty Group retains Personal Information only as long as necessary for the fulfillment of those purposes.

5.1   The Loyalty Group does not give, rent or sell Collector lists from the AIR MILES Reward Program to any organization or individual other than business units of The Loyalty Group, Sponsors of the AIR MILES® Reward Program, and companies contracted to process and manage Collector transactions, redemption requests and communications.

5.2   The Loyalty Group may disclose Personal Information to comply with legal and regulatory requirements or to ensure compliance with the terms and conditions, and the administration of, the AIR MILES® Reward Program, the AIR MILES for Business Program™ and AIR MILES INCENTIVES™.

5.3   The Loyalty Group retains Personal Information in accordance with documented guidelines and procedures established by The Loyalty Group. The Personal Information of Collectors is retained for as long as they are active or potentially active in the AIR MILES® Reward Program.

5.4   The Loyalty Group has guidelines and implements procedures to govern the destruction of Personal Information that is no longer required to fulfill the identified purposes. Collector transaction records and inactive Collector accounts that exceed seven (7) years are deleted from the AIR MILES databases.

Principle 6 – Accuracy

The Loyalty Group keeps Personal Information as accurate, complete and up-to-date as necessary for the purposes for which it is to be used.

6.1   The Loyalty Group updates Personal Information as it is made available by Collectors and Sponsors.

6.2   Collectors and Sponsors are responsible for informing The Loyalty Group about changes to Personal Information, as appropriate.

6.3   The Loyalty Group does not routinely update Personal Information unless such a process is necessary to fulfill the purposes for which the Personal Information is collected.

Principle 7 — Safeguards

The Loyalty Group protects Personal Information with security safeguards appropriate to the sensitivity of the Personal Information.

7.1   The Loyalty Group protects Personal Information against loss or theft, as well as unauthorized access, disclosure, copying, use or modification with security safeguards appropriate to the sensitivity of the Personal Information. The Loyalty Group protects Personal Information regardless of the format in which it is held.

7.2   The methods of protection for Personal Information include:

   a) physical measures, for example, locked filing cabinets and restricted access to offices;

   b) organizational measures, for example, employee confidentiality agreements, security clearances and limiting access on a "need-to-know" basis; and

   c) technological measures, for example, the use of passwords and encryption.

7.3   Personal Information is stored in secure and confidential databases in Toronto, Ontario and Dallas, Texas.

7.4   When The Loyalty Group uses a third party to process information on its behalf, legal agreements require the third party to protect the privacy and confidentiality of the Personal Information. Further, these agreements ensure that the Personal Information is retained only as long as necessary to complete the assigned task and that the third-party organization only uses it for the specified purposes for which it is given.

7.5   The Loyalty Group has appropriate training programs and provides employees with information about its policies and procedures for protecting Collectors' Personal Information and the importance of maintaining the confidentiality of Personal Information.

7.6   Personal Information is disposed of or destroyed with care to prevent unauthorized parties from gaining access to the information.

Principle 8 — Openness

The Loyalty Group makes specific information about its policies and practices relating to the management of Personal Information readily available to Collectors.

8.1 The Loyalty Group is open about its policies and practices with respect to the management of Personal Information.

8.2 The Loyalty Group makes information about its privacy policies and practices readily available to individuals and its Collectors through written materials, its Web site (www.airmiles.ca) and other electronic means, its Interactive Voice Response system, and its Customer Service Centre. In addition, copies of the AIR MILES® *Privacy Commitment* are available to individuals and Collectors upon request.

Principle 9 — Individual Access

Upon request, The Loyalty Group gives Collectors access to their Personal Information and an account of its use and disclosure.

9.1 Collectors can request access to their Personal Information held by the AIR MILES® Reward Program by writing to AIR MILES Privacy Office, P.O. Box 602, Station A, Scarborough, Ontario M1K 5K7, by email to privacyoffice@airmiles.ca or by calling the AIR MILES Customer Service Centre (1-888-AIR-MILES). Upon request, The Loyalty Group informs the Collector whether or not it holds Personal Information about that Collector, and discloses details of that Collector's Personal Information, including, where available, the source type, its use, and Sponsors and research organizations to which it has been disclosed.

9.2 The Loyalty Group may request sufficient information from the Collector including passwords to verify the identity of the Collector and the existence, use and disclosure of Personal Information held by the AIR MILES Reward Program. The Loyalty Group will assist any Collector who informs The Loyalty Group that he or she needs assistance in preparing a request for access.

9.3 The Loyalty Group responds to a request for information within thirty (30) business days of receipt of request.

9.4 Responding to a Collector request for information will usually be done at no or minimal cost to the Collector. However, a fee for reasonable costs incurred may be charged in responding to more complex requests, provided the Collector is informed of the fee in advance. The Personal Information requested is provided to the Collector in a form that is generally understandable.

9.5   The Loyalty Group amends the Personal Information contained in the AIR MILES databases as required when an individual successfully demonstrates the inaccuracy or incompleteness of the Personal Information. An amendment may involve the correction, deletion or addition of information.

9.6   When it is not possible to provide a list of the Sponsors, agents and research organizations to which The Loyalty Group has disclosed Personal Information about a Collector, The Loyalty Group provides a list of the Sponsors, agents and research organizations to which it may have disclosed such Personal Information about the Collector.

9.7   A Collector has the opportunity to challenge the accuracy and completeness of the Personal Information and have it amended as appropriate. When a challenge is not resolved to the satisfaction of the Collector, the Personal Information relating to that Collector shall reflect the unresolved challenge. The existence of the challenge is transmitted to third parties as appropriate.

9.8   If The Loyalty Group is unable to provide access to all the Personal Information it holds about a Collector, the reasons for denying access are provided to the Collector.

Principle 10 — Challenging Compliance

A Collector is able to address a challenge concerning The Loyalty Group's compliance with the above principles with the individual identified in Section 1.2.

10.1   The Loyalty Group has procedures in place to receive and respond to inquiries about The Loyalty Group's policies and practices relating to its handling of Personal Information.

10.2   Inquiries about The Loyalty Group's privacy policies can be forwarded to the AIR MILES Privacy Office, P.O. Box 602, Station A, Scarborough, Ontario M1K 5K7 or by email to privacyoffice@airmiles.ca.

10.3   The Loyalty Group investigates all complaints and responds within ninety (90) business days after receipt of written correspondence. If the complaint is found to be justified, The Loyalty Group takes appropriate measures to resolve the complaint, including, if necessary, amending its policies and practices.

TABLE OF CASES

A.G. Canada v. A.G. Ontario (Labour Conventions), [1937]
A.C. 326 (P.C.) 59

A.G. Canada v. A.G. Ontario (Unemployment Insurance),
[1937] A.C. 355 (P.C.) 59

Alberta Government Telephones v. Canada (Radio-Television &
Telecommunications Commission), [1989] 2 S.C.R. 225,
68 Alta. L.R. (2d) 1, 61 D.L.R. (4th) 193 51

Caloil Inc. v. Canada (A.G.) (No. 2), [1971] S.C.R. 543, 20 D.L.R.
(3d) 472, [1971] 4 W.W.R. 37................................. 57

Citizens' Insurance Co. v. Parsons (1881), 7 App. Cas. 96, 1 Cart.
B.N.A. 265 (P.C.) 56

David Bull Laboratories (Canada) Inc. v. Pharmacia Inc., [1995]
1 F.C. 588 (C.A.).. 108

General Motors of Canada Ltd. v. City National Leasing, [1989]
1 S.C.R. 641, 68 O.R. (2d) 512n, 58 D.L.R. (4th) 255............. 57

Oil, Chemical and Atomic Workers International Union, Local
16-601 v. Imperial Oil Limited and A.G. British Columbia,
[1963] S.C.R. 584.. 59

Ontario Hydro v. Ontario (Labour Relations Board), [1993]
3 S.C.R. 327, 107 D.L.R. (4th) 457, 93 C.L.L.C. 14,061............ 51

R. v. Henderson, [1975] 1 W.W.R. 360 (B.C. Prov. Ct.) 98

R. v. Plant, [1993] 3 S.C.R. 281, [1993] 8 W.W.R. 287, 12 Alta.
L.R. (3d) 305... 75

R. v. Weir, [1998] 8 W.W.R. 228, 213 A.R. 285 (Q.B.) 69

Reference re Application of Hours of Work Act (British Columbia)
to Employees of the Canadian Pacific Railway in Empress Hotel,
Victoria (City); see Canadian Pacific Railway v. British Columbia
(A.G.), [1950] A.C. 122, 1 W.W.R. 220, 64 C.R.T.C. 266,
1 D.L.R. 721 (B.C.P.C.) 59

Reference re Validity of the Industrial Relations and Disputes
    Investigation Act, R.S.C. 1952, c. 152, and as to its applicability
    in respect of certain employees of the Eastern Canada Stevedoring
    Company Limited, [1955] S.C.R. 529, 3 D.L.R. 721 59

Reference re Farm Products Marketing Act (Ontario), [1957] S.C.R.
    198, 7 D.L.R. (2d) 257. 57

Regional Assessment Commissioner and Caisse Populaire de Hearst
    Ltee, Re (1983), 143 D.L.R. (3d) 590 (S.C.C.). 49

Sheldon Blank & Gateway Industries Ltd. v. Minister of the Environment
    (22 November 1999), No. T-1111-98 (F.C.T.D.). 114

Toronto Electric Commissioners v. Snider, [1925] A.C. 396, 2 D.L.R. 5,
    [1925] 1 W.W.R. 785 (P.C.) 59

U.T.U. v. Central Western Railway, [1990] 3 S.C.R. 1112, 76 D.L.R.
    (4th) 1, 91 C.L.L.C. 14,006 51

United States v. Potts, 297 F.2d 68 (6th Cir. 1961) 98–99

Westcoast Energy Inc. v. Canada (National Energy Board), [1998]
    1 S.C.R. 322, 3 Admin. L.R. (3d) 163, 156 D.L.R. (4th) 456,
    aff'g (1996), 193 N.R. 321, 134 D.L.R. (4th) 114, 2 F.C.
    263 (C.A.). 51

Windsor-Essex County Real Estate Board v. Windsor (City) (1974),
    [1975] 51 D.L.R. (3d) 665, 6 O.R. (2d) 21 (Ont. C.A.). 49

INDEX

Access to Information Act, 114

Access to personal information, 40–44, 55, 85–93, 163

    by alternative format, 48, 94

    assistance provided for, 86

    cost of providing, 43, 87, 163

    denial of, 40, 55, 87, 92–93

    exceptions to right of, 88–89

    from government institutions

        notification and response, 89–92

        objection, reasons for, 90–91

            law enforcement, 90

            money laundering, 90–91

            national security, 90

    prohibition of, 91–92

    time for providing, 43, 86, 87, 163

    by written request, 85

Association of Canadian Archivists, 131, 132

Audits of personal information management practices by Privacy
Commissioner, 37, 38, 109–11

    confidentiality of, 111

        exceptions to confidentiality rule, 112–13, 166

    offence and punishment for obstruction of, 121

    report and recommendations, 111

B.C. Civil Liberties Association, 140

Canada Evidence Act, 126

    amendments to, 133–37

Canadian Bankers Association, 84,

    Bank Crime Prevention and Investigation Office, 142, 146, 150

Canadian Charter of Rights and Freedoms, 7, 60, 75

Canadian Direct Marketing Association, 3–5
Canadian Electronic Commerce Strategy, 125, 126
    Electronic Commerce Secretariat, 126
Canadian Human Rights Act, xi, xii
Canadian Standards Association (CSA)
    standard, development of, xiii–xv
    CSA Code, 3, 4, 5, 11, 13, 31, 55, 170
Commercial activity, definition of, 48–49
Complaints to organizations, 164–65
Complaints to Privacy Commissioner
    dispute resolution mechanisms, 99
    Federal Court Review, 104–8, 167
    filing of, 94–95
    investigation of, 97–99
        offence and punishment for obstruction of, 121
    report by Commissioner, 100–4
        remedies, 107
        summary hearings, 107–8
        terms to designate a finding, 101–3
    time limit, 96
Constitution Act, 1867, 50, 56

Direct marketing, 7, 21, 22, 30, 142, 159

Educational information, 9, 49
Electronic documents
    as alternatives for paper, 125–28
    as evidence, 133, 134, 135
    record keeping of, 133, 135
    retention and storage of, 131
    signature on, 128
        digital signature, 130
        public key cryptography, 130
        secure electronic signature, 127, 129–30, 132
Electronic services, 126
    payments, filing, 127
European Council Convention 108, xii, xiii, 2, 10
European Council Directive 95/46/EC, xiii, 2, 4, 14, 31, 227–60
Excise Tax Act, 84

Federal work, 50–52, 159, 160
    atomic energy facilities, 52
    banks, 50, 51

broadcasting, 51
definition of, 50
employees of, 59
gas pipelines, 51
navigation and shipping, 51
offshore drilling, 52
nuclear energy facilities, 51, 52
railways, 51
telecommunications, 51
transportation, air, land, sea, 51
Financial Administration Act, 127
Fish Inspection Act, 129n
Freedom of Information Act (U.S.A.), xii
Freedom of Information and Protection of Privacy Act (Ontario), 140, 268

Human rights legislation, 2, 7

Information Highway Advisory Council, xiv, xv, 5
Insurance Council of Canada
    Insurance Crime Prevention Bureau, 80, 142, 146, 150–51, 165
Internet, 7, 8, 16, 31, 32, 54, 63, 140, 169

Java applets, 170
Junk mail, 161
Jurisdictional limits of the Act
    government institutions under *Privacy Act*, 59
    individual personal or domestic purposes, 60
    journalistic, artistic, or literary purposes, 60, 66

Legislation Revision and Consolidation Act, 137

Medical information, 9, 23, 27, 41, 53, 82, 155–57, 167
Money laundering, 77–79, 90–91

National security, 75, 79, 81, 90

OECD Guidelines (Governing the protection of privacy and transborder
    flows of personal data), xii, xiii, 2, 9, 14, 18, 22, 33, 38, 221–25
Organization, definition of, 50, 52, 153, 160

Patent Act, 127
Personal health information, 122, 159, 161. *See also* Medical information
    definition of, 53

Personal information
    access to. *See* Access to personal information
    accountability within organization for, 15, 16, 44, 62
    accuracy of, 35–36, 163
        amendment of errors in, 43–44, 163–64
        unresolved challenge to, 44
    collection, use, and disclosure of
        justification principle, lack of, 61
        publicly available information, 142
            regulations governing, 142–50, 151–53
        purposes for, 18, 19, 20, 55–56, 61
            commercial activity, 48–49, 56–59
            fundraising, 163
            non-profit activity, 48–49
            research, 154
            third-party use, 41–42, 43, 153, 162
        by Web sites, foreign, 169
            Java applets, 170
            Platform for Privacy Preferences (P3P), 171
    collection without knowledge or consent, 62–63, 64–69, 162
        availability or accuracy reasons, 65–66
        individual's best interests, 64, 72
        journalistic, artistic, or literary purposes, 60, 66–67
        publicly available information, 67–68, 142–53
    consent for collection, 22–27, 62
        express consent vs. implied consent, 28, 29
        method of obtaining consent, 28–30
        withdrawal of consent, 30
    definition of, 53, 139–42, 161
    disclosure without knowledge or consent, 72–84, 166
        archival or historical records, 83
        court subpoena, warrant, or order, 74, 165
        death of individual, 83
        debt collection, 73, 162
        emergency involving health or security, 81
        law enforcement or compliance, 74–81, 84, 90, 165
        money laundering, 77–79, 90–91
        national security, 75, 79, 81, 90
        new purposes for disclosure of previously collected data, 85
        publicly available information, 83, 142–53
        research, statistical or scholarly, 82
        solicitor or notary, 73
    identifying new purpose for previously collected data, 20, 21, 33

limiting collection of, 25–27, 32
limiting use, disclosure, and retention of, 33–35
    destruction of data, 34–35, 38
policies within organizations for protection of, 17, 38,
    challenging compliance, 44–46
policies for openness and accessibility, 38–39
provincial jurisdiction over, 160, 161
"reasonable person" test, 55, 61, 62, 153
security safeguards for protection of, 36–37
    training of personnel, 37
sensitivity of information, 23, 27, 30, 36, 41
transborder dataflow of, 16
use without knowledge or consent, 69–72
    emergency involving health or security, 69–70
    investigation of law-breakers, 69, 72
    new use of previously collected data, 85
    publicly available information, 72, 142–53
    research, statistical or scholarly, 70–72
Platform for Privacy Preferences (P3P), 171
Privacy Act, xii, 1, 50, 53, 54, 59, 78, 83, 84, 101, 102, 103, 111, 118, 139
Privacy Commissioner
    annual reports by, 117
    audit powers of. *See* Audits of personal information management prac-
        tices
    complaints to. *See* Complaints to Privacy Commissioner
    delegation of powers, 110
    establishment of office, xii
    protection of, 114
    role and power of, xv, 49, 58, 60, 70, 84, 96–104, 115–17, 166
    as witness, 114
Privacy impact assessments, 265–73
Proceeds of Crime (Money Laundering) Act, 77–79
Public Key Infrastructure (PKI), Government of Canada, 131, 132

Quebec legislation, xiii, xiv, 3, 4, 5, 7, 9, 14, 18–19, 30, 54, 73, 128,
    154, 160, 161
Quebec Charter of Human Rights and Freedoms, xiv

Record, definition of, 54
Regulations and Orders, 118–19, 132
Research, 60, 66, 67, 70–72
    genealogical, 154, 168
    market, 154–55

medical, 82, 154, 155, 167–68
scholarly, historical, 70–72, 83, 154
statistical, economic, 70–72, 82, 154

"Should," definition of, 61, 169
Standards Council of Canada, 5
Statute Revision Act, 137–38
Statutory Instruments Act, 137

Telemarketing, 5
Trade and commerce powers, federal, 7, 48, 56–58
    validity of, five-part test for, 58

Uniform Electronic Evidence Act, 133, 134, 135
Uniform Law Conference of Canada, 5, 6, 133, 139

Whistleblowing, 120–21

ABOUT THE AUTHORS

Stephanie Perrin is Chief Privacy Officer at Zero Knowledge Systems Inc. in Montreal. Before joining Zero Knowledge, Ms. Perrin was the Director of Privacy Policy for Industry Canada's Electronic Commerce Task Force and led the legislative initiative at Industry Canada, which resulted in the *Personal Information Protection and Electronic Documents Act*. An internationally recognized expert in freedom of information and privacy issues, Ms. Perrin was instrumental in developing Canada's privacy and cryptography policies for nearly twenty years and has represented Canada internationally at the OECD Security and Privacy Committee. Zero Knowledge Systems Inc. is a leading developer of Internet privacy and identity-management solutions.

Heather H. Black is a member of the Department of Justice attached to Legal Services at Industry Canada. She is currently on secondment to the Office of the Privacy Commissioner of Canada. Ms. Black was a member of the Information Law and Privacy Group at Justice from 1982–86, where she participated in the drafting of guidelines for the implementation of the *Privacy Act*, provided legal advice on its interpretation, and litigation support on *Privacy Act* cases. As counsel to Industry Canada from 1994–2000, she worked on the development of Part 1 of the *Personal Information Protection and Electronic Documents Act*. She was involved in the policy development and was instructing counsel on the drafting of the Bill. Ms. Black holds an LL.B. from McGill University and is a member of the Ontario Bar.

David H. Flaherty is a specialist in the management of privacy and information policy issues. He recently completed a six-year, non-renewable term as the first Information and Privacy Commissioner for the province of British Columbia. From 1972 until 1993, he was professor of history and law at the University of Western Ontario, from which he is now a professor emeritus. In 1992–93 he was a Fellow of the Woodrow Wilson International Center for Scholars in Washington, D.C., and a Canada-U.S. Fulbright Scholar in Law. He is currently an Adjunct Professor in political science at the University of Victoria, and a consultant. Dr. Flaherty has written extensively on privacy and information policy and has testified on privacy issues in both the U.S. Congress and the Parliament of Canada. In the fall of 1999, he served as a special adviser to the Deputy Minister of Industry Canada in support of Bill C-6, the *Personal Information Protection and Electronic Documents Act.*

T. Murray Rankin, Q.C., is managing partner of Arvay Finlay Barristers in Victoria, British Columbia, and former professor of law at the University of Victoria. Mr. Rankin has had a long-term interest in freedom of information and privacy protection as a practitioner, law professor, and activist. In 1979 he received the House of Commons "Award of Merit" for contribution to Freedom of Information and was a key adviser to the government of British Columbia on the 1992 provincial *Freedom of Information and Protection of Privacy Act.* He has been involved in public law litigation and complex negotiations for over twenty years. His areas of specialization include information law, administrative law, Aboriginal law, and environmental law. Mr. Rankin holds an LL.B. from the University of Toronto and an LL.M. from Harvard University.